EXTROVERTED FINANCIALISATION

Extroverted Financialisation offers a new account of the Americanisation of global finance through the concept of 'extroverted financialisation'. The study presents German banks as active participants of financialisation, demonstrating how deeply entangled they were with global markets since post-WWII reconstruction. *Extroverted Financialisation* locates the transformation of global banking within the revolution of funding practices in 1960s New York and shows how this empowered US banks to systematically outcompete their European counterparts. This uneven competition drove German banks to partially uproot themselves from their own home markets and transform their own banking models into US financial models. This transformation not only led to the German banks' speculative investments during the 2000s sub-prime mortgage bubble but more importantly to rising USD dependency and their contemporary decline.

Mareike Beck is an assistant professor of international political economy at the University of Warwick. Her research focuses on the global and everyday politics of finance, including transformations of global banking, real estate and asset-based inequalities.

STUDIES IN MACROECONOMIC HISTORY

Series Editor: Michael D. Bordo, Rutgers University

The titles in this series investigate themes of interest to economists and economic historians in the rapidly developing field of macroeconomic history. The four areas covered include the application of monetary and finance theory, international economics, and quantitative methods to historical problems; the historical application of growth and development theory and theories of business fluctuations; the history of domestic and international monetary, financial, and other macroeconomic institutions; and the history of international monetary and financial systems. The series amalgamates the former Cambridge University Press series Studies in Monetary and Financial History and Studies in Quantitative Economic History.

Other Books in the Series:

Jon Moen and Mary Tone Rodgers, *Before the Fed, J.P. Morgan, America's Lender of Last Resort* (2025)

Mareike Beck, *Extroverted Financialization, Banking on US Dollar Debt* (2025)

Per H. Hansen, *There Will Be the Devil to Pay: Central Bankers, Uncertainty and Sensemaking in the European Financial Crisis of 1931* (2024)

Simon Amrein, *Capital in Banking: The Role of Capital in Banking in the 19th and 20th Century: The United Kingdom, the United States and Switzerland* (2024)

Stephen Quinn and William Roberds, *How a Ledger Became a Central Bank: A Monetary History of the Bank of Amsterdam* (2023)

Simon Hinrichsen, *When Nations Can't Default: A History of War Reparations and Sovereign Debt* (2023)

Barry Eichengreen and Andreas Kakridis, *The Emergence of the Modern Central Bank and Global Cooperation: 1919-1939* (2023)

Alain Naef, *An Exchange Rate History of the United Kingdom: 1945–1992* (2021)

Barrie A. Wigmore, *The Financial Crisis of 2008: A History of US Financial Markets 2000–2012* (2021)

Max Harris, *Monetary War and Peace: London, Washington, Paris, and the Tripartite Agreement of 1936* (2021)

Kenneth D. Garbade, *After the Accord: A History of Federal Reserve Open Market Operations, the US Government Securities Market, and Treasury Debt Management from 1951 to 1979* (2020)

Harold James, *Making a Modern Central Bank: The Bank of England 1979–2003* (2020)

Claudio Borio, Stijn Claessens, Piet Clement, Robert N. McCauley, and Hyun Song Shin, Editors, *Promoting Global Monetary and Financial Stability: The Bank for International Settlements after Bretton Woods, 1973–2020* (2020)

Patrick Honohan, *Currency, Credit and Crisis: Central Banking in Ireland and Europe* (2019)

William A. Allen, *The Bank of England and the Government Debt: Operations in the Gilt-Edged Market, 1928–1972* (2019)

Eric Monnet, *Controlling Credit: Central Banking and the Planned Economy in Postwar France, 1948–1973* (2018)

Laurence M. Ball, *The Fed and Lehman Brothers: Setting the Record Straight on a Financial Disaster* (2018)

Rodney Edvinsson, Tor Jacobson, and Daniel Waldenström, Editors, *Sveriges Riksbank and the History of Central Banking* (2018)

Peter L. Rousseau and Paul Wachtel, Editors, *Financial Systems and Economic Growth: Credit, Crises, and the Regulation from the 19th Century to the Present* (2017)

Ernst Baltensperger and Peter Kugler, *Swiss Monetary History since the Early 19th Century* (2017)

Øyvind Eitrheim, Jan Tore Klovland, and Lars Fredrik Øksendal, *A Monetary History of Norway, 1816–2016* (2016)

Jan Fredrik Qvigstad, *On Central Banking* (2016)

Michael D. Bordo, Øyvind Eitrheim, Marc Flandreau, and Jan F. Qvigstad, Editors, *Central Banks at a Crossroads: What Can We Learn from History?* (2016)

Michael D. Bordo and Mark A. Wynne, Editors, *The Federal Reserve's Role in the Global Economy: A Historical Perspective* (2016)

Owen F. Humpage, Editor, *Current Federal Reserve Policy Under the Lens of Economic History: Essays to Commemorate the Federal Reserve System's Centennial* (2015)

Michael D. Bordo and William Roberds, Editors, *The Origins, History, and Future of the Federal Reserve: A Return to Jekyll Island* (2013)

Michael D. Bordo and Ronald MacDonald, Editors, *Credibility and the International Monetary Regime: A Historical Perspective* (2012)

Robert L. Hetzel, *The Great Recession: Market Failure or Policy Failure?* (2012)

Tobias Straumann, *Fixed Ideas of Money: Small States and Exchange Rate Regimes in Twentieth-Century Europe* (2010)

Forrest Capie, *The Bank of England: 1950s to 1979* (2010)

Aldo Musacchio, *Experiments in Financial Democracy: Corporate Governance and Financial Development in Brazil, 1882–1950* (2009)

Claudio Borio, Gianni Toniolo, and Piet Clement, Editors, *The Past and Future of Central Bank Cooperation* (2008)

Robert L. Hetzel, *The Monetary Policy of the Federal Reserve: A History* (2008)

Caroline Fohlin, *Finance Capitalism and Germany's Rise to Industrial Power* (2007)

John H. Wood, *A History of Central Banking in Great Britain and the United States* (2005)

Gianni Toniolo (with the assistance of Piet Clement), *Central Bank Cooperation at the Bank for International Settlements, 1930–1973* (2005)

Richard Burdekin and Pierre Siklos, Editors, *Deflation: Current and Historical Perspectives* (2004)

Pierre Siklos, *The Changing Face of Central Banking: Evolutionary Trends since World War II* (2002)

Michael D. Bordo and Roberto Cortés-Conde, Editors, *Transferring Wealth and Power from the Old to the New World: Monetary and Fiscal Institutions in the 17th through the 19th Centuries* (2001)

Howard Bodenhorn, *A History of Banking in Antebellum America: Financial Markets and Economic Development in an Era of Nation-Building* (2000)

Mark Harrison, Editor, *The Economics of World War II: Six Great Powers in International Comparison* (2000)

Angela Redish, *Bimetallism: An Economic and Historical Analysis* (2000)

Elmus Wicker, *Banking Panics of the Gilded Age* (2000)

Michael D. Bordo, *The Gold Standard and Related Regimes: Collected Essays* (1999)

Michele Fratianni and Franco Spinelli, *A Monetary History of Italy* (1997)

Mark Toma, *Competition and Monopoly in the Federal Reserve System, 1914–1951* (1997)

Barry Eichengreen, Editor, *Europe's Postwar Recovery* (1996)

Lawrence H. Officer, *Between the Dollar-Sterling Gold Points: Exchange Rates, Parity and Market Behavior* (1996)

Elmus Wicker, *The Banking Panics of the Great Depression* (1996)

Norio Tamaki, *Japanese Banking: A History, 1859–1959* (1995)

Barry Eichengreen, *Elusive Stability: Essays in the History of International Finance, 1919–1939* (1993)

Michael D. Bordo and Forrest Capie, Editors, *Monetary Regimes in Transition* (1993)

Larry Neal, *The Rise of Financial Capitalism: International Capital Markets in the Age of Reason* (1993)

S. N. Broadberry and N. F. R. Crafts, Editors, *Britain in the International Economy, 1870–1939* (1992)

Aurel Schubert, *The Credit-Anstalt Crisis of 1931* (1992)

Trevor J. O. Dick and John E. Floyd, *Canada and the Gold Standard: Balance of Payments Adjustment under Fixed Exchange Rates, 1871–1913* (1992)

Kenneth Mouré, *Managing the Franc Poincaré: Economic Understanding and Political Constraint in French Monetary Policy, 1928–1936* (1991)

David C. Wheelock, *The Strategy and Consistency of Federal Reserve Monetary Policy, 1924–1933* (1991)

Extroverted Financialisation

Banking on US Dollar Debt

MAREIKE BECK
University of Warwick

CAMBRIDGE
UNIVERSITY PRESS

CAMBRIDGE
UNIVERSITY PRESS

Shaftesbury Road, Cambridge CB2 8EA, United Kingdom
One Liberty Plaza, 20th Floor, New York, NY 10006, USA
477 Williamstown Road, Port Melbourne, VIC 3207, Australia
314–321, 3rd Floor, Plot 3, Splendor Forum, Jasola District Centre, New Delhi – 110025, India
103 Penang Road, #05–06/07, Visioncrest Commercial, Singapore 238467

Cambridge University Press is part of Cambridge University Press & Assessment, a department of the University of Cambridge.

We share the University's mission to contribute to society through the pursuit of education, learning and research at the highest international levels of excellence.

www.cambridge.org
Information on this title: www.cambridge.org/9781009411813

DOI: 10.1017/9781009411790

When citing this work, please include a reference to the DOI 10.1017/9781009411790

First published 2025

A catalogue record for this publication is available from the British Library

A Cataloging-in-Publication data record for this book is available from the Library of Congress

ISBN 978-1-009-41181-3 Hardback

Meinen Eltern

Bankraub ist eine Unternehmung von Dilettanten. Wahre Profis gründen eine Bank.
(Bank robbery is an undertaking of amateurs. True professionals start a bank.)

Berthold Brecht

Contents

Figures

Acknowledgements

In writing this book, I have accrued more debt than I can ever repay. Neither can these acknowledgements ever get close to properly acknowledging all the brilliant people that have brought this book to life. I am hugely grateful to all.

Firstly, I must acknowledge Sam Knafo who has first seen the value of my initial thoughts and did not grow tired of nurturing them along. He has provided invaluable guidance, support, and inspiration in all those years. Thank you! Earl Gammon has taught me much about academia and kept finance in perspective. I am also grateful to Andreas Antoniades, Lara Coleman, Ben Selwyn and other colleagues at Sussex that have given me a first intellectual home for this project. The reading group that originated at the Open House has provided a hugely important space to test, chat, learn about but also discard thoughts on history, finance and neoliberalism. Besides Sam, Kate Cherry, Manu De Girolamo, Sahil Dutta, Julian German, Michaela Hamilton, Ian Lovering, Nils Peters and Stefano Sgambati have read drafts and/or provided hugely important insights and support.

The colleagues at the Department of European and International Studies at King's College London have provided useful comments and feedback on ideas that made it into the book, including Joseph Baines, Magnus Ryner and colleagues at the International Political Economy (IPE) research group. Johnna Montgomerie has taught me valuable insights into how to academia works. I joined PAIS, University of Warwick, when this book was mostly written. But Mat Watson has supported me in this book endeavour since my viva which – conducted together with Andreas Antoniades – was as challenging as it was fun, and a critical motivation to develop this book.

Revisionist history such as done in this book depends, naturally, on research that came before. Even if I am critical of concepts or assumptions, that work has been important to building my own theorisations about global finance. Various colleagues and friends have commented and asked questions during conferences, workshops and other events. There are too many of them to be named but you are not forgotten. Iain Hardie, Daniel Mertens and Charlotte Rommerskirchen were insightful discussants. Marina Hübner and Caroline Metz have been great colleagues to navigate academia and (male dominated) IPE. The MaxCPE seminar series organised by Björn Bremer, Arianna Tassinari and Lucia Baccaro was a useful first forum to present my concept of extroverted financialisation to a comparative political economy audience based in Germany while Mark Schwartz provided motivation to keep centring the USD world.

The Brighton Aerial Circus community provided the best distraction from writing this book. I also want to acknowledge the many osteopaths, Pilates and yoga teachers who have sustained a combination of many hours at the desk with many hours high up in the air – neither of which has been gentle on the body. Friends, housemates and comrades have been equally important to weather the years of research that went into this book. To everyone, thank you!

I thankfully acknowledge the financial support of the Leverhulme Trust that has enabled me to bring my PhD research to new conclusions. For the first three years of this project, the Foundation of German Business has allowed me to avoid personal debt and leverage whilst researching the business of global banking. I also thank Robert Dreesen and the Cambridge University Press production team for making this book possible.

A huge thank you goes to my parents and my brother who have provided unconditional support. I owe a special thanks to Edward who has often complained about the many hours going into this book but in the end supported every one of them.

1

Introduction

The Puzzle of Contemporary Banking

The global financial crisis (GFC) in 2008 still conjures a dark image of the dangers of banks' innovations and their destructive potential. This memory is still in the foreground during recent financial disasters. And since 2008, there have been many. While European financial regulators and pundits had started to claim that the financial sector had cleaned up its act and became more resilient, the default of Silicon Valley Bank in March 2023 and subsequent emergency takeover of Credit Suisse yet again brought about a sense of déjà vu and panic. Credit Suisse defaulted, and its rescue represented another instance of a public bailout of a European bank that was 'too big to fail'. Just three years earlier, in March 2020, the COVID-19 pandemic threatened an equally large financial calamity when the extent of the economic fallout became apparent and financial markets almost collapsed.

What combined the financial mayhems was a US dollar (USD) funding problem and a subsequent supply of USDs by the central banks. When the Swiss bank Credit Suisse collapsed, central banks quickly provided short-term USD funding – not Swiss Francs (SFr) nor Euros (EUR) – to stop other banks following suit. In March 2020, financial institutions across the globe rushed to equip themselves with USD, selling off long-term Treasuries to be able to meet their income shortfall and nearly causing another global credit crunch. To the financial community's benefit, the Fed also stepped in to meet USD demand, much quicker and to a larger extent compared to the GFC. These barely averted global crises raise the question of why, despite major financial and regulatory efforts since the GFC, so many banks are still so precariously dependent on short-term USD funding. Why is there still such a dangerous USD bottleneck for the functioning of global financial markets?

One obvious answer is that the USD is the global reserve currency. Financial markets and money are hierarchical structures, and financial agents will rush to the apex of the pyramid – the USD, a global financial safe haven – whenever financial turmoil looms. During crises, the USD is in demand while other currencies are sold. US capital markets are the deepest and most liquid markets globally so that they not only provide the safest assets such as Treasury bills, but they ensure steady demand and a variety of other financial securities that can serve as collateral in case an investor needs to monetise their assets during liquidity shortages. One can easily imagine the design flaw of a global system in which every agent suddenly requires the same currency at the same time.

This, however, rather confirms the problem at hand and raises the question of how we ended up in this situation. The fact that European banking giants were dependent on USD funding and could only be rescued with USD – and hence by the US Federal Reserve (Fed) – is historically new. European banks used to enjoy large-scale institutional and public support and were seen as bulwarks within European political economies. What is often seen as a key characteristic of US banks' power – the fact that they have become megabanks, joining commercial and investment banking to provide a huge range of financial services – the European banks long had. In fact, US banks historically envied European banks for their power and influence over European corporate governance, economic activity and policymaking (Danielson, 2016; Kobrak, 2007). Why have European banks embarked on this radical transformation in which they became so deeply dependent on US financial markets?

To answer this question, this book reaches into history to analyse processes of financialisation outside the US. I develop the concept of extroverted financialisation (EF) to reframe the transformation of European banking and to develop analytical tools to analyse the causes of and motivations behind financialisation. I put forward the argument that beyond the well-known run up to the GFC, there has been a more fundamental transformation since the 1960s when European banks attempted to root themselves into global USD markets. At that time, European banks had to respond to the rise of new US funding practices that made US banks astonishingly powerful. To be able to compete with US banks, I show that European banks had to partially uproot their operations from their own home markets to institutionalise themselves into US money markets. This shift required a fundamental transformation of the core of their own banking models towards US-style finance. The adjustments and innovations these banks made in the process produced unforeseen changes of their operations that are closely related to their contemporary problems.

This book's key protagonists are Deutsche Bank and Commerzbank, Germany's two biggest private universal banks. Focusing on how they have tried to compete with US banks, I trace their transition towards global investment banks and the fundamental problems this has produced for the global financial architecture. Most accounts of German finance locate its transformation domestically in the 1990s when, no longer able to resist the global pressures of rising securities markets, Germany embarked on a project of financial liberalisation. By contrast, the book relies on a longer trajectory that extends back to the 1960s when the banks began to operate in the Eurodollar markets, the first major USD offshore markets proliferating in Europe at the time.[1] This long-term global outlook reveals important turning points in their international history which have not yet been accounted for: of the 1970s when the banks began to centralise their operations in London to learn US finance and of the 1980s when they started to arrive in US money markets. Based on this history, I show how German political economy is deeply intertwined with global financial markets. I argue that key to German financialisation has been the banks' extroverted strategies that forced them to significantly uproot themselves from their home markets and to find ways to establish themselves into US wholesale markets.

From the banks' perspective, I reassess where financialisation originated, how its processes redrew the boundaries and practices of global finance, and how this translated into Europe. As powerful European financial institutions, German universal banks provide a useful case study for this revisionist history. As such, the book tells the story of the rise and decline of key capitalist institutions – large universal banks – that are often seen as the founding fathers of the European industry and social model. This belief in a European financial system that was different to the US, and somehow more 'social', came crashing down during the GFC. Financialisation seemed to have finally caught up with a European political economy that was previously considered immune to the worst of the speculative bouts of global financial markets (Schelkle & Bohle, 2020).

Scholars, experts and politicians alike were quick to proclaim the GFC as a US problem when the crisis first appeared. It was supposedly a product of an 'irresponsible rise of the laissez-faire principle' according to Peer Steinbrück, Germany's federal finance minister at the time (cited in

[1] Eurodollars are deposits of large sums of USD that are created outside the US by any institution not resident in the US. This can include the foreign branch of a US bank or a foreign bank that is non-resident in the US. Thus, when a US bank shifts USDs to its London branch and receives in return a deposit, it has created a Eurodollar deposit. The Eurodollar markets grew quickly. The Eurodollar Certificate of Deposit (CD) market, for example, was more active in 1990 than the market for CDs in the US (Stigum, 1990, pp. 56, 199ff).

Hardie & Howarth, 2013a, p. 104), confined to the outcome of inadequate regulation and runaway financial markets infused with too much greed and speculation. Less than a week later, he announced the biggest public bailout of a German financial institution to date, €35 billion to Hypo Real Estate. Subsequently, Commerzbank, the now second biggest commercial bank in Germany after its takeover of rival Dresdner Bank in 2008, received a public bailout of around €18 billion (Buch et al., 2011) with the German state still owning a 15 per cent stake in it.[2] Barclays, ABN Amro, Royal Bank of Scotland, UBS and Société Générale all experienced similar fates and public bailouts. They fell down the ranks and mostly out of the top twenties (Danielson, 2016). The involvement in US finance brought Europe's national champions to their knees and they are yet to get up.

German banks in particular have been struggling. Commerzbank disastrously took over Dresdner Bank in 2009 (Paul et al., 2020) but Dresdner's investments in the US mortgage industry produced extensive write-downs so that Commerzbank had to withdraw its US money market activities. It is now trying to redefine itself as a 'European' investment bank but is in constant danger of a foreign takeover. Deutsche Bank – often seen as the most successful US investment bank amongst the European lenders – has perhaps fallen furthest. John Cryan, head of Deutsche from 2015 to 2018, emailed his employees modestly: 'we have ambitious goals, but the numbers do not add up just yet' (cited in Willmroth, 2018, own translation). Post-GFC, Deutsche (co-)produced many scandals (cf. Enrich, 2020). In 2016, the world waited aghast for the outcome of Deutsche's court hearing as the US Department for Justice threatened to ask for USD 14 billion to settle claims connected to Deutsche's alleged mortgage fraud (The Economist, 2016). The deal was settled for a manageable USD 7.2 billion (The Economist, 2017), but this showed that the US could bring down the German giant (Tooze, 2018, p. 16). What followed was a back-and-forth between expanding and contracting its US business, common amongst the European universal banks attempting (miserably) to keep a foot in lucrative US financial markets[3] (Noonan, 2020). The public credit program of the COVID-19 pandemic brought some relief to the German lenders, and they withstood the 2023 turmoil surrounding US-based Silicon Valley Bank. However, their position remains

[2] The entire bailout of the German banks amounted to roughly a quarter of German GDP (Hüfner, 2010).

[3] Compare Gibadullina (2023) for a breakdown of the phenomenal profits of the US finance industry.

precarious. A few days after UBS' emergency takeover of Credit Suisse in March 2023, Deutsche's shares tumbled, and financial commentators were quick to wonder if Deutsche was next in line.

German banks represent a useful example of the pressures and constraints that global European banks faced not only during the crisis but also during the decades preceding the GFC, including USD dependency, the rise of global financial markets and regulatory challenges. I maintain that financial systems have recognisable national and regional coordinates that are important to keep in mind to understand extroverted strategies of individual banks. Other scholars classify European finance or banking as one category (Bayoumi, 2017; Schelkle & Bohle, 2020) because European universal banking models possess similar characteristics. This has recently been verified when Credit Suisse's obituaries in 2023 described similar histories to memorials of Dresdner Bank or a biography of ABN Amro after their falls from grace during the GFC. Incorporating practices of other European banks throughout the book, I show that German banks have often collaborated or acted directly in competition with other European banks when trying to cope with the power of US finance. Based on this history, I can confidently make claims about important imperatives and constraints that European banks faced during financialisation and the precise responses that Commerzbank and Deutsche Bank came up with.

In choosing two different banks, I demonstrate that banks have responded differently and produced distinct paths of EF. I use the terms German banks, Deutsche Bank or Commerzbank, respectively, when I examine their distinct reactions and when those differences matter. Because Deutsche and Commerzbank significantly diverge in their extroverted paths from the late 1980s onwards, I dedicate Chapters 6 and 7 to their individual transformations and show how the forces of EF were dealt with differently according to the banks' embeddedness in their local context. While the history in this book shows that the rise of US finance posed new imperatives for global markets, causing similar tensions for European banking models, I leave more in-depth research about other European banks for a future project. But in tracing the German transition, I develop broader theoretical conclusions about the US Americanisation of global finance and how we might research its impact in Europe.[4]

[4] Comparing EF with the concept of subordinated financialisation (Bonizzi et al., 2019; Kaltenbrunner & Painceira, 2017), it is the constraints and imperatives with respect to USD funding that are similar for financial institutions in the Global South. A key difference is the powerful starting point that European banks have because the Eurodollar

THE US AMERICANISATION OF GLOBAL FINANCE

The phenomenal expansion and globalisation of financial markets alongside their multiple crises has been termed financialisation. The term has become ubiquitous in scholarship far beyond political economy. But as as we often find with terminology used to describe large-scale processes, financialisation has become a comprehensive but vague concept used to describe all types of market developments and expansions where a financial investor or practice is involved. An influential description states that financialisation depicts the 'increasing importance of financial markets, institutions and motives in the world economy' (Epstein, 2005). The phenomenon of the expansion of markets has come to define one of the key characteristics of financialisation. Indeed, scholars have come to accept that 'financialisation is marketisation' (Braun, 2020; Godechot, 2016).

This phenomenon has historically been associated with the US. Since the GFC, however, scholars more widely began to associate financialisation with European economies that were previously considered immune to the speculative nature of global financial markets. The increasing use of short-term practices and speculation have raised questions about European's own shift to financialisation (Schelkle & Bohle, 2020). Thinking of German banks – or at least its biggest players – as resembling US banks represented a big shift in analytical approaches because German banks were traditionally seen as prudent financial actors that provide long-term funding for industrial production rather than engage with financial speculation (Baccaro & Höpner, 2022; Hardie & Howarth, 2013a; Heires & Nölke, 2014; Streeck, 2009). In political economy scholarship, German finance has often served as a paradigmatic case study because it was the quintessential ideal type of a coordinated market economy (CME) with a bank-based system. Germany was seen as providing optimal conditions for high quality production (Streeck, 1991) because patient capital (long-term loans by banks) supported corporations' long-term investment to build the necessary long-term capacities such as workers' education, research and development, rather than having to respond to the short-term pressures of financial markets such as paying out dividends and shareholder

markets developed in Europe with the British, German and French banks amongst its pioneers, as this book will show, including substantial institutional support for USD funding. Moreover, their own home currencies have themselves been imperial money, for example, the Franc (Koddenbrock & Sylla, 2019).

value (Lane, 2003; Lazonick & O'sullivan, 1997; Vitols, 2005). From this perspective, banks monitor and control corporate performance relying on insider information and close relationships, ensured by many cross-shareholdings and supervisory seats. German banks' own funding relied on stable customer deposits instead of financial securities. Short of bank runs, deposits were seen as more reliable because retail customers tend to be loyal, and bank runs rare.[5]

German finance was termed 'bank-based' because banks were relatively more important for corporate funding than financial markets. Banks' assets are 127% of GDP on average from 1992 to 2011 compared to the stock market (39%) and the private debt market (44%) (Baccaro & Höpner, 2022, p. 256). Equity and securities markets are seen as 'underdeveloped', which often serves as evidence to illustrate the dominance of banks over market-based finance. As the regulatory framework made it difficult for other financial institutions to enter the credit market, the large German banks were powerful not only in the credit business but in the German political economy more generally (Baccaro & Höpner, 2022; Fohlin, 2007; Sablowski, 2008; Vitols, 1998; Zysman, 1983).

By contrast, US finance is commonly characterised as market-based with short-term financial practices that most closely resemble the ideal type of a decentralised 'free market'. US financial markets are deep and liquid compared to European markets, and they are seen as competitive as many financial actors must compete for business. Funding on financial markets is associated with an 'arms-length' or 'transactional' approach to lending. Instead of bank credit, scholars emphasise that corporations often use capital markets to fund themselves. Financial actors would rely on impersonal market metrics to assess non-financial corporation's performance, instead of insider information that German banks could rely upon (Lütz, 2000). Consequently, it was more difficult to form monopolies and banks lent short-term because they are reluctant to assume the risk of long-term lending via volatile financial markets (cf. Zysman, 1983). As a result, US banks traditionally lacked the power that were attributed to German banks.

Political economy scholars identified a change in these stark national differences from the 1990s onwards, arguing that Europe might be converging to the US market-based framework, though the extent is still

[5] The Silicon Valley Bank (SVB) represents a recent bank run, but SVB had an unusual composition of high-value depositors that could be seen as investors rather than traditional depositors (Saeidinezhad, 2023).

debated. Increasing competitive pressures of global (or US) financial markets vis-à-vis coordinated political economies slowly eroded institutional and regulatory frameworks. Scholars refocused their attention to how global transformations affected national economies (Baccaro & Höpner, 2022; Callaghan, 2018; Heires & Nölke, 2014; Jackson & Sorge, 2012; Lane, 2008; Maxfield et al., 2017; Streeck & Thelen, 2005). Global trends such as the removal of capital restrictions and growing international trade started to transform national financial frameworks because regulation gave in to market-pressures and global financial flows. Often, it was useful for certain agents or sectors, either public or private, to give in, adopt or use forms of marketisation so that many jurisdictions experienced a partial form of marketisation (Massoc & Benoit, 2023), even in sectors we would not necessarily expect, such as German public savings banks (Schwan, 2021).

Scholars have thus refocused their attention to examining how banks performed within the apparent growing importance of financial markets. This was a crucial question because the literature had previously relied on a broad-based consensus that the absence of markets was key to banks' power. But increasingly since the GFC, scholars found that market logics have impacted banks during financialisation: Instead of providing long-term loans and taking in deposits, banks buy and sell short-term securities in financial markets as a way of funding themselves and corporations, a fundamentally different way of credit provision to the economy. These financial innovations have been recognised as important to large-scale transformations originating in the US and their expansion into Europe (Gabor, 2016b; Konings, 2008; Thiemann, 2018). Banking is an important feature in understanding those issues because the shift away from deposit banking towards trading liabilities as a way of funding produced profound changes in finance (Knafo, 2022). Banks' business models have been associated with financial globalisation and crisis (Bell & Hindmoor, 2015; Gabor, 2015; Schenk, 2020), an important analytical update because prior to the GFC when financial globalisation was mostly seen as beneficial for global banks.

In response, scholars of political economy have advanced new concepts such as market-based banking (Hardie et al., 2013), market-based finance (Gabor, 2018; Mertens & Thiemann, 2018), shadow banking (Ban & Gabor, 2016; Nesvetailova, 2018; Pozsar et al., 2010) or deal-based finance (Deeg, 2012; Jackson & Deeg, 2012) to depict the fact that banks have marketised their own balance sheets and shifted away from their original purpose of long-term credit provision to the productive sector.

This shift has important implications for the stability and risk within the global financial architecture: As European banks do not have to assume the risk of holding long-term loans anymore, they can play with short-term value and speculative practices on capital markets, just like the US investment banks. While financialisation is associated with marketisation, banking is seen as the marketisation of banking practices, and banks turned into market-based banks (Hardie et al., 2013; Hardie & Howarth, 2013a).

What is surprising about this development is that European banks seem to be doing so much worse than US banks. If European banks became more market-based like US banks, why were US financial institutions not more affected by the GFC than their European counterparts? In the US, the shift from financing patient capital to market-based securities has all but increased the share of profits of financial institutions (Gibadullina, 2023). While Deutsche, Commerzbank and co. have had to significantly withdraw from their US activities, US banks have been striving, reaping profits above and beyond anyone else, not only in the US but also in Europe. In 2016, the top three banks in Europe in terms of investment banking revenues were US banks (Danielson, 2016, p. 9). London, still Europe's most important financial centre, depends on the European subsidiaries of Goldman Sachs, Morgan Stanley, JPMorgan, Bank of America and Citigroup – all US banks (ibid.). The big four US banks have left their European counterparts far behind (Danielson, 2016, p. 58). Apart from a brief interlude in the early 2000s, why have the biggest European banks fared so much worse than their US rivals in this market-based world? What is it about financialisation that has produced this outcome?

I argue that the difficulty in understanding the US Americanisation of finance stems from our inability to grasp the nature of financialisation. There is remarkably little historical inquiry into the significance of banks as major capitalist agents, the contributions of foreign agents to US-led financialisation and the corresponding mechanisms of US financial power. Beyond simply representing a gap of historical inquiry, I will show in Chapter 2 that this analytical problem stems from a limited understanding of the processes of financialisation as a qualitative change in the social relations of finance.

I agree with the sentiment that financialisation describes a large-scale transformation that has led to expanding and globalising financial markets, and that this process has deeply affected how banks, and anyone else for that matter, can navigate financial markets. But the outcome (expansion of markets) rarely sufficiently explains its driving mechanism.

Therefore, the chief aim of this book is to explain why and how that came to be, a question often assumed rather than explained. I ask *why* the expansion of global finance has been built predominantly around US financial practices, rather than acquiring any other potential characteristics. This is important because, firstly, history is unpredictable and complex. European banks have had many international relations and ambitions, financial globalisation could have gone a different way. This book thus examines why the banks adopted US financial practices, with all the difficulties involved, and, importantly, why those practices have had such a transformative impact.

Secondly, marketisation as a concept cannot account for the wide-reaching qualitative change of financialisation. In this spirit, I show that financial markets are nothing new in Germany. In Chapter 3, I use the example of the *Pfandbrief* (covered bond) to show that German housing finance has a long tradition of funding with market-based products, much more developed than the US market-based system. Chapter 4 reveals the German banks' global market-based practices on the Eurodollar markets in the 1960s and 1970s and argues that these were part and parcel of financing the post-WWII German political economy.

The significance of these early market-based practices for theorisations of financialisation is easy to miss if we continue to focus on German finance as a national bank-based system which transformed in response to external markets as a 'national variety'. Scholars rarely analyse how German banks have engaged with global financial markets *before* 1990s when their impact became no longer ignorable. As a result, political economy scholarship has largely overlooked both traditional domestic and early global market-based practices in their theorisations of banking and financialisation. This is because conceptualising US finance's impact as the rise of markets vis-à-vis social institutions makes it difficult to understand how specific market practices have affected banks differently and how, consequently, banks act *in* financial markets. As this book will show, rather than being bulwarks against markets, banks have historically attempted to use markets for their own ends.

How about recent analysis of banking since the GFC? While German banks' have been sidelined historically, scholarship since the GFC have investigated the interconnectedness of US and European balance sheets to decipher the outcomes of the Americanisation of finance. And yet, while the US and European banks' responsibility for the GFC is much debated, most political economy accounts rarely move beyond the banks' investment into speculative sub-prime mortgage-backed securities

(Bell & Hindmoor, 2015; Fligstein, 2021; Hardie & Howarth, 2013a) or their lobbying behaviour since (Hardie & Macartney, 2016; D. J. Howarth & James, 2023). Paradoxically, the scholarship portrays a tendency to read issues of finance as something tangential or external to the European banks. Curiously, therefore, scholarship working on the banks themselves locates the problems of banking as peripheral or external to the everyday business of the banks.

Representing this paradox is Tamin Bayoumi, currently deputy director at the IMF, and part of an influential group of scholars analysing how the changes in European banking led to the GFC, centring the instability of USD shadow banking between Europe and the US as a key cause (also compare Borio & Disyatat, 2011; R. McCauley, 2018; Thiemann, 2018; Tooze, 2018). Remarkable for an Economist, Bayoumi (2017) conceptualises the speculative investments of European banks prior to the 2008 crisis as a key socio-political problem rather than simply a 'market failure'. It was the European banks' speculative USD practices that made them the epicentre of the GFC. However, somewhat ironically, Bayoumi sees the problem of banking predominantly as a regulatory failure: policymakers failed to restrain or foresee the banks' USD funding bubble. Rather than looking for an internal banking dynamic, he identifies an external problem in which regulators lost against the markets. As a result, we continue to puzzle over why and how European banks brought themselves into a precarious position where a US sub-prime crisis could suddenly drain their funding channels.

The point here is not to argue that regulation does not matter. On the contrary, I will show that regulatory differences between Europe and the US were key to processes of financialisation. There is indeed much to gain from better regulated financial markets. For example, Thiemann (2018) demonstrates how global markets cannot exist without its regulators. Germany's experience of the GFC was much worse than France's because German regulators failed to regulate 'their' banks so that the German lenders shifted further towards speculative practices (Thiemann, 2012). However, the fact that European banks participated in US markets is rarely sufficiently problematised. Rather than searching the culprits in markets or regulation, we need a precise understanding of how financial innovations spread across the globe to establish why these banks participate in those processes. Leaving banks' practices, their motivations, and constraints untouched analytically and politically sidelines the very problem we need to tackle.

Moving beyond ideal types, national institutions, and markets is important because banks often behave counterintuitively to what we assume they would do. Political economists have shown that financial strategies have either pushed the limits of what seemed possible (Bryan et al., 2016; Wigan, 2010) or have spectacularly failed. These extremes do not necessarily create observable quantitative – or marketised – patterns but are nonetheless important for our understanding of financialisation. Recent developments would have traditionally been associated with being conducive to the European way of banking. We have seen an increase in deposit funding, a withdrawal from US and Eurodollar wholesale markets by the Europeans, as well as the return to a more European 'boring' type of banking away from 'markets'. As Bell and Hindmoor (2018) have shown, leverage has fallen across the spectrum of banks in 2015 compared to 2005[6] and so has income derived from non-interest sources. From traditional perspectives, this should usher in another period of European glory – or at least an avenue away from perennial problems. Why, then, are large European banks still in this mess?

To answer this question, the book foregrounds the practices of German banks as central to the making of financialisation and the uneven power relations that emerged with the rise of US finance as a key constraint to the banks' operations. I argue that only by juxtaposing both can we understand the transformative impact that US finance unleashed onto foreign agents. I propose to eschew functional understandings of banking and markets and to differentiate between specific forms of market-based finance so that we can start to identify more precisely the imperatives and constraints of US-led financialisation. This will open the analytical space to take banks seriously as the makers and gatekeepers of debt in a highly leveraged financial system. I thus aim to unpack the motivations and limitations of the German banks to build ever more precarious financial relations in their quest to catch up to US banks. Based on this alternative understanding of finance, the book provides a new account of financialisation outside the US.

EXTROVERTED FINANCIALISATION

The key argument of the book is that European banks underwent a unique process of EF. I propose this original concept to analyse the transformation of banking in response to the rise of US finance. More specifically, EF portrays the rise of US-style finance in Germany as an outcome of a major shift in the way US banks funded themselves from the 1960s onwards.

[6] Apart from ING Bank.

US banks began to use securities issued in US money markets as a systematic way of funding, which allowed them quicker access to larger amounts of funds so that they began to outcompete other banks in global markets. This strategy, called liability management (LM), imposed a novel imperative for non-US banks: gaining more USD debt. This forced the banks to partially uproot themselves from their home markets. In Chapter 4, I show how German banks went to the Eurodollar markets in Luxembourg and in London to respond to the new competitive advantages of US banks. But to operate in those markets they had to learn US-style finance to keep up with the US innovations. To properly learn and execute US financial practices, however, they had to gradually relocate key operations into the US, as I show in Chapters 5–7. This process was a key driving factor of the transformation of the nature of German banking. As I show in Chapter 8, despite attempts to keep US and German financial practices separate, German banks could not help but reform their whole business models according to the liquidity requirements of LM.

EF seeks to account for why banks outside the US have sought to adopt US practices and to establish themselves in US financial markets with the example of the two largest German universal banks, Deutsche Bank and Commerzbank. Rather than being a straightforward translation, these markets rested on fundamentally different financial institutions, practices and norms compared to German and European financial markets. As Chapter 2 will demonstrate, US banks have been developing their strategies organically alongside US financial institutions, but when US banks started to outcompete the Europeans in Europe, German banks had to find ways to bridge the differences. To compete with US banks, German banks had to partially uproot themselves from their home markets and gradually implement the practices of LM themselves. While financialisation was thus an active process shaped by the banks themselves, this process of extroversion was also a key constraint for the banks' practices as they had to reorient themselves towards US finance.

While this eventually allowed some of the European banks to reap phenomenal profits, EF foregrounds the problems encountered by financial agents who seek to imitate financial practices that have been developed in different contexts. In *extroverted* financialisation, the key imperatives for change came from foreign impulses, rather than domestic or internal ones. This process of translation was not easy, and as I will highlight throughout the book, non-US banks encountered many problems. Most importantly, and to the banks' dismay, adopting LM was incompatible with their traditional financial practices. Outside a brief successful period in the 2000s prior to the GFC, the banks' actions resulted into the inherently contradictory and devastating nature of banking and of the global financial architecture as a whole.

I maintain that the problems and tensions of translation are more revealing about the imperatives of financialisation than potential profits or the general increase of financial markets. The currency gap between the dollar and, for example, the euro, the pound, or Swiss franc, is an obvious difference. More important, however, was the fact that European banks had to learn a new way of banking and they must do so within an institutional context that was not conducive to their traditional financial practices, as I will show in detail throughout the book. As a result, much of their financial innovations was geared towards overcoming those hurdles to catch up to US banks that were exploiting financial transformations much more easily. While few people disagree with the claim that something has gone wrong on global financial markets during the last decade, we have come to accept multinational corporations as profit-seeking entities that seem to benefit from globalisation and somehow always win. Powerful agents' problems are seldomly incorporated in our conceptualisations of financialisation. Not negating that some banks and traders have made millions and billions in the process, I show how the German banks' challenges and tensions during EF offer a useful window into the power relations and contradictions of the global financial architecture.

I foreground banks' practices to make the transformations and contradictions of financialisation visible. To this end, I deploy a balance sheet analysis and descriptive statistics. However, while many banking practices are written onto banks' balance sheets, this type of analysis is of limited use in studying financialisation beyond assessing the marketisation of banks' loans because it cannot capture (a) qualitative change, (b) attempted but failed strategies, and (c) banking practices that happen offshore and thus outside banks' balance sheets. Indeed, history does not easily present itself in data, ready for us to read or calculate. Offshore is notoriously difficult to come by (Binder, 2023) and banks commonly prefer to act in secret (Wixforth, 2017). The Eurodollar markets – the biggest offshore financial markets – escape official statistics; scholars of the Bank for International Settlement estimate USD 10.7 trillion 'missing' USD (Borio et al., 2017), and studies on Eurodollar markets regularly issue a notion of caution because of data limitations (McCauley et al., 2015).

Thus, tracing the problems of finance, and banks' responses to them, is somewhat difficult. I circumvent this lack of data by combining a varied mix of academic scholarship, the banks' own publications, specialised financial news articles, in addition to balance sheet analysis, as well as official governmental and monetary authorities' reports. These provide comprehensive material to gather and triangulate publicly available data about banks' strategies and the social relations of finance. Revisiting historical academic analysis and previously unused journalistic and expert practitioner accounts is a valuable resource in grasping the problems the financial world faced at times of their writing and what the banks themselves deemed as problems and solutions at that time. This is a new window into the practices of banks, as these issues are often different from what we now theorise about them from a contemporary perspective. Juxtaposed with critical political economy scholarship, these insights have allowed me to reinterpret the history of financialisation from the German banks' perspective. This, I argue, offers a new methodology for studying corporate business models as sites of financialisation.

This history has led me to develop larger theoretical claims and the concept of EF makes four interventions in how we understand the financialisation of European banks: As part of a growing group of scholars emphasising the importance of LM (Beck & Knafo, 2020; Dutta, 2020; Knafo, 2022) and leverage (Baines & Hager, 2021; Sgambati, 2019) for financialisation, firstly, EF underscores that financialisation is foremost driven by LM – a funding practice developed in the 1960s in New York that revolutionised funding and caused significant problems for banks' traditional strategies of funding with deposits. EF secondly draws attention to the fact that this shift in funding methods (as US banks started to expand into Europe via the Eurodollar markets) implied a shift in the dollar's role for non-US banks. The book shows how this was a key prompt for a change in traditional banking practices towards extroverted strategies that were geared towards foreign markets and, therefore, finding novel methods of USD acquisition. Thirdly, the concept accounts for the influence of institutions that organise financial markets and enable the practices of LM and leverage. US money markets uniquely accommodate practices of LM to which German banks had to adapt if they wanted to participate in global financial markets. Originally, LM could only be developed in the US, as European money and capital markets were not suitable to the fast-paced requirements of LM. And finally, EF reads global finance's capacity for crises as substantial internal and external contradictions caused by the managerial and operational changes that LM implied for banks operating from the periphery to US money markets.

Using EF, the book throws new light on how the macro-processes of US-led financialisation interact with the micro-processes of Deutsche's and

Commerzbanks' business models. German banks operate from a peripheral position to US financial markets, and overcoming this outsider position was a key driver for their financial innovations since the 1960s. This history shows that they have been much more international than hitherto recognised and, therefore, have been key contributors to financialisation, if from a peripheral position. By key contributors, I mean that they actively responded to the imperatives of LM and thereby forged new financial relations in on - and offshore USD markets. While they intentionally tried to empower themselves within these new competitive pressures, the banks did not deliberately create the conditions for their own demise. Chapter 7 shows Commerzbank as attempting to perform a half transformation to avoid losing control of its 'European' business. Chapter 8 highlights how unlikely it was initially for Deutsche to transform so thoroughly. But aiming to successfully take advantage of US money markets, it could not help but to integrate the practices of LM, which deformed its German financial practices. US banks on their part did not consciously suck European banks into this new way of banking. They, too, reacted to the rise of US money markets in the 1960s, a development initially not of their own making. But they subsequently discovered the power of LM, a global competitive advantage few escaped. No one could have known how deeply this would affect the financial world in the following decades.

EF thus frames financialisation as a long-term transatlantic historical process. I locate the start of financialisation before the fall of Bretton Woods in the early 1970s, before large-scale initiatives of financial liberalisation in the 1980s, and before the 1990s or 2000s, decades that are commonly seen as the cornerstones of financialisation in Europe and in banking. I do not dismiss these transformative moments, but key dynamics of financialisation go amiss if we limit ourselves to that periodisation. This rethinking of financialisation and its inherent contradictions is, so is my hope, my analytical contribution to start thinking about a more fundamental way forward to an alternative financial future.

The book joins a growing political economy scholarship that foregrounds power relations and financial claims in offshore and onshore markets (Braun & Koddenbrock, 2023). From that perspective, the politics of finance are located within financial relationships themselves, rather than relegated to issues of governance, (de-)regulation or macroeconomic recycling mechanisms. Based on EF's re-conceptualisation of financialisation, this book advances the theoretical claim that financialised market power rests on agents' ability to use LM to leverage USDs. The book thus portrays financial markets as uneven institutions that are made and remade as banks compete over resources. Financial agents outside the US therefore operate from a peripheral position and must deal with uneven power relations that benefit US banks. This is a necessary theoretical reorientation to specify the imperatives of financialisation in global markets, and to make it traceable from the perspective of key financial conglomerates.

It is vital to note that while uneven global financial markets might appear as solid structures, they have historically developed. I show in Chapter 2 that the structural constraints that drove European banks to adopt US-style finance, the reasons for foreign banks' systemic reliance on USD liabilities, and, consequently, the rising structural power of US finance developed from the fundamental changes in US funding practices that are traceable back to the 1960s' rise of US money markets that led US banks to develop LM. Importantly, the history presented in this book shows financialisation as a process of the unintended consequences the German banks' attempts and failures to empower themselves. The concept of EF, then, emerges as an analytical tool to frame US-led financialisation so we can trace how changes in financial practices can result into a large-scale structural transformation. These have allowed some financial agents to exploit financial markets to no end while it had devastating outcomes for all those who must live with finance's influence in our social and economic lives.

SYNOPSIS

The book is divided into two parts and nine chapters. The first part of the book revisits and revises common historical and theoretical accounts of (German) banking and finance. Chapter 2 takes up the preceding discussion by debunking three myths that dominate political economy accounts of financialisation: (a) that financialisation is best understood as a process of marketisation; (b) that financial systems transform in response to external drivers (i.e., liberalisation) as 'national varieties' conceptually outside the global economy, rather than as embedded within it; and (c) that German finance is best conceptualised as a bank-based system which transformed into a hybrid from the 1990s onwards. I show how the concept of marketisation captures the expansion of markets but struggles to identify fundamental transformations within markets. As a result, political economy scholars rarely study banks in their own rights and underestimate the power and weaknesses of banks as agents of financialisation.

Instead, I propose an alternative reading of financialisation. I provide a recalibration of banking which zooms in on the rise of LM in the 1960s as a central origin of processes of financialisation. I document how the practices of LM arose out of the restricted financial system in the US but allowed US banks to increase their power almost unhinged. Building on this historical reorientation, I outline the concept of EF, which frames the analysis of the book. EF has four features that each represent a new imperative for European banks: (a) the rise of LM; (b) the need for USD; (c) the institutional specificity of US money markets; and (d) the contradictions of contemporary banking. This chapter thus provides the key theoretical building blocks and explains how focusing on financial practices allowed me to conceptualise the response of European banks to the rise of LM as EF.

Chapter 3 starts the recalibration of banking by telling an alternative history of German banking. We cannot assess change if we do not understand its origins. Therefore, this chapter zooms in on the struggles over deposits to provide the historical and institutional backdrop of German finance. This will allow the reader to appreciate the key differences and overlaps in US and German financial markets, and to understand those financial developments that set them apart from the 1960s onwards. I go back to the nineteenth century to examine the development of the *Pfandbrief* (covered bond) to establish that market-based funding practices have a long history in Germany. After the devastation of the Seven Years' War (1756–1763), banks and the state (the Prussian price and its gentry) together sought new ways to boost lending and borrowing with the help of financial securities and collateral. This history challenges a core assumption about German finance: that there is a distinct dichotomy between market-based and bank-based finance. In fact, German housing finance was historically much more market-based than in the US.

The *Pfandbrief* has been a key financial security promoting long-term lending and relationship banking. To understand its significance in the story of financialisation, however, I differentiate between financial agents: The *Pfandbrief* was predominantly used by specialised mortgage banks and public savings banks. Universal banks only entered the fray in the 1970s, at a time when their corporate deposits declined. This chapter thus locates the origin of financialisation within a more precise historical context: German banks' strategies were geared towards market-based practices, but different ones to those that emerged in the US with the rise of LM. While US banks turned to US money markets to compensate the drop in liabilities, German banks tried *Pfandbriefe*. Contrasting covered bonds with

US mortgage-backed securities, I underscore that not all market-based practices necessarily lead to processes of financialisation. This historical grounding allows me to specify the precise imperatives and constraints of financialisation and thus to better understand the impact of US finance.

Doing just that, Chapter 4 situates the beginnings of EF at the time when US banks started to build the Eurodollar markets from the 1960s onwards. The Euromarkets are an important turning point for financialisation but their impacts on European banking are rarely examined. During this global rise of US finance, German banks had their first contact with the new US innovations. While Chapter 3 revisits a very early domestic financial history, this chapter examines the links of the German post-WWII reconstruction era with global markets. These connections reveal a vital impact of US funding practices on German financial strategies very early on, and significantly before the 1990s when many accounts date the impact of globalisation. Instead, I argue that the making of the German CME was already bound up with global financial markets.

The reason was that Germany's financial architecture was ill-equipped to fund the growing export sector. Public support for corporate governance was geared towards promoting the export sector, wage restraint and *domestic* capital markets. As a result, domestic funding was available but German banks lacked USD to lend to internationalising corporations. This was an important internal push factor for the large banks to seek USD in foreign markets. US banks aggravated this shortcoming with their competitive advantages through the practices of LM. The European banks attempted to pose a counter-strategy against the US takeover of their corporate loans: joint European bourses. However, due to different strategic interests amongst the French, Swiss and German banks, this strategy did not materialise. Instead, European banks grudgingly embraced Eurodollars to catch up to US banks and tried another strategy: club banking in Luxemburg. They joined resources to expand their leverage and split the risk involved in these unknown markets. Despite initial successes, however, a more radical change in strategies – rather than simply pooling – was needed to keep up with US banks. European banks had to shift to London – the US financial innovation channel – to embrace US financial practices more comprehensively. Through this history, I argue that the transformative impact of US finance is not market expansion or regulatory evasion through offshore per se. Instead, financialisation has posed distinct imperatives in relation to LM that induced a *qualitative* change as LM fundamentally differs from previous international strategies, and started to require a relocation of banks' key operations.

Having established a different understanding of US finance and its initial global impact, the second part of the book traces how German banks attempted to adjust to the rise of LM. I use the concept of EF to explain why banking turned out to be a specifically US form of banking – an outcome that is well-recognised in political economy, but without its causes being historically interrogated outside the marketisation thesis. I call this form of banking 'financialised banking' to stress the difference between previous forms.[7] Zooming in on Deutsche Bank and Commerzbank, this part reveals the rise and fall of the German banks by tracking their aims and the problems they encountered in transforming towards financialised banking. Part II thus exposes the ways in which the micro processes of changing business models can produce the macro process of financialisation.

Chapter 5 lays out the institutional grounding for global financial markets and their currency, the USD. This provides an answer to an ongoing puzzle on the origins of the 2008 financial crisis. Scholars of the 'global banking glut hypothesis' recognise *that* European banks were deeply connected to US finance but do not fully account for *why* this was the case. By contrast, I demonstrate that, despite their global nature, US and Eurodollars are still thoroughly grounded in US financial institutions.

The connections between New York and the Eurodollar markets gave US banks an additional competitive edge over other banks. The complex institutional infrastructure made US financial markets exceptionally deep and liquid so that US banks could flexibly fund their practices and arbitrage between both markets. US money markets were a rare financial resource at the time allowing US banks to tap endless USD, a key reason why LM was uniquely suitable to US markets. By contrast, European banks faced heavy restrictions on international capital flows and foreign entry from policymakers until the 1970s. This posed a key constraint to the international practices of the European banks. Instead, German banks had to expand their offshore USD funding practices.

Chapter 6 delves into the heart of Deutsche Bank's transformation towards a US investment bank by situating the changes of its business model within its play of catch with US banks. To compete in Eurodollar

[7] When scholars talk about agents or relationships to be 'financialised', they often mean that financial markets have come to affect something that was previously disconnected from financial markets. From that perspective, financialised banking might sound like a paradox because banks have always been financial agents and were deeply enmeshed with financial markets. I use the term financialised banking to emphasise how financial agents themselves have changed during financialisation.

markets, German banks had to find a way to access US financial markets beyond their offshore networks in Luxemburg and London, and thereby institutionalise their connections to US money markets. The attempts to adopt LM thus drove Deutsche's partial uprooting from its home markets to relocate to the US. This challenges the dominant narrative of a US imposition, instead recognising that the trajectory of change was driven by Deutsche's strategies of extroversion. Tracing the specific changes of Deutsche's foreign acquisitions and US financial strategies on US money markets, I demonstrate how Deutsche progressively had to change its traditional practices to accommodate the imperatives of LM. This transformation went from a change in funding strategies to acquire more USD to the subsequent adaptations on its asset side – from corporate loans to US residential mortgage-backed (or 'toxic') securities. This chapter thus presents Deutsche's move away from the centre of Germany Inc. towards a US investment bank as an outcome of its progressive institutionalisation in the US.

Chapter 7 traces Commerzbank's trajectory of financialisation to highlight how its strategies with respect to LM differed from those of Deutsche Bank. Commerzbank is a less-likely actor of financialisation as it is a smaller bank and has historically focused on the European SME sector. While all major German and European banks were impacted by imperatives and constraints originating from the US, and therefore transformed their banking strategies by acquiring British or US financial institutions and traders, they did so in different ways. In contrast to Deutsche, Commerzbank attempted a transformation without major relocation, and redirected fewer resources to its extroverted strategies. While it established the first German foreign branch in the US in 1971, it never bought a major US or British institution.

Commerzbank's more hesitant approach meant that the bank failed to uphold itself in US money markets several times. While Commerzbank initially also expanded to London in the 1970s and 1980s, it subsequently spent fewer resources to advance its USD wholesale integration. Its renewed attempts in the 2000s failed, and Commerzbank's significant immersion happened during the GFC when, ironically, it bought another German not US bank. It purchased the larger Dresdner Bank during the 2008 financial crisis but could not manage Dresdner's heavy investment into USresidential mortgage-backed securities (RMBS), eventually resulting in a public bailout. Commerzbank's story is different from that of Deutsche, demonstrating that the rise of US finance made LM a significant but differentiated concern for non-US banks.

Chapter 8 reemphasises that the transition to financialised banking was no easy shift and only saw huge profits for a limited amount of time for European banks – at least if compared to US banks. I document the problems and contradictions that banks experienced internally and externally. I thus lay out the reasons for why I think the transition to LM is better understood as a necessity to accommodate the higher costs, risks and logics of banking in US money markets, rather than a straightforward shift towards higher profits compelled by securities markets. To emphasise how unlikely it was initially for Deutsche to transform so thoroughly towards LM, I trace the resistance of Deutsche's own bankers towards the new practices in the 1990s and early 2000s, which they saw as a loss of their traditional power and autonomy over banking practices. Nonetheless, it took the financial calamity of 2008 to propel a rethinking of Deutsche's path.

And yet, financialised banking is not easily reversed. I underscore this argument by tracing the German banks' efforts to get out of their malaise. Since the GFC, German banks have been struggling because German banking is now caught between two opposing logics – German patient capital and LM – within neither of which German banks seem to be able to (re-) gain strengths. Having built expensive USD funding networks and a significant of USD-denominated assets in their books, they must sustain their USD needs as well as accommodate their costs. As such, regulators and analysts alike would be well advised not only to worry about banks' funding gap, the gap between (bank-based) deposits and market-based securities to refinance their assets, a common worry that replicates the trope of opposing banks to markets. Instead, emphasising the history of EF, I show how the *USD* funding gap (the gap between EUR as home currency and USD as foreign currency) is a key source of vulnerability and risk. At the same time, some US banks have excelled in mastering LM so that, for them, the ability to flexibly (mis-) match their assets with US money market funding is a source of power and strength. This chapter thus underlines how the unevenness of an LM-centred global financial architecture has only been entrenched by the Europeans' extroverted strategies. It is for this reason that recent attempts to build 'national champions' either as proactive or rescue merger fail to yield their geopolitical promises of strong global banks regaining control over global markets. What regulators and analysts alike have missed is that the key to global market power is not the size of balance sheet per se, but the banks' capacity to leverage beyond ends by exploiting large, deep and flexible pools of capital, something only USD wholesale markets can currently supply, and LM can exploit.

The conclusion summarises the book and further reflects on what is at stake in reconceptualising the transformation of European banking as EF. I contemplate other recent financial endeavours to 'improve' our global financial architecture and find them – unsurprisingly given the history I outlined here – somewhat lacking in their ability to introduce a global financial system that serves social rather than financial ends. In fact, missing the implications of EF, some of these endeavours have the potential to worsen, rather than improve, the threats of credit crunches and crises. Alternatively, we might be better off to contemplate more radical solutions that tackle the very nature of USD credit creation and the financial architecture itself.

2

Extroverted Financialisation

A Political Economy of Global Finance

INTRODUCTION

'Financialisation is marketization!' (Godechot, 2016). Few scholars working on the question of how financialisation has impacted contemporary capitalism would disagree with this statement, even if it is rarely exclaimed with such force or explicitness. The phrase describes a near consensus about one of the key transformations of financialisation: the phenomenal rise of financial markets since the 1980s. International capital flows, trends of liberalisation and privatisation, and technological advances have led to the fact that financial markets grew out of proportion compared to the 'real economy' on which they were previously based. Definitions usually involve the growing importance of financial markets for non-financial entities, including households, states and corporations, and their deep effects on the inner working of our industrial and digital economy, on everyday life and our democratic society (cf. Epstein, 2005; Van der Zwan, 2014). Another important aspect of financialisation is that profits increasingly accrue through financial channels rather than production or trade (Krippner 2005).

The origins of these financial phenomena are often located in the US, and the debate on the US Americanisation of global finance is rich. Particularly since the GFC, scholars have shifted towards assessing the impact of US finance outside the US, and US financial innovations have been recognised as deeply impacting Europe (Gabor, 2016b; Konings, 2008; Thiemann, 2018; Wansleben, 2023). In particular, the shift from long-term finance for productive and social purposes to short-term financial logics associated with speculative activity has captured the attention of scholars.

Germany is often seen as having followed this trend since the 1990s. Banks in particular are often seen as quintessential agents in these shifts because they used to be bulwarks against the vagaries of speculators, issuing long-term loans to the productive sector, rather than engage in proprietary trading for their own benefits (Hardie et al., 2013; Hardie & Howarth, 2013b). Banking is indeed an important feature in understanding these issues because the shift in funding from deposits towards trading liabilities produced profound changes in global financial markets (Knafo, 2022). Banks' business models have been associated with financial globalisation and crisis (Bell & Hindmoor, 2015; Gabor, 2015; Schenk, 2020) – an important analytical update since, prior to the GFC, financial globalisation was often seen as beneficial for global banks.

While US and European banks' responsibility for the GFC is much debated, most political economy accounts employ a limited historical horizon and rarely move beyond the banks' investment into speculative sub-prime mortgage-backed securities in the 2000s (Bell & Hindmoor, 2015; Fligstein, 2021; Hardie & Howarth, 2013a) or their lobbying behaviour since (Hardie & Macartney, 2016; Howarth & James, 2023). Early processes of financialisation are seldom considered, and German banks' key contribution to global offshore markets remains obscure. As a result, the scholarship tends to read issues of finance as something tangential or external to European banks, and not something they have co-produced. Because the sub-prime mortgage industry has collapsed since the GFC, the 2008 crisis is seen as an *exception* to the banks' strategies of financialisation (Fligstein, 2021; Fligstein & Habinek, 2014). Rather than representing an outcome of the fundamental changes that financial relations have undergone in the past decades, the mortgage bubble is often presented as excessive speculation that eventually had to realign itself with 'normal' economic foundations, in part evidenced by the recent decline of the European lenders' US investment banking activities.

In this chapter, I argue that the tendency to sideline banks' practices is an outcome of reading financialisation as a process of marketisation. By contrast, the central argument of my book is that German financialisation is better conceived as a process of extroverted financialisation (EF). As Chapter 3 will show, market-based practices have a long history in Germany and are therefore insufficient as a signifier of financialisation. Instead, key to the US Americanisation of German finance has been a process of internationalisation that forced banks to relocate strategic resources into global and US markets to catch up with US banks. But because scholars have mostly sidelined the role of European banks in processes of financialisation, they have underestimated the impact of new funding practices originating in US money markets in the 1960s, which triggered financialisation much earlier and in a different way than usually assumed.

This chapter is divided into three sections. The next section introduces what came to be known as the differences between the German and US financial system and sympathetically critiques the marketisation of finance hypothesis. I examine five key theoretical innovations through which political economists made sense of the complex transformations of financialisation. I show that despite efforts to overcome the binary of market-based versus bank-based systems, it still dominates current conceptualisations of finance and banking. For an alternative conception, the second section establishes a specific funding practice, called liability management (LM), as defining feature of the rise of US finance. Section three introduces the concept of EF that seeks to capture the precise imperatives of US-led financialisation, constraints that the marketisation metaphor is ill-equipped to capture.

THE MARKETISATION OF FINANCE HYPOTHESIS

Financialisation describes a recent period of capitalism during which financial markets gained dominance over other areas of socio-economic life (Van der Zwan, 2014). There is widespread consensus that this transformation originated in the US but has turned into a global phenomenon with differentiated effects. The question of how much US finance has impacted everywhere else is often linked to marketisation (Callaghan, 2018; Godechot, 2016; Hardie & Howarth, 2013b), even as scholars differ in their theoretical dispositions and areas of focus. From that perspective, the question has been about to what extent US financial markets have replaced banks as primary financier of non-financial corporations (NFCs) and how far their actions have become market-based (Hardie, Howarth, et al., 2013; Maxfield et al., 2017).

As I will show, the idea of marketisation usually rests on at least one of the three following theoretical assumptions. Firstly, scholars see this process as a US imposition, often implying that something like a 'US financial disease' has infected German financial institutions with its market logics, so that German banks have become more like US banks. From that perspective, scholars see the original German system as bank-based, with market-based practices and speculation playing little role. Before the US disease, German lending was seen as characterised by more 'social', non-market aspects. Patient capital, a long-term credit relation between banks and companies, was based on insider information to monitor firm performance, which allowed banks to have a voice in corporate decision-making processes. This is often portrayed in stark contrast to the US system in which firms fund themselves on capital markets, rather than via banks. There, market logics would determine capital allocation because credit relations were 'transactional' rather than 'relational'.

Secondly, the notion of marketisation often implies that banks are financial intermediaries that lost out during financialisation. Banking is theoretically contrasted with financial markets. From that perspective, scholars often characterise the role of German banks based on their lending activities vis-à-vis corporations, rather than on what they do in financial markets. Banks are often conceptualised as financial conduits, passing on liquidity from savers (including institutional investors) to their corporate clients for long-term productive investment. When firms started to raise funds in financial markets, banks lost the voice they had in companies and therefore ceased to provide patient capital. From this perspective, the marketisation of lending practices dissolved the power of German banks as they could no longer influence corporations and instead became subject to market forces.

The third feature concerns the reasons why banks would pursue this shift. The explanation given is that market-based practices offer higher profits compared to the traditional long-term financial practices of German banks. Scholars either foreground the dissolution of institutions and restrictions that had previously prevented banks from following their global ambitions or the fact that the banks' clients would seek funds in capital markets and thereby eradicated their previously profitable lending business. From either perspective, German banks became more like US investment banks because they pursue a strategy of maximising profits in global financial markets.

While there has been a rich debate over the diverse impact of financialisation on Germany, notions of marketisation offer weak conceptual tools to understand the role of banking within this process and its nature. Firstly, conceptually opposing financial markets and banks makes it difficult to grasp how banks act within financial markets. As a result, political economists have largely overlooked traditional and global market-based practices in their theorisations of German finance prior to financialisation. This means that they have overemphasised market-based practices as a novel imperative. By contrast, Chapter 3 shows that market-based banking (MBB) has a long tradition in Germany, and cannot therefore act as a catalyst of financialisation. Chapter 4 shows how global financial practices have been a crucial part of the rise, rather than demise, of the German post-war economy. As such, rather than representing a US disease, financialisation has been actively contributed to by German banks.

Secondly, and consequently, the idea of marketisation cannot account for the qualitative shift of financialisation. If this transformation was about German banks becoming more like US banks and making more profits with market-based practices, why are they currently struggling so much more than US banks? Political economists have ignored the novel imperatives and constraints that the rise of US finance has imposed on others from the 1960s onwards and therefore underestimated the profoundness of the transformation of financial practices. From that perspective, it was not the profit lure in the 1990s that drove non-US banks to transform towards US finance, but the necessity to compete with US banks in the Eurodollar markets since the 1960s. Taking into consideration these imperatives, global financial markets become deeply uneven socio-financial institutions that cannot be captured with the concept of marketisation. As the following chapters will show, it was this unevenness that shaped how German banks conducted their international financial strategies.

Markets, Social Institutions and Ideal Types: Divergence or Convergence?

Looking at the origins of conceptualisations of German and US ideal types, John Zysman (1983) has been an influential voice in the academic project to establish a relation between the structures of bank-based and market-based finance and processes of institutional change. His analysis of the different financial systems and the politics of industrial change put in place the conceptual opposition of banks and markets that scholars have found difficult to bridge since. Tracing how different countries respond to external impacts such as financial globalisation, he argues that national systems transform in a way that closely resembles how certain economic interest groups can mobilise financial structure to influence change. Writing at a time when financial globalisation was only in its beginnings, Zysman strongly suggests that national financial systems will remain divergent.

Zysman's work is part of the scholarship that aims to understand the institutional complexity of different economic models, their historical developments and how they led to socio-economic benefits. His typologies reflect a long-standing academic endeavour of rejecting the simplicity of mainstream economic analysis that relied on one-path-fits-all understandings of the economy, such as Rostow's modernisation theory. Relying on authors such as Hilferding (1981 [1910]), Gerschenkron (1962) and Shonfield (1965), Zysman was writing at a time when Japan and Germany were often singled out as better market economies than the US after the decline in Fordism. Their analysis rebuked the idea that the US and its free market approach was the only viable option. Instead, Germany's prosperous economic model was 'coordinated' by institutions and was consensus-seeking rather than 'liberal'.

Zysman was interested in how economic models were structured to finance industrial activity. The binary between bank-based and market-based systems reflected the relative importance of banks and financial markets in providing funding for corporations. The German system was characterised as a 'tutelary banking system' (Zysman, 1983, p. 252), where banks are central to and deeply involved in industrial matters, providing long-term loans to corporations. This is in contrast to a market-based system where firms raise short-term funds in financial markets (cf. Streeck, 2010).

In Zysman's account, the power of banks lies in their capacity to monopolise the issuance and management of corporate debt (Zysman, 1983, p. 264). Equity and bond markets are dominated by banks that hold large shareholdings, while securities markets are limited in size so that corporations have little choice but to get their funding from banks. Banks also assert their voice in corporate decisions via several channels. They have a disproportionate amount of voting rights during annual corporate meetings because of 'proxy votes' through which they represent shareholders who deposit their shares with them. Bankers also sit on supervisory boards of the largest companies. Extensive deposit bases provide banks with a stable source of funding, allowing them to fully concentrate on their assets and influence in corporate governance.

By contrast, the power of exit is not available for German banks. German banking is very competitive and less concentrated than other financial systems. Competition for the big three universal banks, Commerzbank, Dresdner Bank and Deutsche Bank, came from a large network of regional banks (public savings banks and cooperatives) that had public support and regional connections and expertise. Thus, while the power lies with banks, 'no single bank can exercise power by denying a client access to finance' (Zysman, 1983, p. 263).

By contrast, US banks have very limited power vis-à-vis corporations because of strong US securities markets so that 'power is diffused into the market' (Zysman, 1983, p. 269). Access to securities markets is provided by nonbank intermediaries, including brokering houses and large institutional investors such as pension funds. Commercial banks primarily provide short-term industrial finance relying on short-term deposits, because they do not want to commit to long-term support. Legal rules for equity holdings further limit bank intervention (their voice) in corporate affairs, they cannot hold influential amounts of equity. In lieu of personal networks and insider information, financial institutions rely on external 'objective' factors (Zysman, 1983, p. 269), such as market prices, to monitor their assets' performance; they use the power of exit if these performance indicators do not match their expectations. Because of the high level of competition for corporate finance, funding markets are more 'perfect' and more 'efficient' (Zysman, 1983, p. 270), allegedly preventing financial actors from being able to monopolise credit conditions and set distorted prices, compared to the German model.

A decade after Zysman's writing, these stark differences were increasingly questioned. A flagging German financial sector, a stagnating economy and accelerating global financial innovation made scholars sceptical that Germany could withstand the impact of markets. Globalising securities markets seemed to draw banks, financial regulation and corporations into their orbit and US market forces were more transformative than originally thought. German economic and political authorities embarked on the promotion of securities markets and financial liberalisation in Germany – labelled 'Finanzplatz Deutschland'[1] – to adjust to the growing market pressures of US finance. Scholars began to wonder if the expansion of US finance would lead to global convergence after all (Beyer & Hassel, 2002; Lütz, 2000, 2005b).

Yet, as I will show later, the ideal-typical distinction between banks (Germany) and markets (US) have made it difficult to conceptualise the influence one might have on the other, beyond the binary of convergence or divergence. While opposition is useful to highlight differences, it hinders the analysis of change outside that structural binary. One key problem has been the type of difference that Zysman (building on others) established between decentralised US financial markets and German socially organised financial institutions. While his typology has long been criticised as too coherent (cf. Hardie et al., 2011), scholars aiming to bridge the divide were often left with few analytical devices to track the impact of US finance

1 Many European countries had similar initiatives, for example, the Netherlands (cf. van Meeteren & Bassens, 2019).

outside the understanding of convergence. Instead, scholars have searched for general evidence of 'more markets' to assess how much Germany became financialised. But the more market-based practices arrived in Germany, the less authors paid attention to the changing practices of banks.

The Marketisation of Social Institutions: Capitalist Convergence

With the rise of global liberalisation, multinational conglomerates and transnational capital flows, scholars have argued that national boundaries became more porous than Zysman's typology would allow. Instead, the economy is best conceptualised as a global market that has submerged previous national coordinates, questioning the basic assumption that they were ever as important as Zysman made them out to be. Exemplary for this case is Wolfgang Streeck (2009, 2011, 2014, 2016), who has argued that divergence was a myth, a momentary snapshot in time, while institutional change is gradual and endemic, bringing out the internal capitalist drive to move beyond national barriers. Looking at internal change, Streeck turns Zysman around, arguing that Germany is, in fact, a great example of the unifying force of the capitalist logic instead of proving persistent difference.

For Streeck, the driving force for marketisation is not so much the external impact of US finance on static national regimes, but rather the logics of capitalism inherent in those national systems. Streeck shows how Germany was, in fact, one of the most internationalised economies in the 1960s (Streeck, 2009, p. 187f). It did not exclude global financial markets, but German institutions forced actors operating upon them, such as banks, to share the corresponding profits equally amongst 'Germany Inc'[2] and to mutually take responsibility for overall economic wellbeing and equality.[3] Corporate actors had to make compromises – such as accepting lower profits and workers' rights in exchange for institutional support for stable business and protection from international competition (Streeck, 2009, p. 189f). Germany's institutional logic embedded actors in consensus-seeking processes that contained the capitalist drive to maximise profits.

2 'Germany Inc' ('Deutschland AG') is often used to describe the tightly knit network of German corporations and banks that sometimes are seen to work in unity and 'harmony'. Corporations are interlinked in an expansive criss-cross of shareholdings, personnel and insider information, including institutional channels for workers' unions (Thelen, 2014).

3 See Melinda Cooper (2017) for an excellent feminist critique of how this 'equality' was quite male-centred.

However, with the globalisation of US financial markets, it became increasingly difficult for states to contain the interests of private capital. Financial actors were only institutionally embedded for so long as institutions were able to force them to be. Decreasing public resources due to declining revenues and higher unemployment after the decline of Fordism (and later German unification) made it increasingly difficult for the state to mobilise enough resources to ensure the corporative class compromise in Germany. Growing public debt empowered German investors, which made it easier for them to push for their own interests. This enabled them to successfully demand financial liberalisation, in other words, the dismantling of their institutional shackles.

Growing global financial markets changed the interplay of forces because German banks could use them as exit strategies. Now equipped with market power, banks escaped the tutelage, pulling their capital into global markets and joining their more profitable US counterparts. Change, for Streeck, is thus a historical process in which the forces of free markets reveal themselves across the globe when states can no longer contain them because of economic stagnation. As the US represented the closest version of a 'free market' economy, the process started from there. And because German finance used to operate on different logics, its marketisation offers, for Streeck, proof that the process denationalises economies (Streeck, 2009, pp. 225–226). 'Marktvolk' now trumps 'Staatsvolk' (Streeck, 2014, 2016) and threatens democracy as a whole. In that sense, financialisation is a global process in which the logics of capitalism, rather than specifically US finance, impose their imprint on the previously more social German system.

For Streeck, capitalist actors are underspecified 'analytical carriers' of power relations (Freye, 2015, p. 408) and he does not examine how markets can empower some actors over others. Difference and unevenness within markets, so important in Streeck's earlier work, do not carry explanatory power. Streeck thus displays a common tension in the literature: While German banks seem to be core actors in this process and somehow interested in global markets (cf. Beyer, 2003; Lane, 2003; Streeck & Höpner, 2003), their role is too often underspecified and banking practices rarely closely examined. By contrast, taking banks' practices into account, I show that German banks have in fact struggled with the expansion of global securities markets. While the GFC is often seen as a defining moment highlighting the great extent of capitalist convergence, in Chapter 8 I show how the GFC rather represents a turning point of the great crisis of German banks while some US banks once again surge in power. While for Streeck all capitalists hold power over non-market agents, I argue throughout the book that the unevenness of global financial markets has been a defining factor of financialisation.

The Marketisation of Corporate Control

The rise of shareholder value (SHV) and the transformation of non-financial firms have been debated as a key frontier of financialisation (Aglietta, 2000; Froud et al., 2000; cf. Höpner & Jackson, 2006; Stockhammer et al., 2021).[4] As such, scholars identified a similar trend of growing market power to Streeck since the 1980s, but this literature has also identified specific social agents that mobilise their resources to influence – but not necessarily overdetermine – social and economic outcomes. Scholars have wrestled with the question of how shareholders as capital givers have influenced and transformed the 'real' economy towards financial logics. Scholars have discussed to what extent the 'shareholder revolution' – the rise of equity firms, venture capitalists and other financial investors – has restructured corporate governance (and the real economy as a whole) in a way that prioritises investor pay out over industrial or social developments (Lazonick & O'Sullivan, 1997; Mazzucato, 2019; Orhangazi, 2008). The more firms depend on external capital, the more shareholders can direct corporate decisions towards prioritising short-term financial motives, such as SHV, over long-term investments. There is a rich debate about how shareholders (and which ones) have been able to do that, but the general process is described as marketisation that allowed financial investors to take over corporate control (Callaghan, 2018).

In Germany, the breakup of Germany Inc. is the most prominent example of this development (Ahrens et al., 2013; Berghahn & Vitols, 2006; Cioffi & Höpner, 2006; Lane, 2003; Streeck & Höpner, 2003). With the rise of markets as part of firm finance, German corporations wanted to be listed on the New York Stock exchange, the most central exchange for shareholder investment. To do that, firms had to adopt transparent standards and stop insider trading, which meant reducing those personal relationships. This shift from relationship banking to transactional banking (Lütz, 2005b; Röper, 2018; Vitols, 2005) implied that German banks as credit givers became less important.

[4] SHV depicts the amount of dividends paid to shareholders or the increase in stock price. SHV often implies that the measure of corporate success is the extent to which it increases the wealth of its shareholders.

Sigure Vitols' work in understanding this transformation is a great example of scholarship aiming to move beyond Zysman's legacy. Vitols aims to show how the rise of shareholders did not simply reflect the market-based model (in which shareholder interests dominate) or the German bank-based model (where shareholders were mainly absent so that stakeholders could implement their long-term, productive interests) (Vitols, 2004b, 2009).[5] Combining markets and institutions, he was one of the first to argue that Germany developed an 'augmented stakeholder system' that represented a hybrid arrangement, a now commonly accepted characteristic of the German model (cf. Röper, 2018).

From that perspective, Vitols maintains that the impact of US finance has changed the German long-term corporate governance system to an extent, but the German 'augmented stakeholder system' is a variant that is still negotiated through a network of complex institutions. SHV does not over-determine the metrics of firm performance, and other stakeholders, such as labour, managers and banks, still have a say. Patient capital, handed out by banks, has been the crux of the interplay of these institutions because it has allowed corporations to invest in high-quality production, enabling long-term and secure labour contracts and protecting managers from following short-term market logics (Vitols, 2004b). Vitols' account (2003, 2004b, 2004a, 2009) questions the fact that marketisation has led to convergence. He instead argues that institutional obstacles against full marketisation persist, representing a long-standing argument that German institutions still work like a bulwark against too many market forces.

For Vitols, Germany's complex institutional setup is in stark contrast to the much simpler US system where firms fund themselves on short-term capital markets (2004b, p. 362). This market dependency allows shareholders to engrain their interests in NFCs through threat of exit, as already described in Zysman's typology. Transparent financial practices ensure external monitoring of financial investment so that US shareholders avoid a complex negotiation process with a coalition of multiple interests (Vitols, 2004b, p. 368). Foreign institutional investors were previously reluctant to invest in Germany because its insider model would not allow for much market influence in corporate decisions.

Relying on the now-familiar argument of the growing impact of integrated financial markets enabled via liberalisation, Vitols argues that Germany's insider model had to change to stay competitive and attract

[5] Callaghan (2018) provides a very interesting updated and comparative history on the marketisation of corporate control in Germany, Britain and France.

enough capital: more and more corporate funding was reoriented towards SHV as corporate rationale for refinance and performance (Vitols, 2004b, p. 358, 2004a). Major firms announced the sale of their long-term holdings, reduced their seats on supervision boards and adopted US-based accounting methods. Corporations enhanced transparency and frequent trading of shares, which were core shareholder demands. This transformation caused large banks to shift their strategies towards the higher profits associated with global equity trading and capital markets at the expense of patient lending.[6]

This has not led to convergence for Vitols. Despite increasing market pressures, banks have continued to lend long-term. For example, the institutional investor of Deutsche Bank, DB investor, invests in large corporate stakes, rather than small ones that would be easier to trade (Vitols, 2004b, p. 367). Access to patient capital has allowed corporations to resist shareholders' priorities for short-term dividends to some extent, so that German corporate governance has not fully been marketised (Vitols, 2009). This leads Vitols to argue that the German model turned into an augmented stakeholder system, rather than unfolding into a straightforward adoption of all SHV practices. In that sense, Vitols aims to overcome the shareholder (market) vs stakeholder (social institutions) dichotomy that often attributes too much significance to markets in dominating corporate decision making.

It is not clear, however, if Vitols has escaped a binary understanding of the shareholder and stakeholder systems. While the impact of marketisation turned into a hybrid in which US and German logics coalesce, the problem is the binary understanding of the starting point and the subsequent change. Having identified US finance as a simple social network of market forces that remain underspecified beyond short-term profit imperatives, the impact of US finance remains caught within a binary understanding of more or less markets, or more or less shareholders. While social institutions play a role in shaping market outcomes, financial change is reduced to a linear process of growing markets, kept in check by stakeholders. In that sense, Vitols remains trapped in the coordinates of the convergence debate, allowing change towards market-based systems or divergence if bank-based finance can persist against market forces.

Within these conceptual parameters, banks are stakeholders who shield corporations from short-term market pressures by providing patient

[6] See Callaghan (2018, p. 68ff), Lütz (2005a), or the book 'Alle Macht dem Markt' (eds. Streeck & Höpner, 2003) for an extensive analysis, but in German.

capital. Banks are crucial actors only in their role in allowing other actors to perform long-term interests. The point here is not to challenge the idea that patient capital provides long-term horizons for firm planning; the problem in this perception is that the dichotomy provides only a stylised picture of the interests of market agents as short-term and German agents as social and long-term. Change is orchestrated by foreign investors that infuse market pressures into Germany's system, while the banks' role is to fend it off. Vitols therefore posits the process of marketisation outside of what German banks would do. Within this typology, it becomes very difficult to trace the practices of banks within financialisation because banks' role is limited to corporate finance and diametrically opposed to financial markets.

The Marketisation of Corporate Loans

Since the GFC, scholars have paid renewed attention to the changing role of banks during financialisation and debated to what extent banks have moved beyond their original roles as bulwarks against markets and in providing finance to the real economy (Bayoumi, 2017; Dafe et al., 2022; Deeg & Hardie, 2016; Hardie & Howarth, 2009; Lehrer & Celo, 2016). Richard Deeg is an influential scholar of German finance. For him (2010a), the process of marketisation represents the extent to which banks do 'deal-based', rather than relationship, finance and he attributes banks with a leading role in transforming the German model in response to the rise of US finance. Deeg (1999, p. 86) argues that banks have not become superfluous as common understandings of financialisation suggest. Similarly, rising market pressures are not necessarily a sign that financial actors have become homogenous capitalists with structural market power. Instead, for Deeg, practices reflect banks' unique institutional dispositions and adaptations that are different in time and space. From this perspective, banks have responded in innovative ways that cannot be directly read off ideas of market logics.

Deeg alerts us to the fact that banking practices make a difference for the competitive positions of banks and how they manage their balance sheets. Similarly to Vitols, Deeg challenges Zysman's dichotomy, revising common interpretations of German banking as tutelage, putting too much emphasis on bank–firm relationships as a core enabler for long-term credits. German banks have never controlled firms so much because supervisory boards have limited access to information and firms' decisions. Large corporations on their side have never been so reliant on patient capital as they used internal and market-based funds (Deeg, 2012). Instead,

Deeg (1999) suggests that the characteristic feature of traditional German finance was the provision of a wide range of financial services such as securities and corporate loans.

His revision highlights that the relationship between banks, the way they position themselves vis-à-vis other banks, influences their role within a corporate governance regime and how they conduct their practices, perhaps more so than the corporate–bank relationship. For example, specific funding conditions of public banks made them a relevant contestant to the big banks. Public state banks can draw from a large pool of cheap savings deposits, which allowed them to effectively compete against the big banks (Deeg, 1999, p. 81). According to Deeg, this was a key reason for why big banks already lost their influence and their share in corporate lending in the 1960s and 1970s, right at the time when the model of German finance started to emerge. This led them to provide such a wide range of financial services, including patient capital, to keep their business.

For Deeg, these competitive dynamics changed with the growth of US securities markets. Because of growing profit opportunities in investment banking, German banks reoriented themselves to become more like US investment banks from the mid 1980s onwards (Deeg, 1999). German institutions and investors, by contrast, were sluggish to adjust and could not be expected to invest enough into banks' securities. According to Deeg, this motivated German banks to push for changes in domestic markets to accommodate their shift (Deeg, 2005). The big banks themselves thus started to attract foreign investors and lobbied to change German market regulations and norms to accommodate investors' interests (Deeg, 2005; Deeg & Lütz, 2000). Deeg, alongside colleagues, shows how banks were internal driving factors for German markets to change towards US financial logics. In that sense, Deeg shows how the banks aimed to transform their domestic institutional base to fit their global banking practices.

In Deeg's account, banks drive this transformation in their own interest, but this is not a straightforward process. The growth of securities markets has led to disintermediation because corporations switched to global market funding, away from bank credit (Deeg, 2010b, p. 478; Braun & Deeg, 2019; Deeg, 1999). In Deeg's words, 'the traditional Hausbank system has weakened, as securities markets have become more important for both borrowers and savers' (Deeg, 2010a, p. 116). It is this observation that determines Deeg's assessment of the power of banks. Exposing insightful data on changing corporate demand for bank loans, Braun and Deeg (2018) claim that the loss of bank loans made them 'victims' of the rise of securities markets. As such, Deeg asserts that banks are key agents of market transformation, but banks' power is conceptualised as banks' capacity to control firms, which, once again, diminishes with the increasing marketisation.

Deeg displays the tensions within the literature that results from understanding financialisation as a form of marketisation most interestingly. Deeg has made important contributions to show how German finance is more complex than Zysman's ideal-typical understandings of bank-based systems. Nonetheless, when assessing financial change, he reverts to Zysman's binaries as comparative boundaries, and uses the idea of marketisation that brings the German ideal type closer to the market-based one. While Deeg contends that global finance is 'intricately linked to institutional change in domestic financial systems' (Deeg, 2010b, p. 469), he puts too much emphasis on the contrast between the traditional bank-based model and global finance. While he describes in depth how German banks have pushed for change within Germany to accommodate global transformations (Deeg, 2005, 2009, 2012), banks' historical practices in global markets do not receive the same attention. As a result, changes in global banking practices go amiss, and it becomes very difficult to decipher a qualitative change in the trajectory of German banks' international practices.

A crucial problem is the conceptualisation of power during financialisation. Key indicators of financialisation for Deeg are, firstly, that deal-based finance replaced relationship banking and, secondly, the growing distance between bank–corporate relationships. Banks' power remains their influence over corporate governance, even though Deeg himself argues banks never had that much control in the first place. While Deeg shows that banks' role in German finance has been complex and nuanced, pushing beyond common ideal types, when he examines the impact of markets, banks' active role is narrowly defined as pushing for markets for profits. An account of their changing power relations in financial markets and vis-à-vis corporate finance is absent beyond banks' diminishing influence. In this sense, his analysis reflects common understandings that derive banks' diminishing role from growing financial markets, positing financial markets as at odds with bank-based practices. As a result, the paradox between the idea of powerful banks as drivers of marketisation that simultaneously became victims of that very same process cannot be solved. Missing a more complex appreciation of banks' changing practices, we are left wondering why they would engineer their own decline.

The Marketisation of Banking

The most recent attempt to overcome the distinction between markets and banks resulted in exploring how banks themselves display market features. Moving beyond their role as gatekeepers of corporate loans, there is a flourishing literature looking at banks' entanglements with markets through shadow banking, disintermediated credit processes, trading, etc. In fact, rather than simply being impacted by, scholars have argued that European banking was the key driver of growing financial markets between the US and Europe in the run up to the GFC (Bayoumi, 2017; Tooze, 2018). Termed the rise of market-based banking (MBB), the traditional Zysmanian distinction between market-based and bank-based systems has become obsolete (Hardie et al., 2013). Hardie and colleagues argue that MBB provides a conceptual solution to the paradox lingering in the financialisation literature: banks have continued to be core actors in European economies even though financial markets have become dominant.

Analysing how banks take positions in different markets, MBB shows that the impact of US finance changes banking itself, rather than there being a shift towards more markets and less banks.[7] MBB builds on Deeg's idea of deal-based finance and allows us to analyse banks' practices beyond firm finance towards broader market-based activities. Focusing on changing banking practices, Hardie and Howarth (2013a) can disprove the explanatory power of concepts such as SHV or short-term profit motives associated with the rise of financial markets because the impact of foreign investors in Germany was rather small – as, for example, foreign bank branches held only 6.4 per cent of total bank assets in 2003 (Hardie & Howarth, 2013a, p. 108). SHV is also inadequate to assess the extent of marketisation because banks with and without shareholders were engaged in MBB in the 2000s.

Rather than representing an external impact, German banks have themselves internationalised and marketised their own activities. Since the 2000s, German banks' international subsidiaries have bought huge volumes of assets, refinancing on financial markets (Hardie & Howarth, 2009, p. 1021, 2013a, p. 109f). Beyond simply demonstrating the presence of markets, Hardie and colleagues show the importance of differentiating between markets and the distinct pressures they create. For example, bonds as a method of funding allows banks to refinance long-term, giving

[7] See an extensive – and incisive – critique of the market vs. bank dichotomy by Erturk and Solari (2007).

them some buffer for lending, a key reason why German banks continued to lend despite heavy losses during the GFC (Hardie & Howarth, 2013a, p. 115f).[8] However, increasingly involved in financial trading, banks' activities are now subject to market pressures, which diminished their oligopolistic status as lenders. With marketisation, according to Hardie and colleagues, banks turned into price takers because short-term market pressures determine rates of financial securities. In contrast to their traditional role, German banks are now reduced to being financial intermediaries simply passing on competitive market prices to their customers. MBB thus contradicts Streeck's account in which financial agents gained unprecedented market power by turning themselves into market agents.

From the perspective of MBB, the extent to which banks have lost their power can be discerned through the funding gap. This is a useful method to understand the extent to which banks have inserted themselves into markets, and thus the extent to which they are subject to short-term pressures. The funding gap is the volume between the value of assets and customer deposits, which represents the amount of debt that must be financed by market-based products. Assessing the need of market-based funding in this way allows for a differentiated picture of individual banks or groups of banks in the aggregate. It is useful to discern the shift away from deposits to other ways of funding that are often more short-term.

However, as I have argued elsewhere (2022a), MBB only partially removes the problem of bridging ideal types that the literature has been wrestling with for the past decades. MBB allows us to assess banking within the two static Zysmanian ideal types: In traditional bank-based systems, banks are price makers, monopolising credit relations. After sufficient volumes of marketised loans, banks become price takers, embedded in decentralised markets. As a result, Hardie and Howarth identify the 2000s as the key period of the internationalisation of banks' practices, because their marketised loans and securities are highest in numbers. But, as Deeg has already argued, German banks have always combined loans and securities within their own business models. What, then, has changed? If neither corporate-bank relations nor the impact of foreign financial investors can explain this transition, what triggered financialisation instead? While Deeg attributes to banks some power to determine their own fate in markets, MBB proposes that banks could

8 They also attribute this phenomenon to the prevalent existence of the large regional networks of the cooperatives and savings banks that continued lending to corporations.

not once they significantly moved down the path of marketisation. As a result, MBB does not provide us with new tools to understand the tension already present in Deeg's work: Why and how would German banks turn themselves into market agents if they thereby lose their power?

To move beyond dichotomous understandings of banks and markets, we must appreciate markets as uneven institutions with differentiated imperatives. Eschewing functional understandings of traditional German and US ideal types, this book foregrounds qualitatively new imperatives linked to the rise of US finance in the 1960s, which changed global competitive pressures and securities markets. This will allow me to decipher more precisely what banks are doing in markets, as well as the power and weaknesses they have. As this book will explore in detail, an early change in US funding practices triggered a reassessment of non-US banks' market-based practices, their power, and the long trajectory through which they played catch up with US banks, leading to the US Americanisation of global finance. To this end, the next two sections develop the concept of extroverted financialisation used in the remainder of the book to trace the financialisation of German banking.

BEYOND MARKET-BASED BANKING: THE RISE OF LIABILITY MANAGEMENT

The rise of US finance has its origins in a fundamental change of funding practices towards LM. LM refers to funding practices that tap US money markets, rather than relying on deposits from individuals or corporations. Buying and selling securities, LM allowed financiers to dynamically raise and manage funding in much higher volumes compared to their traditional deposits that accumulated steadily but slowly, with banks doing rather little to attract them. A change in funding practices might sound small, but as this book will show, it played a key role in how US banks were able to outcompete German banks and why German lenders had to uproot themselves from their own home markets to learn the practices of LM in the US. Focusing on the financialisation outside the US, I rely on partly co-authored work of colleagues that emphasises how LM played a decisive role in the phenomenal rise of financial transactions, finance's turn to proprietary trading and its extensive leverage power (Beck & Knafo, 2020; Dutta, 2020; Knafo, 2022).

LM was originally a pragmatic response to a funding crisis in the US from the 1960s onwards. Post-WWII, large savers such as corporations started to move their deposits away from banks into other securities – in part because the Federal Reserve's (Fed) interest rates rise made them more attractive, in part because US corporations had started, since the 1930s, to sideline commercial banks to get away from their control. Money market securities such as Commercial Papers (CP)[9] and Certificates of Deposit (CDs)[10] would fetch the cash that was previously parked at the banks. This started to create a tension between the banks' capacity to raise funding and the rising interest rate in markets, which set in motion far-reaching transformations (Konings, 2011).

The problem was that existing interest rate ceilings aimed at limiting competition between banks, such as Regulation Q, prohibited them from offering higher rates to reattract savers. Suddenly, non-bank financial institutions such as money market funds (MMFs) found that their short-term securities became very attractive. Banks' reduced funding meant that they cut down on corporate loans, leading more corporate actors to turn to money markets. Because banking regulation was highly restrictive, banks could not easily reverse this trend. Bans on regional expansion and Glass–Steagall prevented them from setting up widescale branch networks to gain more customer deposits. This liquidity squeeze turned into a wider problem for their previous strategies because deposits were a convenient way of funding, not only because of their security but also because they were traditionally a cheap source of funding. Previously, banks waited for deposits to accumulate, seeking stable sources and concentrating their efforts on investing in and managing assets.

The losing battle against MMFs meant that banks had to change their funding strategies. In response, they also sought money market funding, with the help of CDs (Cerpa Vielma et al., 2019; Stigum, 1983, p. 53f). The CD market grew so much that the Fed became concerned about its inflationary pressures, but by the time the Fed considered serious action, it had grown so integral to funding circuits in New York that it had become too difficult to shrink it (Konings, 2008b, p. 47). While CDs were also subject to interest ceilings, banks were allowed to set a rate similar to other market-based products because they were time bound. To improve attractiveness for CDs, banks started to work towards the creation of secondary markets so that CD-holders could easily sell them. The first CD tradable

[9] A CP is a short-term, unsecured debt security used by corporations to gain funding for a specific length of time.

[10] A CD is a savings account with a set period before the saver can access that money. The time limit can range from a few months to years, with up to a year being a short-term time deposit, anything longer is long-term.

on a secondary market was issued by Citibank in 1961, and CDs became a major money market instrument throughout the 1970s and 1980s (Stigum, 1983). Banks turned themselves into market makers to generate the liquidity needed to sell their own securities. In that way, banks were actively engaging in the marketisation of debt to attract funding.

At the same time, the market for corporate funding, the CP market, doubled from 1966 to 1970s as corporations flocked to the money markets (Thiemann, 2018, p. 81). US banks were able to integrate themselves as a central part of those funding channels by issuing standing credit lines to CP issuers. This effectively backstopped the CP market as corporate borrowers could turn to banks in case of a squeeze in funding. This further integrated the CP market into banking practices, but also into the safety net of Fed funds, which commercial banks in turn could access in case CP issuers activated these credit lines (Sissoko, 2017; Thiemann, 2018). This made the CP market more liquid and ensured banks kept a central role – even as corporations increasingly developed the means to exploit the rising CP markets with growing success.[11] The rise of money markets thus kickstarted a host of innovations by banks to regain cash lost to money markets and to re-integrate themselves into corporate funding channels. Banks did not lose out against financial markets as a stylised account would predict (Zysman, 1983). Instead, US banks responded to the process of bypassing traditional credit relations by going directly to the money markets themselves. Of course, some banks were better at this than others.

Funding on money markets opened many possibilities but also created new pressures. CDs carried higher interests than deposits and therefore funding became more expensive. Money market securities are short-term, can be sold easily in case investors need cash, and are therefore more volatile and riskier as a funding strategy. Banks thus had to worry about their funding and, because it was more insecure, manage it much more dynamically. This turned the management of liabilities into a central concern for overall banking strategy. As a result, banks became increasingly concerned but also innovative about the costs, timing and liquidity of their funds.

The innovations of LM led banks to a re-evaluation of their traditional practices. Because liabilities absorbed much more of banks' resources, banks started to align their strategies of investment with their

[11] See Knafo and Dutta (2020) for an incisive account on how corporations exploited the CP market for funding and leverage.

liabilities. Beyond developing secondary markets to sell their securities, banks invested in higher-yielding assets with shorter maturities, reducing the costs of capital that assets would trap on the balance sheet. This unleashed a surge of financial innovations to securitise and trade debt as it gave US banks unprecedented capacity to expand their balance sheets (Knafo, 2022).

Bankers Trust's business model is a useful example of this transformation. In the 1970s, Bankers Trust was increasingly devastated by losses and rising funding costs. In the 1960s, the commercial bank was one of the most prominent banks to invest internationally (Kobrak, 2007). By the 1970s, however, it ran huge losses and was in severe trouble, barely a second-tier commercial bank anymore. In response, Sanford, then an employee in the resource management department, started to change its funding strategy with an innovative risk management tool that would come to dominate finance in the 1990s. Sanford developed risk-adjusted return on capital (RAROC) (Guill, 2016).[12] RAROC was a statistical tool to price and measure the performance of loans by considering their risk and the capital they would absorb – the costs of the funds needed to invest into the asset. That way, RAROC evaluated if a loan or security was an efficient use of the bank's expensive and scarce capital (Sanford, 1996).

Accounting for capital is common practice now, but, in the 1970s, this started to call into question a fundamental practice of banking: holding loans on its own books. RAROC visualised a phenomenal insight into lending: if costs of funds were considered, corporate loans were in fact highly expensive and risky so that interest as compensation for a long-term loan was no longer sufficient to cover the costs. If things go wrong, getting rid of a loan is usually much more difficult than selling a security. In response to this new awareness, Bankers Trust started to find new ways to sell its loans to third parties, such as other banks or institutional investors. Bankers Trust shifted its focus from growing assets to selling them, shrinking its loan portfolio to half its value in the 1980s (*The Economist*, 1993, p. 19) transforming away from its traditional nature as a corporate credit institution. Underwriting and then selling loans (e.g., corporate bonds) was previously done by other financial institutions. But Bankers Trust quickly used its innovations to underwrite loans and bonds of non-investment grade clients, excelling in junk bonds and highly leveraged buyouts, winning deals despite having less capital than some of its

[12] For a critical political economy analysis of risk models such as RAROC, see de Goede (2004).

bigger competitors. Bankers Trust became one of the most competitive firms in the leveraged finance league tables by the 1990s (Sanford, 1996).[13]

LM quickly spread in the US as other banks needed to keep up with rising US money markets and their competitors' growing funding powers (Battilossi, 2010). Because of the practices of LM, US banks started to trade with each other more to optimise their funding and loan portfolios, relying increasingly on other financial intermediaries to raise funds, instead of depending on depositors. At the same time, they started to craft assets in a way that they resembled deposits – a financial instrument that you can cash in quickly if needed (Knafo, 2022). This propelled a huge increase in the volume of financial transactions and the speed at which US banks could issue loans. Securitisation, the construction of tradeable securities out of illiquid loans and future income streams, further fuelled the rapid increase in financial transactions.

Rather than diminishing banks' power to issue corporate loans, this development showed how LM allowed some banks to exploit growing financial markets. US banks mastering LM were in many ways freed from the constraints of accumulating deposits. Instead, they could actively manage their debt to unprecedented volumes. Banks had embarked on a radical reversal of their strategies, buttressing their funding capacity to fund their ever-growing balance sheets, and supporting the increasing liquidity by building new financial connections and markets. Banks reinserted themselves into key nodes connecting the growing and increasingly more integrated financial markets (Sissoko, 2015a, 2015b). While initially developed to address a crisis in funding, LM turned into an important practice of funding power. LM is thus the first of four features of EF. The remainder of the chapter develops the other three features, which frame how this new funding practice travelled into Europe and which account for how European banks became internal agents of US-led financialisation from a peripheral position.

THE CONCEPT OF EXTROVERTED FINANCIALISATION: FINANCIALISATION OUTSIDE THE US

How did the rise of LM affect finance outside the US? While the US is dominant and can influence global financial and socio-economic outcomes (Norrlof, 2014; Schwartz, 2010), it is not immediately obvious how

[13] Of course, RAROC was only a statistical tool comparing historical data of risk and return, and Bankers Trust lost several million dollars despite the aim to account for the risks involved (*The Economist*, 1993).

a specific change in US funding practices represents a transformative concern for German banks. How then did LM translate into European finance? US banks were able to put pressures onto their global competitors because of the developing Eurodollar markets. As the CP and CD markets were growing in New York, the Eurodollar markets became their global outlet (Seabrooke, 2001; Stigum, 1983). This produced a new imperative for European banks: the need to access USDs – which is the second feature of EF.

(Euro-) Dollars

The Eurodollar markets represent the initial global impact of the rise of LM (Battilossi, 2010). A Eurodollar is a deposit that is created outside the US by any institution non-resident in the US. This can include foreign branches of a US bank or a foreign bank. Thus, when a US bank shifts US dollars to its London branch and receives in return a deposit, it has created a Eurodollar deposit. The Eurodollar markets are now key offshore markets at the centre of credit creation. Initially, however, they were not very popular. When the foreign branches of US banks started to receive 3–6 months USD deposits, their parents were uninterested because those deposits did not fit their books, so that the foreign branches started lending them to other banks and commercial customers, independent from the US markets (Stigum, 1990, p. 207ff). International capital flows were usually managed through foreign correspondent banks that handled bills of trades and other international trade-related papers, rather than through offshore deposits (Mayer, 1976).

This changed with the rise of LM. When US banks were forced to reorient themselves towards money market funding for themselves and their clients, US banks' funding capacity exploded. This made the Eurodollar markets much more attractive to them because they provided additional resources and outlets for securities-based funding and lending, and banks were not bound by interest rate ceilings (Schenk, 1998). In the 1960s, US banks substituted four-fifths of the decline of their domestic CDs with Eurodollars and, in 1966, Eurodollar funding reached 50 per cent of domestic CDs (McCauley & Schenk, 2020). US financiers quickly started to fund not only their own internationalising corporate sector but also European firms (Gindin & Panitch, 2012). This soon had a fundamental impact on the global financial architecture and European finance: using LM, US banks were in a position to capture Eurodollars much more easily than other banks, a competitive advantage I will further explain in Chapters 4 and 5. Because US banks outcompeted European banks on their home turf, this had an impact on the kind of currency the latter could use to conduct their financial strategies. European banks had to get USD and for that, they had to go to USD markets.

This had crucial implications for what kind of resources would become central to conducting international banking. Counter the Zysmanian understanding, financial markets are inherently hierarchical. Different kinds of currencies rest on geopolitical and financial power relations and produce dependencies between countries and within financial markets (Bonizzi et al., 2019). Global finance is centred on USDs, which has created dependencies on Europe (Cafruny & Ryner, 2007) and globally, incorporating both financial and NFCs into USD credit creation (Schwartz, 2019).

This started with the Marshall Plan, which infused US capital into European political economy right after WWII. As a Fed study confirmed, historically, once a country begins to use dollars, its financial system has tended to require more of them, particularly after financial crises (Judson, 2012). This posed a novel problem to German banks: they had easy access to DM deposits, but not USD. This currency mismatch represents a distinct market problem for German banks in contrast to US banks because they had to find new ways to gain USD. This strained the cosy relations between the industrial sector and German universal banks as early as the 1960s, when German companies started to borrow cheaper Eurodollar loans, as I will detail more thoroughly in Chapter 4.

The imperative to get USD is thus the second feature of LM. But beyond the hegemonic position of the USD, EF foregrounds that the rise of the Eurodollar markets meant that European banks met LM, which changed the way they did foreign currency and international finance. This imperative is important not only to understand the internationalisation of banking, but also to appreciate the new competitive dynamics and the socio-economic fabric of global financial markets that emerged. The Eurodollar markets are often treated in a negative sense; for example, a space of 'nowhere' (Palan & Nesvetailova, 2014), 'free' of regulation or as part of an 'evasive' strategy by corporate actors. In contrast, I want to foreground how the competitive dynamics unleashed by the rise of LM weaved a specific money relation that US banks produced and exploited much more easily. This integrally fused together banking on global markets with financial practices geared towards accessing USD, shaping how non-US banks were able to compete on global markets in new ways. This was a key trigger point for German banks to change their international strategies, prompting them to enter new offshore markets to innovate and engineer new ways to leverage their limited USD resources, long before they used their offshore SPVs to get access to US markets in the 2000s.

I do not claim that LM was the only factor that led to the spread of the Eurodollar markets. Other key global factors for their rise and impact on European finance were petrodollar recycling in the 1970s and the Global South debt crisis of the 1980s, with European banks as key agents. After the fall of the Bretton Woods, the Eurodollar markets swelled because the US freed itself from the need to provide gold in exchange for USD, which unchained a material restriction on the global circulation of USD. When Nixon defaulted on the Gold Standard, cementing the end of the international agreement, the Eurodollar markets increased from USD 60 billion to USD 400 billion in the first half of the 1970s (Burn, 1999, p. 19).

Nonetheless, EF foregrounds USD as a novel imperative for non-US banks because it was the power of LM that allowed US banks to outcompete European banks, a fact that started the latter's process of extroverted financialisation in the 1960s. Because of the revolution in funding, US banks could capture liabilities and assets on global markets much more easily than non-US banks. Financialisation thus became an internationally connected process from the moment European banks had to enter the Eurodollar markets to catch up with US banks. As such, the rise of LM helped to nurture USD hegemony by giving US banks a competitive edge. But, as the book will show, the hegemonic role of USDs also acquired a new quality as USDs became inseparable from the everyday funding practices of non-US banks. As such, contemporary USD hegemony is itself partly an outcome of the extroverted strategies of non-US banks.

Money Markets

The third feature of EF accounts for the specific financial institutions in which the practices of LM are embedded: US money markets. While the rise of the Eurodollar markets meant that European banks became central agents of USD creation and USD became a global currency, the way USD claims were managed, originated and engineered still depended on their institutional context. Global banking is not only deeply influenced by which kind of currency one can raise and mobilise as a home-based deposit, but also how one can raise and manipulate that currency. US money markets were key to global banking because their institutional framework was organically linked to LM. From that perspective, MBB is misleading because US banks were well aligned with US money markets, while non-US banks were initially excluded and had to innovate in all sorts of directions to reduce their peripheral position.

LM could originally only be successfully used in the US because it has very specific liquidity requirements. LM derives its flexibility from funding with short-term, sometimes overnight, securities. While inherently volatile, LM allows banks to manage money market funding much more precisely, compared to customer deposits or longer-term liabilities. For this to work, deep and liquid financial markets are needed to buy and sell enough liabilities with very short-term maturities. US money markets were core institutions that enabled banks to manage those new liquidity requirements inherent in leveraging and trading CDs, CPs and offshore funding. Cash-rich corporations and other institutions in the US would channel their surplus funds through the money markets to the banks (and other institutions) (Stigum, 1990). As a result, banks and other financial actors could trade billions of US dollars on money markets every day.

US money markets have been at the heart of financialisation (Gabor, 2016b; Konings, 2011; Wansleben, 2020). They are exceptionally deep and liquid, attracting cash from both households and large institutional investors and therefore provide a key context for the practices of LM. US money markets were very useful for US banks to raise debt, manage their balance sheets and leverage to the extreme (Sgambati, 2019). By contrast, debt markets in Europe were smaller and capital markets more fragmented, which is not only less suitable for LM but also less suitable to build alternative practices that could rival LM's funding power. Money markets outside the US are rather small and mainly provide funds for the inter-banking market instead of mediating larger pools of funds between various financial institutions, retail customers and banks. Historically, they have been mostly used to bridge funding squeezes rather than being systematically tapped on an everyday basis (cf. Mai, 2015). Fearing competition from other financial agents, some European universal and central banks did in fact heavily lobby against the introduction of money market funds, stifling their expansion (Tanega & Baklanova, 2018; Wansleben, 2023). LM did not develop outside the US and was not supported by a European financial landscape.

The unique embeddedness of LM in US money markets thus caused a new imperative for non-US banks: to keep up with US banks' growing leverage and to participate in new financial innovations, non-US banks had to establish themselves in US money markets. Despite the large volume of US dollars that flowed globally, dollars in the US still represented the most crucial source of funding because of LM, and have been a core anchor point in the global financial architecture since the 1960s, as I will detail further in Chapter 5. This was a key trigger that forced non-US banks to transfer parts or all of their strategies to the US. This path was non-linear as many banks first moved to London – a key offshore US financial hub because it institutionalised itself in US money markets. But, importantly, if banks wanted to compete in global markets, they needed a large presence in the US. It is this constraint that caused more fundamental transformations in global banking: To operate in US money markets, non-US banks had to transform their banking strategies towards the practices of LM. As I will show in Chapters 6 and 7, in the late 1980s and throughout the 1990s, these transitions represent key turning points for Deutsche Bank and Commerzbank towards US-style finance.

Problems and Contradictions

EF aims to account for the US Americanisation of German finance by framing the changing practices of German banks in response to the rise of US finance. As feature one to three highlight, the rise of new funding practices triggered the need for non-US banks to leave their home markets behind, find roots in US financial markets and therefore develop the practices of LM. The fourth feature relates to the specific problems and contradictions that non-US banks faced in developing LM. The feature accounts for the fact that integrating strategies of LM in the overall banking strategy was complex and caused many problems beyond initial adjustment costs. Because it organically fitted US financial logics, adopting LM caused tensions with previous funding and investment strategies, including risk management, compensation and banking culture, which resulted into power struggles over the new directions within the banks themselves. Beyond bridging the currency gap, banks had to overcome institutional and operational differences, which produced a unique set of intra-institutional controversies for German banks, as I will show in Chapter 8. The fourth feature thus highlights that the impact of US finance is best understood as a socio-financial dynamic shaped by struggles between and within the banks over their strategies to accommodate LM.

As I have shown, LM reshaped the coordinates of global financial competition. While LM allowed many European banks to build institutional on and offshore roots into US money markets, it also entrenched this way of banking into the global financial architecture. As I trace through the book, the practices employed by European banks to catch up to US banks further entrenched money market funding in their everyday operations. LM provided the banks with huge potential to leverage their limited USD funds and particularly Deutsche Bank made large profits in the 2000s. However, when access to US dollars becomes more limited, as it has for European banks since the GFC, the reliance on LM made its deep-seated USD dependency an intractable problem. As Chapter 8 will highlight, common attempts to reduce US market dependency post-GFC – to get back to previous, more European positions of power – only fuel further the dynamics of LM and therefore the reliance of global banking on US financial institutions. The fourth feature thus foregrounds the tensions and contradictions non-US banks face and must try to resolve after having adopted the practices of LM.

EF thus portrays the politics of markets and processes of financialisation in a different light compared to the idea of marketisation. Overcoming unevenness has been a key driver for European banks to build on and offshore USD funding channels to get closer to US money markets and the funding power of LM. The rise of LM was a key trigger for the European banks to uproot themselves into foreign financial markets, and the imperative of US money markets caused a change in banking and the attempts to relocate into the US. As such, their attempts made them important agents of US-led financialisation, albeit from a peripheral perspective. But as I problematise in more detail throughout the book, it was a lack of funding power, not the lack of market power per se, that triggered the qualitative changes in finance that characterise extroverted financialisation.

CONCLUSION

Ideal types can be useful to make sense of our complex world. However, when conceptualising financialisation, stylised accounts have sometimes obscured more than they have revealed because they prevented a more nuanced engagement with financial change. Because of a lack of historical inquiry, political economy scholarship often falls back on conceptualisations of financialisation as marketisation, often seen as the quantitative increase of markets vis-à-vis other social relations. This has made it difficult to track qualitative changes within markets and their uneven nature. Scholars have widely criticised Zysman's ideal-typical understandings of bank-based and market-based finance, but too often found themselves replicating his typology when trying to understand the rise of US finance.

By contrast, this book develops the concept of EF to understand financialisation outside the US. EF thus aims to capture the problems of financial agents seeking to adapt to financial practices in a different context. From this perspective, financial practices are better understood by examining how they are geared towards overcoming specific imperatives and constraints within market contexts, rather than in opposition to markets. This will open the analytical space to take banks seriously as gatekeepers of liquidity in a highly leveraged financial system and to differentiate between specific forms of market-based finance. To do that, EF frames the transformation of non-US banks according to four imperatives that triggered fundamental changes in the competitive dynamics of global finance. These imperatives forced non-US banks into foreign markets and to operate in those markets, non-US banks had to adopt US-forms of finance and to uproot significant parts of their own business models. In that way, the rise of LM in the US generated a global dynamic much earlier than commonly assumed. Importantly, these dynamics have imprinted globally uneven power relations within banking. Overcoming them has been a key driver for non-US banks' strategies of building USD funding channels to connect to US money markets.

In sum, this chapter established the conceptual grounding for an examination of how German banks have actively navigated the impact of US finance. Chapter 3 applies EF to refine what is commonly understood as German finance to place financial change on a more solid historical footing. I show how German banks' early market-based financial practices that have their origins in the nineteenth century. In Chapter 4, I then examine how the imperative of LM came to impose its pressures on German banking in the post-WWII decades, making German banking much more international than commonly assumed. The rest of the book then sets out to show that US Americanisation of German finance is not about marketisation per se, but instead about a problematic transfer of key parts of the banks' business models to the US.

3

The *Pfandbrief*

Securitisation Made in Germany

Michael Philipp said they had something really innovative: asset-backed securities. They could securitise mortgages. I responded: we do this for the past 150 years in Germany. It is called Pfandbrief.

A Deutsche Banker in 2001. Michael Philipp was of Bankers Trust[1]

The massive write-downs on the structured asset-backed securities make it painfully clear: mortgage-backed securities, CDOs etc. have no similarities with the Pfandbriefe, yes, indeed, they represent striking differences.

Axel Weber (2009), president of the German Bundesbank during a conference talk to the Association of German mortgage banks

If we perceive the fundamental problem of the financial system as one of ABS, we miss an opportunity to come to grips with the larger systemic problems inherent in finance

(Amato & Fantacci, 2012)

INTRODUCTION

The *Pfandbrief* literally means 'letter of pledge'. 'Pfand' refers to 'deposit' or 'security', now most often associated in Germany with empty glass bottles (*Pfandflaschen*) that fetch 15–25 cents when returned to a store. A 'brief' is a letter, which in the Middle Ages was used to describe an economic document. *Pfandbrief* in English is often called a covered bond, suggesting it is like a bond, but one with a cover, an extra security.

As the quotes above reveal, people perceive the *Pfandbrief* in a rather controversial, even contradictory manner. The first quote highlights the underappreciated role of the *Pfandbrief* within German political economy and global finance. The Deutsche banker stresses that the *Pfandbrief* is

[1] Personal conversation with a Deutsche banker who recollected this exchange, own translation; Mr. Philipp was only the second US investment banker who joined the management board of Deutsche in 2000.

in fact, an asset-backed security (ABS). This quote similarly attests to the common neglect of this age-old security that allows commentators, analysts and practitioners alike to portray ABS as something entirely innovative. The second quote represents another strand of financial experts who contrast both securities and vehemently stress that they are completely different. These experts think the *Pfandbrief* is a quintessential German financial product indicative of the German relational, secure, and long-term lending logics. The third quote sums up the analytical purpose of this chapter: to avoid seeing financialisation as a quintessential problem of ABS investment only (brought about by marketisation). In this spirit, I highlight why it is important to differentiate between different processes of marketisation: some ABS have led to financialisation, others have not. This chapter thus provides the historical grounding to appreciate what is at stake with German financial markets on the one hand, and financialisation originating in the US on the other so that we can start 'to come to grips with the larger systemic problems inherent in finance' (Amato & Fantacci, 2012).

In line with the second quote, the *Pfandbrief* is often treated as typical of the German bank-based financial system, as its legalities make it a stable, long-term refinance option (Hardie & Howarth, 2013a) as I will further describe later. Apart from mentioning the *Pfandbrief* as the most established covered bond, few scholars have delved into its complex history. In Germany, it is a well known financial practice, and yet, it is under-researched (Skyrman, 2023; Spangler & Werner, 2013). *Pfandbrief* seems to confirm the ideal type of German finance. Its long-term nature based on a collateral predominantly supports the productive industry instead of experiencing excessive credit growth based on speculation. It is part of relationship banking because banks needed to monitor their borrowers to ensure long-term economic viability. *Pfandbrief* has long been used for public finance, providing municipalities with long-term and cheap capital (Mertens, 2015). *Pfandbrief*'s important role in housing finance has prevented mortgage speculation and excessive housing bubbles in the 2000s (Mertens, 2015, 2017; Van Gunten & Navot, 2018; Wijburg & Aalbers, 2017). This is in stark contrast to high levels of mortgage debt in the US, often identified as key features of financialisation (Schelkle, 2012). As a result, *Pfandbriefe* (plural for *Pfandbrief*) are often seen as having helped to prevent financialisation trends in Germany.

This chapter agrees with arguments asserting the long-term orientation of the *Pfandbrief*. However, this chapter portrays the significance of the *Pfandbrief* less according to its fit with German ideal types but instead in its potential for financialisation. In other words, rather than searching for covered bonds' role in counteracting financialisation, I turn this issue on its head and examine what it allowed financial agents to do and how it was mobilised as a practice of market-based funding. Revisiting *Pfandbriefe's* history from this perspective, I assess what practices concerning the *Pfandbrief* might tell us about German finance, and about those market-based practices that have led to financialisation and those that have not.

Historicising the *Pfandbrief*, I argue that it undermines common assumptions about German finance and about the role of 'markets' in changing the trajectory of German banking. Counter to common acceptance, I show that German financial agents have practiced securitisation long before the 2000s. The Prussian Prince Friedrich II started to promote asset-based funding in the nineteenth century, while the City of Ulm promised the future rents of their city gate as security for a loan in 1378 (Jäger, 1831). Noble and wealthy people used *Pfandbriefe* to borrow money, guaranteed by the underlying asset. While anecdotal evidence does perhaps not prove a widespread trend, *Pfandbriefe* trouble understandings that see market-based issues as a problem for finance from the 2000s onwards (cf. Hardie & Howarth, 2013a).

Indeed, this chapter demonstrates that *Pfandbriefe* played a vital 'market-based' role in nineteenth century housing finance. German banks were relatively successful in securitising financial assets to tap anonymous, centralised capital markets in Berlin. By contrast, US financial markets were local, personal, decentralised and much more limited in scope. In the 1970s, *Pfandbriefe* came in handy yet again when German universal banks sought to take advantage of growing household income and retail finance. The big lenders' use of covered bonds blurred the boundaries between the three-pillar German banking system. While initially sceptical about extending credit to small borrowers in the 1960s, *Pfandbriefe* represented a convenient way for the big banks to use an existing market-based institution to manage long-term lending and compensate for the loss of corporate deposits. It is here that crucial different trajectories emerge: while German banks turned to the *Pfandbrief*, US financial institutions turned to money markets to (re)capture growing household debt and savings, and corporate deposits. *Pfandbriefe* only lost their strategic appeal once German banks were more connected to US money markets from the 1980s onwards. While never really becoming a central strategy of large universal banks, *Pfandbriefe* finally diminished against US-based mortgage-backed securities (MBS) in the 1990s.

It is only since the GFC that covered bonds have experienced a revival in Europe, not least through EU initiatives to revive corporate funding.

By highlighting Germany's history of securitisation, I do not mean to suggest that nineteenth century MBS are the same as the US RMBS of the 2000s. On the contrary, the *Pfandbrief* has had distinct features that are different from US MBS. Historicising market-based practices, however, reveals that the understanding of financial change as 'marketisation' is of limited use to come to grips with German financialisation. By tracing concretely how and why big German banks got involved in the *Pfandbriefe*, I aim to provide a more nuanced understanding of the relationship between funding and securitisation in Germany. As such, the predominant role of this chapter is to cast doubt about what we have come to see as 'normal' about the German financial system and to put its financial system on a precise historical footing.

Appreciating this history means that we have to be much more nuanced about what exactly changed, and which financial practice might indicate the rise of financialisation. If financialisation was about growing markets and market-based exposure, German lenders could have developed that in their local home markets. Why, then, did big German banks not engage with *Pfandbriefe* more? Or asked differently, after the big banks adopted the *Pfandbriefe* in the 1970s, why did they not adjust *Pfandbriefe* to their needs but instead went through the trouble of entering US markets to invest in US-based MBS[2]? Caroline Fohlin (2007) aptly argues that German universal banks have always been about both, securities *and* loans, this chapter adds that they have historically been much more successful in plumbing 'markets' than US banks.

The rest of the chapter is divided into three more sections to show that *Pfandbriefe* never quite fit the classic German model as scholars often assume. The second section briefly introduces the unique characteristics of *Pfandbriefe*. Section three examines how these characteristics emerged historically to establish its distinctive role in the German financial landscape, and to show that Germany had a well-functioning marked-based financial system at the turn of the twentieth century. Section three delves into a more recent turning point of the *Pfandbrief* when the universal banks discovered the *Pfandbrief* as a useful funding strategy and to capture the growing retail sector of the 1960s and 1970s.

[2] Of course, banks cannot simply change a financial practice from one day to the other. However, German banks have been attributed with significant power so that we could have expected some changes if they were interested in expanding market-based practices.

PFANDBRIEF: A BRIEF INTRODUCTION

Pfandbriefe have been a convenient security for capital market funding (Kohl, 2017, p. 92; Seabrooke, 2007). It is commonly represented as a secure, fixed income and long-term financial paper, a quintessential example of Germany's bank-based financial system and its coordinated market economy. It is part of so-called plain-vanilla finance as banks live off the interest difference between the credit and the covered bond. *Pfandbriefe* stay on the balance sheet rather than moving to an outsourced legal entity, and banks are liable to their investors in case of default of the underlying asset. *Pfandbriefe* therefore represent mutual responsibility, neither party can easily walk away from their commitments and secondary markets did not develop. The *Pfandbrief* thus reflects well the institutional landscape of the traditional German banking sector with relational rather than transactional finance at its core.

The collateral value can only be 60 per cent of the property that covers the *Pfandbrief*. This value is calculated more conservatively than, for example, in the USA, or in fact many other countries. *Pfandbriefe* are therefore often seen as 'over-collateralised' and have a small profit margin as a result. By contrast, pre-GFC RMBS were sold on to Special-Purpose Vehicles (SPVs), traded on secondary markets, and the underlying house grossly overvalued. For this reason, most authors use the *Pfandbrief* as a contrasting device to the short-term speculative practices of contemporary US RMBS and because of its role in providing stable funding (Hardie & Howarth, 2013a; Skyrman, 2023). Its long-term and conservative characteristics, so scholars argue, have been crucial in restricting international capital from investing in Germany (Einzig, 1969).

These rules have been tightly regulated for a long-time by the 1899 *Hypothekenbankgesetz* (mortgage bank act) which has experienced very little change since then. Receiving an overhaul in 2005 only, scholars see this as part of the evidence that there has been no major change in German finance until the turn of the century (Behr & Schmidt, 2015). The *Pfandbrief* is indeed part of the three-pillar German system in which different financial agents provide distinct financial services. Only specialised banks, the mortgage banks or *Hypothekenbanken*, can issue *Pfandbriefe*. The specialised banks hold 25 per cent of assets in Germany, of which mortgage banks hold most (Mertens, 2015, p. 166). Banks issuing *Pfandbriefe* must gain prior permission from BaFin (the federal financial authority). Until 2005, this was only granted to *Hypothekenbanken* according to the *Hypothekenbankgesetz*. Apart from the Landesbanken, only very few mixed mortgage banks (Eurohypo, HRE, and HVB) were exempt. This was because their parent banks or predecessors were the big universal banks that issued covered bonds before the Mortgage Bank Act came into existence. They were allowed to continue, and this right was transferred into their subsidiaries (Golin, 2006, p. 134).

Pfandbriefe were deeply institutionalised, often provided long-term funding and the German universal banks enjoyed institutional privileges with the *Pfandbrief*. It therefore represents a financial security that can reliably point to the on-going difference between US and German markets. And yet, the next two sections will show that these differences are often overstated in our theorisations of German and US finance, which has led to an overstatement of the coherence of the German financial system as non-market. In fact, relying on the conceptual starting point of a non-market financial system that does not trade with risky assets has prevented scholars from appreciating Germany's market-based history. The history will validate that we need to be very careful in drawing any deductive conclusions from ideal types, and that instead, an analysis that starts with financial practices to trace structural transformations can be very fruitful.

MONEY FOR THE PRINCES: THE ORIGINS OF SECURITISATION

To specify the role of *Pfandbriefe* in expanding banks' debt, this section examines two crucial features of financial securities. The first is their function in expanding banks' balance sheets, that is, providing the capacity to raise more funds. To recall, leverage is the potential to increase your resources beyond your own means. Much of financialisation has been about increasing the capacity to leverage financial resources (see Chapter 2). For this, the ability to access and use other people's money is key. The second attribute is managing and sustaining the risk involved in doing so, including insurance or the ability to pass on that risk to others. Long-term investment projects are notoriously risky and difficult to finance, regardless of whether they are 'industrial' or 'financial' because banks must manage the maturity mismatch involved. As Mark Schwartz (2020) indicates, people providing long-term capital are usually fewer in number than people seeking long-term debt.

To understand how banks have used *Pfandbriefe* in managing those two issues, I explore, firstly, the emergence of the *Pfandbriefe* to fund the reconstruction of Prussia in the nineteenth century, and, secondly, its role in Germany's housing finance infrastructure at the turn of the twentieth century. This history demonstrates that German banks were very successful in securitising financial assets and in plumbing a financial infrastructure in which they refinance with the help of 'impersonal', marketized debts.

One of the first *Pfandbriefe* was established by the Prince of Prussia to raise money for the reconstruction of Prussia after the Seven Years' War (1756–1763). Friedrich the Great wanted to motivate bankers to lend to the state despite several bankruptcies. To finance wider reconstruction efforts, he wanted to increase access to capital for the countryside gentry (Frost & Raab-Rebentisch, 2005). He forced local landholders to enter debtors' associations, the *Landschaften*, in which every member had the right to obtain credit by selling a mortgage bond that members jointly guaranteed. To protect themselves as guarantors, the *Landschaften* established strict rules for the collateral of the mortgage bond – debentures that had very similar rules to the *Pfandbrief*.

Constructing a financial infrastructure based on collateral lending worked. In contrast to other landowners, this allowed the members to raise substantial volumes of debt. The *Landschaften* held one fifth of the mortgage market in Germany (Kohl, 2017, pp. 290–291) and were very successful in financing rural construction by enabling agrarian landowners to get cheap credit (Seabrooke, 2007).

Pfandbriefe's history partly confirms its reputation as fostering personal, long-term and secure relationships to channel finance into public, housing or agrarian sectors. The value of financial collateral was prudently and conservatively estimated, and personal networks played a large role in making the system work. State agents took a leading role in supporting the long-term financial relations, something the German state still relies upon as public *Pfandbriefe* take a major share in contemporary covered bond markets. Indeed, the public *Pfandbrief* has been significantly used by municipalities and federal states as a tool for refinancing their debt, and by public state banks and *Sparkassen* (regional savings banks) as long-term debt papers with stable fixed interest rates. Variable interest rates are often associated with the toxic US assets of the 2000s that have thrown public treasuries in Germany into horrendous volumes of debt when interest rates rose (Hendrikse & Sidaway, 2014).

And yet, *Pfandbriefe* signified impersonal capital market lending as well. Urban housing finance was predominantly provided by Hypothekenbanken (mortgage banks). While housing finance today is seen as one of the most secure assets, mortgage finance at the end of the nineteenth century was seen as 'too risky' for 'normal' banks (Hughes, 2016). It was specialised mortgage banks developed in the second half of the nineteenth century that took up the task. While they were previously seen with suspicion by the state – lest they intercepted capital that could be flowing to public projects – they were able to grow substantially from 1850s onwards, from 66 million marks in 1865 to 6.9 billion in 1900, overtaking the *Landschaften* that expanded from 470 million to 2.2 billion only (Redenius, 2009, cited in Kohl, 2015, p. 291).

Mortgage banks operated trans-regionally and refinanced with the help of *Pfandbriefe*. The banks were not obliged to remain regionally, and they did not have a localised branch network operating on interpersonal networks such as the *Sparkassen*, the other main agent in the mortgage – *Pfandbrief* sector. While *Sparkassen* attracted smaller borrowers with their large branch networks, mortgage banks preferred large mortgages. Cross-regional mortgage banks relied on well-constructed assets to sell to distant investors in Berlin and therefore favoured standardised construction projects such as larger apartment blocks. They were a crucial part of German urbanisation, and in contrast to individual homes, generated higher income (Kohl, 2015, p. 273). Apartment blocks were easier to monitor and manage, and monthly rental income was important because the law obliged mortgage banks to pay continuous interest on their loans. As a result, Imperial Germany financed most of its apartment buildings with the help of the *Pfandbrief* (ibid.).

German mortgage banks used these bonds regularly to refinance themselves on the formal securities market (Snowden, 1987, p. 688). While financing of agricultural reconstruction was based on localised debt networks, urban housing finance connected the *Hypothekenbanken* to capital markets. *Pfandbriefe* eventually traded on the Berlin stock exchange. This is nothing else than a sellable financial product based on a securitised mortgage (Schwartz, 2020, p. 492).

While securitisation worked well in Germany and supplied mortgage banks with capital from securities markets, the US has a more complicated history with asset-backed securities. In the US, mortgage banks were not well capitalised and only held two percent of total banking capital at the end of the nineteenth century. It is not like they did not try. They attempted mortgage securitisation six times between 1870 and 1940, but every attempt failed (Kohl, 2015, p. 293). There are various reasons for failure, but one is the lack of institutional support and harmonised regulation for markets. Private mortgage banks in the US often used the riskiest types as underlying assets for the bonds. While the market grew rapidly for a few years, it collapsed quickly (Lea, 1996).

In contrast to German cities, lending in US urban areas happened to a large extent informally. As late as 1930, 38% of mortgage lenders were non-institutional. Savings & Loans (the US savings banks) held less than a quarter, rising from 16% in 1896 (Quinn, 2019, p. 93 based on Snowden) while commercial banks only provided 5% of the residential mortgage market in 1896, rising to 10% in 1930. Urban mortgages were short-term investments and attracted small savers. They were part of localised networks, allowing the S&Ls (as well as buildings and thrifts) to monitor their borrowers. While national mortgage providers existed, they had very little market share overall. Without 'social' or 'cooperative' mandates, their monitoring practices were difficult to enforce. Most mortgage business went to local institutions while nationals had to contend with second mortgages (Quinn, 2019, pp. 95–98). Between 1887 and 1897, nationals' assets were worth USD 250 million, while the buildings and loans' assets totalled about USD 1 billion.

Because of the local orientation, expanding debt to fund mortgages was limited to the local pool of debt. Areas in Western parts of the US, and farmers in rural areas, paid a lot of money for their mortgages (Quinn, 2019). US housing advocates looked to Germany for inspiration (Snowden, 1987). One of the first systematic legal systems defining the securitisation of US land partly replicated the German *Landschaften*, as the Farm Loan Act of 1916 allowed voluntary credit associations. Federal or state-level public support only came in significantly during the housing crisis after WWI (Quinn, 2019).

This brief comparative history emphasises how Germany had a fruitful starting point for extensive market-based finance and the securitisation of housing, commonly associated with US-led financialisation. Germany's financial infrastructure was much more advanced than in the US. Significant parts of it were based not on personal and insider networks but on cross-regional or distant capital markets. The Prussian prince and mortgage banks were key agents in engineering asset-backed securities. While we came to associate private mortgages and homeownership with financialisation, rental apartments in large building blocks are in fact ideal material for the securitisation of mortgages, at least in the late nineteenth century (and increasingly again now after the GFC). Up until today, German covered bonds have provided banks with 'convenient direct or indirect access to the capital market' (Deutsche Bundesbank, 2006, pp. 39, 43). Indeed, often rated AAA, they usually carry a higher yield than state bonds and have provided an attractive alternative to corporate bonds (Kohl, 2017, p. 93). If the possibility to expand balance sheets with the help of market-based finance were key, the *Pfandbrief* would have been a prime candidate, if not in itself, then as a base to be developed further by the German banks.

However, by 2010, the nineteenth century trend has completely reversed. About 66% of mortgages went through capital markets in the US, whereas only 20% of Germany's outstanding mortgage loans were funded by capital market funding. German mortgages are predominantly financed by bank deposits (IMF, 2011, p. 5). To start exploring this reversal, the next section examines another important turning point in the history of the *Pfandbrief* to show that the large private lenders got involved for a particular reason, but lost interest quickly when other, more pressing financial dynamics required a different kind of innovation. This will highlight that the large universal banks engaged with *Pfandbriefe* to expand their own financial reach, which actively blurred the boundaries between the division of labour amongst the German banking sectors. More importantly, however, their investment into *Pfandbriefe* in the 1970s represents an important distinction in the trajectories of financialisation between US and German banks with respect to managing their liabilities.

THE MOB OF THE STREET: RETAIL FINANCE AND THE STRUGGLE FOR DEPOSITS

This section examines a third pillar of all finance – retail finance. The *Pfandbrief* had an important role within the competitive pressures arising with the rise of retail finance in Germany in the 1960s and 1970s, and in shaping the German banks' funding options. I contrast here the differences in the competitive 'market' pressures German banks faced in contrast to US banks. While German banks opted for the *Pfandbrief* to tap the decentralised branch network of the *Hypothekenbanken*, US banks developed the strategies of LM to tap US money markets.

During the post-WWII economic boom, there were two sectors providing potential new financial flows for the German universal banks – retail finance and construction finance. Firstly, household savings increased significantly from the 1960s onwards (Mertens, 2017, p. 6).[3] Next to rising incomes due to the economic boom, savings were promoted via a number of tax benefits and regulatory initiatives. Secondly, construction increased massively in Germany (cf. Kohl, 2017). Construction financing consisted of 50 per cent of all credit to private persons. In finance's three-pillar

[3] Similarly to the US (Hyman, 2013), but to a lesser extent and in different ways.

organisational structures, the savings banks and cooperatives were well placed to capture retail and housing debt because they were strong locally and had extensive branch networks (Deeg, 1999; Mertens, 2015).

Financing home ownership as a new sector, however, became interesting for Deutsche and the other big banks. Some scholars argue that German banks only became universal banks in the 1950s and 1960s when they started to advance into retail banking (Wixforth, 2010, p. 103). Tapping household savings was, in fact, considered a 'revolutionary' step and the three big banks traditionally financed big business. Not only were they founded to do so in the second half of the nineteenth century by industrial leaders themselves, but bankers were also traditionally suspicious of retail clients; they particularly shunned giving out small credits. In 1959, a Deutsche Bank employee complained that the 'mob of the street' would take over the branch (Frost, 2009, p. 13) but he was not referring to some large protest against the bank, a robbery or a bank run. Those were customers wanting to enquire or even take out the first 'Kleinkredit' (small loan). While the big banks were continuously sceptical of retail business because it might look like they had degraded themselves to a lesser bank, the banks had to approach the 'small customers' for business if they wanted to engage with the rise in construction finance (Frost, 2009).

Moving into household finances was somewhat accelerated by the decline in corporate deposits that started in the 1960s. While banks continued to be responsible for firms' internal debt management, including restructuring internal pension funds and how to manage retained earnings (Sattler, 2010), banks had to find new sources of funding when corporations started to discover financial markets as both a source of funding and as a way to invest their cash. This was a rather slow development that accelerated during the 1980s and 1990s (Braun & Deeg, 2019; Deeg, 1999) but the banks knew they could not rely on growing corporate deposits anymore. Generating private customer deposits was a response to improve banks' refinancing (Frost, 2009; Sattler, 2020). This was so new that Deutsche Bank sent one of its board members to London to learn from Midland Bank how to engage with private households. Anglo–American banks had more experience with this kind of funding, which the big banks had previously considered far beyond their pride (Frost, 2009).[4]

[4] The move from elite finance to the 'small' everyday customer (or debtor) was equally once considered beyond the banks' pride and interest in the US, but the shift happened in the first half of the twentieth century (Ott, 2014).

This shift was not easy for the big banks in Germany. German finance rests on the three-pillar system in which each banking sector has 'their' own financial expertise. The extensive regional branch networks of the smaller savings and cooperative banks, and their traditional expertise in retail finance, placed them at an advantage to capture growing household savings and debt. The larger commercial banks, by contrast, struggled. While the balance sheets of the three big players tripled during the 1960s, their returns stagnated because the costs of establishing widespread branch networks and the competition against decentralised savings and cooperative groups kept income low (Ahrens, 2010, p. 75ff). Overall numbers increased, but the share of the private banks in retail business declined in relation to the savings and cooperatives from 20% in the 1950s to 11.3% in the 1960s and to 10% in the 1970s (Ahrens, 2010, p. 75).

Retail deposits, however, were needed firstly to extend the length of their heretofore short-term credits into the famous patient capital handed out to manufacturing (Büschgen, 1995, pp. 687, 790). In 1950, the share of long-term loans of Deutsche Bank, Commerzbank and Dresdner Bank from overall credits was 3.6% (6.6% for all commercial banks) (Vitols, 1998, p. 81), a fraction of their credit business.[5] Corporate deposits were increasing, initially, but stagnating from the mid 1960s and banks needed to find alternative deposits.

The importance of *Pfandbriefe* was thus in creating a diversified portfolio through which the universal banks could rival the smaller banks (Büschgen, 1995). Rather than reinventing the wheel, they tapped well established funding markets and bought stakes in the *Pfandbrief* institutions in the post-war years (Mülhaupt, 1977, p. 101). At the beginning, Deutsche Bank, Commerzbank and Dresdner Bank bought about 25 per cent shares, often in the same bank (Büschgen, 1995, p. 781). While mortgage banks mostly continued their own refinancing models independently from their owners, the big banks used this expertise to change their own product portfolio to offer different kinds of credit to individuals. From the 1960s onwards, the big lenders combined their 'traditional' bank loans with their newly obtained *Pfandbrief* funding to build a comprehensive portfolio of construction finance (Frost, 2009).

When the German lenders discovered the *Pfandbrief* for themselves, they slowly increased their capital market funding. They agreed to swap

[5] Mortgage banks had a staggering but unsurprising 97%, savings banks 36% and regional and national savings banks 48%. In 1994, this share was 61.1% (the big three), 95% (mortgage), 81% (savings) and 86% (regional and national savings banks) (Vitols, 1998, p. 81).

their shareholdings so that they increased their shares to controlling stakes at their respective *Hypothekenbank*. The volume of construction finance for the large banks increased exponentially from almost nothing in 1965 to about 32 million DM in 1990 (Büschgen, 1995, p. 780). While the competition over retail deposits has been a continuous challenge for the big German banks, with the help of *Pfandbrief*, they managed to increase their long-term credits and advance into construction finance.

This historical juncture of German finance meant that the big German banks experienced competition from savings and cooperatives, whereas US banks chased funding in US money market funds. Money market funds were non-existent in Germany at the time (Baklanova & Tanega, 2014). This difference is important for the differentiated transformations of banking. The big German banks use of *Pfandbriefe* provided an opportunity to rival Sparkassen and cooperatives, and get funding and retail business without having to change their strategies much as they could tap existing structures. The big lenders could simply acquire another institution – a mortgage bank – that would run mostly in parallel to their own. By contrast, as Chapter 2 established, US banks had to compete against money market funds, which led to a fundamental change in their strategies at the time.

And yet, compared to their retail and industrial finance business, *Pfandbriefe* remained a small part of the universal banks' business, rather than turn into to fundamental aspect of their banking – and thus perhaps an opportunity for financialisation. One reason for the stagnation of covered bonds is historically low homeownership rates in Germany. This has been skillfully linked to the institutional framework of the German model that does not encourage individual homeownership but instead provides institutional support for household savings, rather than rising household debt (Mertens, 2015). No homeownership, no mortgage, no *Pfandbrief* of course. By contrast, in the US, state support was channelled into household mortgage debt (Quinn, 2017; Schwartz, 2010), and where saving was encouraged, it went into pension funds as the main avenue for family savings (Hyman, 2013, p. 224), providing capital to large institutional investors, rather than to decentralised Sparkassen. The wider institutional setting is important for why the private German banks did not turn this into a financialised business model.

Another obstacle in the expansion of *Pfandbriefe* as a market-based funding tool was the well known shipping crises in the 1970s, which put a significant dent into the development of shipping *Pfandbriefe* to fund the shipping industry. Ships provided another common collateral for capital market funding, and the big lenders had their own shipping *Pfandbrief*banken, similarly to the Hypothekenbanken. But those banks (almost) went bankrupt during the oil crises in the 1970s. North Germany's shipping industry benefitted substantially from the booming global economy post-WWII. Influenced by another detrimental war, the Six Day War in 1967, there was a massive increase in demand for tankers. More big German tankers shipped oil globally, and the corresponding funding needs were covered through *Pfandbriefe*. However, due to the 1973 oil crisis and the reopening of the Suez Canal in 1975, the demand for tankers and trading ships dropped rather suddenly. Globally, this resulted into a huge drop in ship values to as little as 10 per cent (Büschgen, 1995).

As a result, *Pfandbriefe's* collateral decayed dramatically, and borrowers faced default. The Hypothekenbanken had to downgrade their assets and used up all their reserves. They only avoided a larger crisis that hit many banks investing in shipping through heavy state involvement. Deutsche Bank bailed out its own Hypothekenbank, integrated it into its own balance sheet to avoid complete default and to held up the image of the *Pfandbrief* (Büschgen, 1995, p. 719). The *Pfandbrief* and other long-term assets and liabilities allowed German banks to withstand international crises such as the Volcker shock in early 1980s (Wixforth, 2010), at least better than their peers. Banks often failed in the 1980s because they had to refinance their long-term positions with short-term liabilities whose interest rates suddenly shot up. Nonetheless, the shipping crisis confirms that German banks had to contain the market-based risk of *Pfandbriefe*. *Pfandbriefe*, counter to common wisdom, can – and have – failed.

CONCLUSION

To understand financial change, we need to know where it starts from. In this spirit, this chapter argues that the *Pfandbrief* is an important practice that we can learn from in our conceptualisations of financialisation. *Pfandbriefe* represent Germany's long history with market-based practices, as this deep dive into the origins of securitisation shows. Banking and housing finance at the turn of the nineteenth century have been the opposite of what is commonly assumed to be the characteristics of German and US finance. While the US relied on local deposit banks and localised personal networks, German mortgage banks channelled money into housing from anonymous capital markets (cf. Kohl, 2015). The history of the *Pfandbrief* thus challenges traditional accounts of German ideal types characterised by a stable financial system based on non-market and 'boring' features.

This chapter's history also reveals that the idea of the *Pfandbrief* as a long-term, stable financial security with long roots in the three-pillar German financial system should be taken with caution. Rather than representing a never-failing bond, the oil crises of the 1970s showed that they can default similarly to any other financial practice. Similarly, big banks' investment into the Hypothekenbanken (Klein, 1995, p. 9; Wijburg & Aalbers, 2017, p. 980) blurred the boundaries of the three pillars of German finance. If we only focus on its role as an ideal typical financial practice that has prevented the rise of markets, we miss an opportunity to analyse how German financiers have actively used and changed market-based practices according to their funding and investment needs. If German banks had been well accustomed to tapping markets, more so than US banks, markets are an insufficient signifier for the transformative change of financialisation. *Pfandbriefe's* nature requires us to develop a more precise understanding of what financialisation consists of, and what it does not.

Apart from debunking the myth of German finance as non-market-based, why do I spend a whole chapter on a financial practice that did not lead to financialisation? After all, investment in and funding by *Pfandbriefe* have played a rather small role within the overall strategies of the protagonists of this book. According to Daniel Mertens (2015), *Pfandbriefe* have had more of a symbolic role than an actual material impact and this chapter confirms that their significance within the big banks' strategies has indeed been minor. It has been core funding strategy for the smaller mortgage and public banks. But if markets were the go-to ideals for finance, and given universal banks' historical power in Germany (Beyer, 2003; Pfeiffer, 1987; Zysman, 1983), and the large banks' ability to lobby for financial change (Höpner, 2001), why would they not mould *Pfandbriefe* towards a more dynamic and flexible financial practice according to their own needs?

Eventually, the big German banks lost interest in the *Pfandbrief* and left it to the specialised banks. While they actively tried to re-engineer the *Pfandbrief* to fit a more globalised financial world in the 1990s with the invention of the Jumbo-*Pfandbrief*, this endeavour mostly failed. Instead, in the 2000s, German banks, alongside many European financial institutions, became customers of US banks' ABS. Covered bonds, on their parts, were perhaps significant, with outstanding covered bonds amounting to 15 per cent of the European capital market in 2005 (Lassen, 2005). However, they propelled little in terms of the larger banking transformation. *Pfandbriefe* only received more widespread attention after the GFC (Wijburg & Aalbers, 2017, p. 979), when it became too obvious that the US mortgage industry might not have been the best idea.

The significance of this political economy of the *Pfandbriefe* is that it allows us to appreciate the role *Pfandbriefe* played in the history of German finance and to put the contrasting lineages of US and German financialisation into perspective. *Pfandbriefe* were useful for managing and funding long-term investment, for the *Landschaften* to fund construction and agriculture, and later for the universal banks to engineer new strategies to advance into retail finance and housing construction in the post-war years, and to compete against the smaller savings and cooperative banks to do so. It is here that the different trajectories of German and US finance emerged. While German banks adopted new market-based practices to compete against decentralised savings and cooperative banks, US banks started to use market-based practices to compete against US money market funds. And it was this shift in US money market funding that started to prompt a transformation towards financialisation. While German banks have had opportunities for market-based funding in Germany, historically more so than US lenders, there was an important funding resource that the *Pfandbriefe* could not give them to respond to the new global competitive dynamics of the second half of the twentieth century. It was this need that would eventually deeply affect the German banks, as the remainder of the book will show.

4

The Eurodollar Roots of the German Model

INTRODUCTION

Chapter 3 has established the German origins of securitisation and argued that market-based funding was integral to German construction and retail finance. This chapter takes an international viewpoint and finds significant engagement with global market-based finance during the post-WWII years. Tracing German banks' practices on Eurodollar markets, I argue that global offshore markets were not only a significant international dimension of German banking but part and parcel of the German export-led model. This is a key step in the process of extroversion. Commerzbank and Deutsche Bank's Eurodollar strategies reveal how German banks first encountered LM and how this started to trigger a *qualitative* change. As the German domestic institutions required, but could not themselves support, international financial practices, the universal banks must start to orient themselves towards US financial practices.

Political economy scholarship recognises the significance of the Euromarkets – not only for financial globalisation in general but also for the US Americanisation of European finance (Green, 2016; Konings, 2011; Schenk, 1998; 2010; Strange, 1987, 1986). However, most accounts either analyse the role of the Eurodollar markets in the demise of the Bretton Woods system (Helleiner, 1994), in advancing US hegemonic power (Gindin & Panitch, 2012) or in financing the UK trade deficit and advancing the power of the City (Burn, 1999b; Norfield, 2017), predominantly focusing on the states' role in constructing offshore financial relations. Studies concentrating on private agents remain focused on their role in recycling petrodollars (Altamura, 2016). While scholars have argued that the increased globalisation of finance in the 1960s expanded the 'territorial scope of financial activity' (Lütz, 2004, p. 175) and caused tremendous changes (Deeg, 1999, p. 13), they have so far remained vague about their impact on European financial agents, neglecting early transformative entanglements during the 1960s almost entirely.

This chapter recasts the Euromarkets' transformative impact from the perspective of EF in two parts. The first part shows that the connection to international finance was already built into the fabric of the German bank-based model.[1] The next section examines the post-war export model and shows that big banks had convenient business opportunities in Germany but struggled to provide international funds when German exporting corporations increasingly went abroad from the 1950s onwards. The second section reveals that US banks provided further challenges to German banks as the former started to outcompete their European counterparts in financing international corporate loan projects. I examine the different strategies and conflicting intentions of European banks in regaining control of European assets to highlight how the German banks tried, but mostly failed, to fight the US 'American challenge' (Battilossi & Cassis, 2002) on their own ground by building pan-European bourses. The German post-war economic architecture thus made Eurodollar funding a crucial prerequisite for its export model but Eurodollar funding was dominated by US banks.

The second part of the chapter argues that German banks were, in fact, among the pioneers on the Euromarkets and contributed to many of their early innovations. However, they quickly lost out against the financing power of LM. To this end, the third section demonstrates that German banks reluctantly embraced offshore markets where the German exporting sector sought – and US banks provided – USD funding because there was no other way to compete with US banks. All big German banks engaged in European club banks[2] in Luxembourg – an offshore centre less dominated by US banks – to pool their limited Eurodollars and spread the risk of unknown markets. While successful from the mid 1960s throughout the 1970s, I explain in the fourth section how these initial Eurodollar strategies lost out because the rise of LM gave US banks the upper hand in the Euromarkets. If they wanted to compete with US banks, European banks

1 See Andrea Binder (2023, p. 77ff) for a rare account of how German state managers used offshore structures to sweeten the German social compromise for the moneyed elites during the post-war years.

2 European club banks represented formal collaborations between several banks that would pool their capital to mutually issue loans on the Euromarkets. The level of collaboration varied between the club banks. A syndicated loan depicts one-off financing from a group of lenders that jointly provide the funds to the borrower.

had to innovate more. This led them to banking in London, the European centre for US financial innovations and where the practices of LM were proliferating. In this way, the territorial expansion of financial markets as part of globalisation was not a problem for the German banks per se. The real challenge arose instead from the innovations of LM. As the rest of the book will show, this was the beginning of a transformation that forced the banks to reorient themselves towards the logics of US finance.

EXPORT FINANCE IN POST-WAR GERMANY

Any history of German finance must account for the distinct characteristic of the German model that emerged during the post-war years (Deeg, 2001; Neebe, 2004). While the German economy is internationally connected through its export sector, predicated on repressed wages and price stability (Baccaro & Pontusson, 2016; Germann, 2021), the German model is often seen as a coherent institutional framework in which the banks played their functional role in supporting the German export economy – significant change only came in the 1990s with financial liberalisation. By contrast, taking the banks' extroverted strategies into account, I find that they did act according to the German model in the late 1950s, but not in the way that is usually assumed. Instead of simply providing a steady outlet for patient loans, the German export orientation constituted the initial challenges for the German banks' international financial strategies. While the reconstruction of the German political economy provided support for banks domestically, its export orientation made international finance a necessity – but the institutional setup offered little support for issuing international loans.

The centrality of exports emerged during the early post-war decades during what is sometimes termed the German 'economic miracle'.[3] But rather than constituting a truly new beginning, German industry did not suffer as much as might be expected after the deadly war. Industrial capital stock was relatively intact and at a level comparable to that of the mid 1930s. Owing to high wartime investment by the Nazis, its industrial machinery was relatively modern compared to other European nations (Altvater & Hübner, 1988; Carlin, 1996). Because of immigration from the east, there was a steady, relatively highly skilled supply of labour. Sourcing

[3] For a historical discussion on the German '*Sonderweg*' (special path), see Abelshauser, 2016; Kocka, 1988. For an internationally oriented analysis of German 'embedded liberalism', see Germann (2021, p. 62ff).

raw materials and fuel as well as the destroyed rail system were the main problems for capital accumulation. The 1948 Currency and Economic Reform was successful in promoting economic growth because of these favourable preconditions. Post-war macroeconomic policy favoured quick industrial growth and investment through tax incentives and a fiscal system that kept the previous wealth distribution in place. The currency reform and the eradication of previous financial savings excluded industrial capital, which meant that Nazi-era ownership and employment continued, allowing production to resume quickly (Altvater & Hübner, 1988). Moreover, companies had to liquidate their assets to finance everyday business (rather than holding them), which promoted industrial production rather than financial development (Carlin, 1996).

Termed the German economic miracle, geopolitics played an important role in supporting reconstruction. Allowing previous capital ownership and Nazi officers in high positions to continue, US financial support was important in setting up the 'German' model. A huge boost came from the funds of the Marshall Plan, part of the US's European reconstruction efforts that connected the European economy to its own internationalising Fordist regime and to prevent the spread of communism in Europe. The Marshall Plan provided the capital for growth to a significant extent, which funded core industries that did get destroyed, financing about 20 per cent from 1952 to 1956 (Grünbacher, 2004). I will detail later how the Marshall Plan institutionalised one of the core financing institutions of Germany, the Kreditanstalt für Wiederaufbau (Bank for Reconstruction, KfW), but it is important to note that as a result of this capital injection, Germany had a very young and modern industry that boosted its productivity and exceptional growth (Carlin, 1996, p. 467).

The accompanying macroeconomic policy for domestic demand was more restrained, granting geopolitical developments another important input factor. Low demand at home did not match increasing pace of production so that demand abroad would need to absorb a significant share of production, contributing to the internationalisation of the German corporate sector (Abelshauser, 1983; Baccaro & Pontusson, 2016; Neebe, 2004). Termed the 'black irony of history', another deadly war, the Korean War from 1950 to 1953, caused a significant boost in international demand that catalysed the German economy (Altvater & Hübner, 1988, p. 470). German brand names did not suffer much from the Nazi crimes; 80 per cent of goods were sold by previously existing brands and other European countries, such as France and Italy, bought Germany's capital equipment to build up their economies. Demand for German exports was further boosted by orchestrated wage restraint, which was made possible by a combination of weak unions and a growing cohesion of business associations, and a favourable exchange rate for the German Mark (Berghahn & Vitols, 2006; Neebe, 2004).

This export regime was financed by the universal banks, commonly seen as close allies to the manufacturing industry, guiding and benefitting from growth based on 'diversified quality production' (Streeck, 1991). Aside from retained earnings, the main source of funding for business was short-term bank loans. Initially, big German banks were severely restrained in the 1950s (Wixforth, 2010), partly because the Allies divided them into separate entities. More transformative initiatives, however, such as the attempts, favoured by the US, to establish a second Glass-Steagall Act, failed because of the resistance of the German authorities (Carlin, 1996, p. 488). Instead, banks could already reunite in West Germany in 1958, a consequence of the Allies prioritising a functioning German economy over preventing those responsible for World War II from regaining power. A prominent example of this was Hermann Abs, chairman of Deutsche Bank from 1957 to 1967, who, if not a party member, nonetheless held many important positions within the Nazi regime. He was arrested and detained for three months during the *Entnazifizierung* but ended up as an influential architect of the West German political economy (Grünbacher, 2004, p. 30). Commerzbank had similar wartime veterans in its management if they could evidence needed financial expertise (Sattler, 2020, p. 227). While German banks had to build up their balance sheets again, they were up and running by the 1960s.

The distinct socio-economic organisation of the German model meant that banks accumulated capital quickly during post-war reconstruction, but this was supported by the US. A crucial source of funding was thus the Marshall Plan, which provided US capital to reconstruct Europe. This was critical for German banking because it secured the funding of bank loans at a time when capital markets and cash were basically non-existent in Germany (Büschgen, 1995, p. 559; Sattler, 2020, p. 235). The Marshall Plan provided most of KfW's money for reconstruction.[4] KfW passed on transfer credits to the German universal banks that they channelled to corporations (Grünbacher, 2004). While German banks carried the risk of these loans, they had easy access to refinancing (Vitols, 1998, p. 85).

[4] By the end of 1950, KfW was provided with DM 3.2 billion to pass on as loans, of which 762 million came from German sources, the rest from US counterpart funds (Grünbacher, 2004).

KfW was founded in 1947 with the specific aim to provide capital for reconstruction[5] with export finance becoming one of its core tasks. The Marshall Plan provided a significant amount of its equity; by 1953, it had received €1.89 billion. While the Marshall Fund had to be repaid in parts, it was the federal government that repaid the US, whereas the KfW acquired the capital as equity (KfW, n.d.). With the help of KfW, bank loans became increasingly long-term. KfW and other special banks remained important financiers and provided about 25 per cent of long-term refinancing up until unification. It was this easy access to long-term finance that enabled a large amount of long-term loans, rather than the 'tutelage' between German banks and corporations (Vitols, 1998, p. 85). Public provision secured bank funding.

Deutsche Bank particularly benefitted, not least because head of the KfW was one of Hermann Abs influential positions. This facilitated a close relationship between Deutsche and KfW, enabling the former to acquire credit business easily from the public funds (Kobrak, 2007, p. 293). In 1957, Deutsche secured 30% of all export financing, which only declined slightly (to 20–25%) in later years. This remained a growing proportion of assets because the German export sector share of GDP grew from 8.5% in 1950 to 18.5% in 1970 (Büschgen, 1995, p. 726) – from around €4 billion to €64 billion[6] (Statistisches Bundesamt, 2019).

As was discussed in Chapter 3, banks also captured a growing volume of retail deposits from an increasingly wealthy society to refinance themselves, while long-term finance was provided by *Pfandbriefe* and long-term bank bonds. For example, in 1948, Deutsche Bank group could only issue *Pfandbriefe* worth DM 4 million, but has built on its *Pfandbrief* business since, as Chapter 3 showed. While the big three struggled to mobilise sufficient funds initially, capital markets were growing again from the late 1950s with significant state support as capital providers (Sattler, 2020). The Central Capital Market Committee (*Zentraler Kapitalmarktausschuss*) is dominated by banks and has given them privileged access to these markets since 1957[7] (Vitols, 1998, p. 85). Banks also had preferential access to the bond markets, allowing them to generate long-term capital provided by the insurance industry. Bank bonds

5 See Grünbacher (2004) for a detailed history.

6 For comparison, it was just under €1,317 billion in 2018.

7 Joint-stock banks directly issued bonds on the markets; cooperatives and savings banks issued their bonds through regional and national institutions that then refinanced the local banks.

accounted for about half of German insurance companies' investments and provided banks with large amounts of funds. Until unification, two-thirds of publicly traded bonds were bank bonds, one-third public and industrial bonds negligible (Vitols, 1998, p. 85). This was a second route through which they had easy access to funding and were able to capture German retail savings that were increasingly invested in insurance companies. The distinct socio-economic organisation of the German model meant that banks accumulated capital quickly during post-war reconstruction with convenient access to public and private funding. They could have had an easy life.

International finance, however, became a more complicated problem. In contrast to domestic structures, their international assets received less beneficial treatment by the allies and were confiscated. Despite repeated attempts to get them back, Hermann Abs had to give up (Kobrak, 2007, p. 264). And yet, German exports were the biggest driving factor of banks' accumulation of international assets (Streeck, 2009) so that the banks had to become innovative with how to support their internationalising companies. Growing exports posed a specific challenge for banks as there was a USD shortage in the German model. German banks had trouble providing currency exchanges and other international services (Pohl, 1998, p. 80; Sattler, 2020). Even Deutsche, with its largest pool of resources, had to advise its customers to seek funding from foreign local banks when they were internationalising in the 1950s (Kobrak, 2007, p. 294; Pohl, 1998).

While banks' DM liabilities slowly grew through bank bonds, the KfW and *Pfandbriefe* built up their long-term credit portfolio, the world market orientation of the German model lacked equally outward-oriented financial support. In fact, the German Bundesbank (central bank) regarded too much international capital in and outflow with suspicion and attempted to restrain it where possible (Rademacher, 2021). The banks' international assets could not equally rebuild due to their lack of foreign capital and foreign networks in the 1950s. This is a peculiar contradiction of the German political economy: Its bank-based financial system was ill-equipped to provide the finance for its expanding export sector. This was a key steppingstone for the international strategies of German banks: they had to look outwards to find financial resources to continue benefitting and supporting the export sector.

This problem was aggravated by a specific challenge in Europe that arose in the 1960s. One can easily imagine that German banks could grow and learn how to do international finance abroad and thus somehow retain their influence over the exporting sector. Both Commerzbank and Deutsche Bank started to build their international relations with other European banks soon after the end of the war (Gall et al., 1995; Sattler, 2020). However, these international ambitions were complicated by the fact that US banks were advancing into Europe, lead managing European corporate loans, and thus providing a new degree of competition in Europe. As the next section will show, this rendered the building of a more organic European financial architecture difficult. Instead, this challenge would soon push the extroverted strategies of the European banks towards US financial logics.

THE RISE OF THE US CHALLENGE

The Eurodollar markets are large offshore wholesale money markets, but their true size remains unknown. They played a defining role in financial globalisation since the 1960s. To recall, the syllable 'Euro' denotes that a currency is booked outside its own jurisdiction. Whenever a foreign bank or a foreign affiliate of a US bank issued or borrowed USD, they were called Eurodollars. For example, when a US bank shifts USD to its London branch and receives in return a deposit, it has created a Eurodollar deposit at the London branch. The biggest segment of the Eurocurrencies is the Eurodollar, with Eurodollar deposits leading with between 72% and 84% from 1964 to 1984 (Battilossi, 2010, p. 31). EuroDM was the second biggest currency, other currencies outside the Eurodollar were negligible.

The Eurodollar markets most famously proliferated in London from the 1950s when the Soviet Union and other countries gave USD deposits to the US banks and UK merchant banks in London as several foreign investors were reluctant to deposit them in the US directly, lest they were confiscated because of the Cold War (Schenk, 1998, 2002). Another important, if mostly neglected, factor for their growth is post-war European reconstruction and integration, significantly promoted by the already mentioned Marshall USD funds in the 1950s and 1960s (Balaban, 2022). But they quickly outgrew their initial impetus and proliferated also in Luxemburg and other offshore centres such as the Cayman Islands, which rose to fame as tax haven during the last decade. A Eurodollar is a time deposit with a 30-, 90- or 180-day duration and has been used to finance sovereign, corporate and bank debt (Stigum, 1990, p. 68).[8] The Eurodollar

[8] See Schenk (1998) for an account of the historical origins in London ; Palan and Nesvetailova (2014) for its connection to shadow banking.

markets expanded exponentially in latter half of the 1960s and are massive today.[9] The Eurodollar CD market, for example, was more active in 1990 than the market for CDs in the US (Stigum, 1990, pp. 56, 199ff).

The Eurodollar markets introduced new imperatives and constraints for German banks and triggered their contribution to the development of those global markets. As I have outlined in Chapter 2, US banks started to tap money markets when corporations and households began to deposit their cash with money market funds (MMFs). Regulation Q and other limiting financial restrictions meant that US banks additionally started to use Eurodollar markets systematically for funding in the 1960s, particularly during the second half of the decade. In addition to the flexibility of interest rate setting and attracting funds, commercial banks were allowed to be both investment and commercial banks in the Euromarkets – like the Europeans – a key advantage to their home restrictions. With the rise of Certificates of Deposits (CD) and time deposits connected to the strategies of LM, and increased demand from American MNCs, liabilities of US banks exploded (Battilossi, 2010), while corresponding need for liquidity management was ensured by the rise of US money markets (Baker and Collins 2005, p. 255). Their newly gained power through the innovations of LM gave them a key competitive advantage on the Eurodollar markets (Beck, 2022a; Dutta, 2020) that they increasingly used to fund both their international and domestic assets (Konings, 2008b).

This posed a rather inconvenient problem for European financial institutions. The US banks were better placed to provide funding not only for US companies but also for European corporations and international sovereign borrowers that increasingly used the Eurodollar markets (Panitch & Gindin, 2005). The increasing sophistication with which they managed that debt allowed them to dominate European corporate syndicates (Battilossi, 2010) – an attack the Europeans did not appreciate. As Ost (1970) from the associations of German banks recalls, the German banks were concerned that the US banks fostered their foreign networks in Europe. German and other European banks barely served as underwriters of new issues in the 1960s (Bussière, 2005, p. 271ff). They complained bitterly about this disregard of their position and thought they should be the leading banks. The situation was considered 'evil' and Hermann Abs went so far as to claim that it would endanger Germany's national interests as a whole (Roberts, 2001, p. 19).

9 'At the end of 1969, total liabilities of US banks to foreign branches stood at about $13 billion. As late as 1967 they had been less than $2 billion' (De Cecco, 1987, p. 190, cited in Konings, 2008b, p. 48).

The leading European banks aimed to challenge this takeover. German banks wanted to expand on their fledgling partnerships with other European banks to create a pan-European capital market strategy that would allow large-scale loans denominated in DM and other European currencies. With Hermann Abs taking up a leading role among Belgian, Dutch and Swiss bankers, they responded with joint strategies to increase foreign investment in all European bourses and to improve their placement capacity in their home markets (Bussière, 2005, p. 271). While this resulted in increased international issues in the German market in the mid 1960s, foreign investment in Paris and Germany remained marginal (Feiertag, 2005, p. 233f).

The initiative did not last long. In contrast to the German banks, the French financial market was more restricted internationally so that French banks had less interest in this particular European strategy. This was complicated by a French split in interest with respect to cooperating with US banks. The French merchant banks favoured US links for financial engineering, while the deposit banks leaned towards the continental strategy that was better suited to their wide spectrum of clientele and large capital base for syndicated loans. When Deutsche was adamant in refusing to participate in US-led syndicates, French bank Paribas acted as capital provider in a European investment that was managed by US banks. The French banks were able to quickly join US alliances and therefore had less interest in pursuing pan-European strategies (Bussière, 2005, pp. 265–272). Deutsche declared in 1967 that 'it was disagreeable to see two great European companies entrusting their transactions to New York houses' (Bussière, 2005, p. 273).

This left the Swiss and German banks alone in their rejection. The attempts to counter the US influx by fabricating a cross-border European financial infrastructure that would allow them to mobilise their own financial resources failed. While Abs initially claimed that the Eurodollar market 'was transitory and would go away' (Roberts, 2001, p. 19), the German banks had to finally embrace it. The initial joint ventures on the Eurodollar markets were still mainly a defensive strategy against the 'forceful and hardly ethical' aggressive strategies of US banks pushing into German banking (Abs quoted in Ross, 1998, p. 355), but, once offshore, Deutsche Bank started to lead the assault of the German banks in the Euromarkets (Battilossi, 2002) with Commerzbank aggressively expanding a bit later from the 1970s (Paul et al., 2020). It is here that their first extroverted strategies of financialisation were forged, as they had to start relocating to Luxembourg and finally London to compete against US banks.

The next two sections bring to the fore the different roles of Luxemburg and London as financial centres and highlight their institutional context and legacy. I trace the changing extroverted strategies of the German banks as they were motivated and constrained by the increasing global capital flows and US banks' practices of LM. While Luxemburg was not yet overrun by US banks and became the centre for Eurocurrency exchange and club banking, London was crucial for developing practices of LM once the clubs ran out of steam. It is important to note that while I focus on Commerzbank and Deutsche Bank, some forty German banks participated in the Eurodollar markets (Binder, 2023, p. 85), with Dresdner Bank and the public Westdeutsche Landesbank (WestLB, the Westphalian public state bank) being two more leading agents and part of club banks (Roberts, 2001; Trampusch et al., 2014).

CLUB BANKING IN LUXEMBURG

Luxemburg was the first step in the extroverted strategies of the German banks. Initially, the banks tackled Eurocurrency business via the banks' own trade departments and their correspondent banks in Luxembourg, and later London (Battilossi, 2010). However, to meet the challenge of US banks, they increasingly explored cooperations among two or several European banks (Sattler, 2020). And the further the Euromarkets developed, the less able the banks became to manage the growing volumes and currency transactions of the Eurobonds, -credits and -loans on their own. To cope with these unknown markets, raise enough USD and limit the risk involved, they formed club banks comprised of several banks, including the US banks, that pooled their resources and expertise to jointly issue securities (Drach, 2022). As I will show, the initial goal of financing German corporations – the attempt to defend 'their' assets against US banks – quickly aligned the German banks with the broader operations of the Eurodollar markets.[10]

Few European banks had experience in offshore finance or understood precisely what was going on. When attempting to define Eurocurrency markets in 1964, the Bank for International Settlement (BIS) – the main forum for central banks' discussion of the Euromarkets – stated modestly:

[10] Sovereign bonds were also an important business segment for the European banks. For example, Eurocurrency loans to British authorities in 1958 show that foreign banks provided USD 73 million, almost as much as British merchant banks which provided 76 million, while British overseas banks lent 22 million (Balaban, 2022, p. 20).

'There are several difficulties involved in trying to say precisely what a Eurocurrency is' (cited in Balaban, 2022). Deutsche lamented the fact that it could scarcely monitor its clients' projects' credibility, a source of power it enjoyed within the tightly knitted corporate network of Germany Inc. As late as 1974, Franz Heinrich Ulrich (chairman of Deutsche at the time) lamented the comparatively small margins of Eurodollar claims in comparison to the credit risk (Büschgen, 1995, p. 738).

The nature of the US challenge, however, meant that competition was happening on the Eurodollar markets, so that is where the European banks went. Luxemburg as a financial centre gained momentum in the 1960s as the Euromarkets' stock market and as a hub for currencies other than the dollar (Dörry, 2016). The world's first Eurobond was issued and listed in Luxemburg in 1963. It was issued by Warburg, a London-based investment bank, with the help of Deutsche Bank (Burk, 1992; Pohl, 1998, p. 71). The banks issued Eurobonds on behalf of the MNCs and sovereigns so they could sell their debts in foreign currencies, but mostly in USD. European banks were in fact, well-placed for these large issues because they could engineer multi-currency bonds where each bank would do its own currency part. They exploited currency differentials and circumvented capital controls (Battilossi, 2000).[11] Non-dollar currency rose from 15% in 1969 to 35% in 1970s (Baker & Collins, 2005, p. 258).

Luxemburg was dominated by German banks so that its key Eurocurrency was DM (Dörry, 2014, p. 229). Luxemburg's German foreign affiliates financed a large share of their parent banks' Euromarket activities (Büschgen, 1995, p. 737). Of thirteen German banks' foreign subsidiaries, ten were in Luxemburg in 1972, and they were growing fast. German banks' assets in Luxemburg tripled from DM 2 billion to 6 billion in the early 1970s (Kobrak, 2007, p. 289). Initially, Commerzbank's board in Frankfurt attempted to limit the exposure of roll over credits of its subsidiary to DM 4 million, but in vain. Increasing volumes of credit meant that this limit was transcended only a few months later (Sattler, 2020, p. 354).

Another boost for the EuroDM was the European partner banks. German banks relied on their correspondent banks to gain access to USD after their own international subsidiaries were confiscated. Their partner banks in turn demanded access to DM, which internationalised the currency (Büschgen, 1995, p. 746). The growing EuroDM markets and

[11] Eurobonds made an even larger comeback in the 1980s, when different risk techniques allowed single banks to underwrite and sell bonds more easily.

the prominence it afforded German banks also brought them closer to US banks and finally provided a useful recycling mechanism for German exports. By the mid 1960s, using their growing Eurodollar resources by swapping from EuroDM, German banks lent Eurodollar to US banks which in turn passed them on to US corporations to buy imports from Germany (Binder, 2023, p. 85).

While the German Bundesbank opposed the selling of German securities abroad and domestic USD deposits (Germann, 2013) and the state attempted to tighten credit laws (Story, 1996, p. 382), German banks simply cleared their Eurodollar transactions abroad.[12] The Bundesbank introduced some initiatives to shield domestic financial markets and obliged any EuroDM bond issue to have a German lead manager to stay in the loop. Nonetheless, Luxemburg allowed German banks to breach any international capital limits and the Bundesbank did little more than complain about the growing EuroDM and other offshore markets. In fact, the Bundesbank itself started to participate. Besides placing parts of its own USD reserves in the Eurodollar markets, the central bank provided the roughly forty German banks operating in the offshore markets with currency swaps below market rate, facilitating the aforementioned Eurodollar recycling mechanism (Binder, 2023, p. 85).

Deutsche made quick advances in regaining some of its international dominance. According to a Euromarket banker at the time, each time the dollar fell out of favour because of stark fluctuations, financiers sought EuroDM, allowing Deutsche to establish its lead (Burk, 1992, p. 83). Deutsche actively pushed the EuroDM market to reduce its reliance on foreign currencies (Büschgen, 1995, p. 738). While Commerzbank focused on extending Eurocredits to its German clients and fostered bilateral relations, Deutsche established its first subsidiary in 1968 to participate in the wider financial expansions, developing significant currency operations to manage syndicated loans and other large-scale sovereign loans (Büschgen, 1995, p. 373). While Commerzbank's Luxemburg outpost was its most profitable international investment in 1970–1973, returning 6–7 million in profits to its headquarters (Sattler, 2020, p. 318), Deutsche generated billions in revenues and substantial profits in Luxemburg (Kobrak, 2007, p. 297). Luxemburg reflects the initial resolution to build strategies that could compete with the practices of LM.

However, while the DM turned into the second reserve currency, it only represented a minor share compared to the volume of Eurodollars.

[12] By contrast, Italian banks, for example, booked them domestically (Balaban, 2022).

Luxemburg's centrality as a multi-Eurocurrency hub did not remove banks' need to get Eurodollars if they wanted to remain important international players. In that regard, the European banks were in a similar position: they did not have USD as home deposits and therefore lacked reliable funds to operate on the Eurodollar markets, a situation that provided a crucial imperative for the direction of their extroverted strategies (Beck, 2022a). To recall, US banks' use of LM meant that they were able to hoover up much of the USD claims available.

The main way for European banks to challenge the US Americans was club banks (Drach, 2022; Ross, 1998). Those joint ventures allowed them to pool their limited USD resources and share the risk of offshore finance (Pohl, 1998; Roberts, 2001). Club banks were even joined by US and UK banks to conquer the dramatic rise of global MNCs and turbulences such as the 1970s oil crises. The consortium banks were also a way for banks to try to make sense of these new practices (Roberts, 2001, p. 24). The general confusion of the Eurodollar markets and how to respond to it is summarised by a former Eurobanker: 'No one knew what they [Club Banks] were for except that everyone else was doing it' (Roberts, 2001, p. 35). They founded 'study groups' that met regularly to make sense of the Eurodollar markets (Ross, 1998, p. 365). The joint initiatives enabled banks to experiment with currency swaps and securitisation in a safer way. Club banks benefited from a larger pool of capital from their parent banks allowing them to extend credits far beyond of the sum of the individual parts (Roberts, 2001). By the late 1960s, the Euromarkets grew so rapidly that joint managers from at least two different countries were needed for any new floated issue. Through these joint ventures, European banks regained a remarkable influence in corporate financing (Lockhart, 1969, p. 128). German banks, with their constrained international capital resources and embryonic domestic capital markets, were able to participate in complicated financing operations that they otherwise could not have managed (Klein, 1995). They praised these partnerships as a 'new epoch of international activities' (Wixforth, 2010, p. 109).

Besides pushing for EuroDM markets, Deutsche recovered from its loss of international networks by consolidating its club banking networks. It was among the first to form a banking club in 1959 – Club des Celibataires – together with Banque de la Société Générale de Beligique, S. A., the Amsterdamsche Bank N. V. and Midland (which joined in 1963). Renamed in 1963 as European Advisory Committee (EAC) and European Banks International Company (EBIC), it became one of the leading Eurocurrency club banks in 1967 (Ross, 1998, p. 354). As a cooperative group across national boundaries, EBIC was the first 'true' European champion (Drach, 2022). As Luxemburg was still an easier place for European banks to get Eurocurrency, EBIC established a subsidiary there to expand its access to Eurodollars (Büschgen, 1995, p. 832f).

Commerzbank followed a similar strategy, albeit later and less forcefully. Commerzbank tried longer to follow a pan-European strategy as well as bilateral and cross-border lending, including an attempt to be listed in Paris in 1962 – the first German bank to do so – but the French finance minister declined the listing, much to the disapproval of the German banks (Feiertag, 2005, p. 238). Deutsche, in contrast, declined to partner up with French banks after the failed strategy of a pan-European alliance against US banks. No French bank was allowed to be part of EBIC. Commerzbank started a partnership with the publicly owned Crédit Lyonnais in 1970, and its repeated efforts to gain access to the Paris bourse were finally successful in 1971 (Feiertag, 2005, p. 238f; Bussière, 2005, p. 167). Being the smaller bank, Commerzbank had less resources to spend on the Euromarkets amid its strategies to expand retail finance in Germany. However, Commerzbank, too, formed a club bank called Europartners with Crédit Lyonnais, Banco di Roma and Banco Hispano Americano (now part of the Santander Group), which was signed into an official partnership in 1970–1971 (Wixforth, 2010, p. 109). Europartners was more integrated than EBIC, and its main focus was European monetary integration (Ross, 1998, p. 355), pushing for the European economic and currency union, while Deutsche was more oriented to the offshore (Wixforth, 2010, p. 116).

The story of the European banks in Luxemburg is not complete unless I mention the Petrodollars. In the 1970s, Eurodollars experienced a huge push through recycling petrodollars. It was the European banks in Luxemburg that recycled a large amount of the money produced during the oil crisis years (Altamura, 2016, p. 32). The petrodollars were important in increasing the funds available for European banks. Deutsche Bank's balance sheet volume in Luxemburg grew exponentially to DM 9 billion in 1975 and 15.5 billion in 1979 (Büschgen, 1995, p. 739). Petrodollars were commonly used for credits to the Global South, including Mexico and Argentina, which laid the ground for the detrimental 1980s debt crisis. Deutsche was no exception: it coordinated a syndicated loan of USD 1.2 billion, including sixty-eight participants in the loan. To account for the risk, Deutsche had to repeatedly increase its Luxemburg subsidiary's equity in 1973, 1975, 1977 and 1979 (Ibid.).

Nonetheless, Luxemburg as a financial centre is a remnant of a failed attempt to tackle the US challenge. While European banks captured a large share of the Petrodollars, the dominance of the US banks in corporate finance and sovereign bond issues remained. Despite initial success, the club banks and syndicate loans hit their limits in the 1970s and early 1980s because they predominantly relied on traditional lending and funding methods, as I will elaborate below. European banks pooled their Eurodollars to gain leverage but did not fundamentally change their strategies of how they got and managed them. To recall from Chapter 2, the rise of LM meant that a radical change in the management of funding was afoot in the US. The competition over Eurodollar deposits could not be won without a more dynamic management of liabilities to finance long-term assets (Battilossi, 2010). Reliably tapping wholesale funding to manage liquidity and time constraints became a crucial aspect of international banking. To manage their corporate funding – which was increasingly long-term and transnational in the 1970s – Eurobanks introduced floatable interest rates and roll over credits that again had implications for the management of liabilities: these joint ventures, where several banks had to coordinate, had little chance against the flexibility of LM on US money markets. To gain more control over the management of their balance sheets, they realised they needed to raise and leverage Eurodollars in a different way: the way that was practiced in London.

THE SHIFT TO LONDON AND THE LIMITS OF CLUB BANKING

London was a strategic location in the development of the Eurodollar markets (Gindin & Panitch, 2012; Konings, 2008). As I mentioned, they enabled US banks to finance their own internationalising conglomerates that restrictions in the US prevented, giving the City a strategic anchor point between the US and Europe. London saw a phenomenal rise in financial transactions in the 1970s. US banks were flooding the markets, introducing new ways to plumb financial systems. In response, UK merchant banks increasingly adjusted their practices, which fostered the development of secondary markets and new financial multinationals. (Dutta, 2018).

US banks had an institutional advantage in comparison to European banks in London. While European banks had advanced in the multi-currency transactions in Luxemburg, US banks were able to exploit Eurodollar deposits as well as the growing New York money markets, as I will detail more thoroughly in Chapter 4. US banks had ample resources for short-term funding to manage increasingly large, long and transnational loans. Radically new practices to engineer and place securities such as derivatives and CDs afforded the US banks incredible funding flexibility (Konings, 2008). This was an uneven playing field for the German banks attempting to gain deals on the Euromarkets. While the increase in volume of EuroDM in the 1970s gave the German banks a powerful niche, and the club banks were allowed to share USD resources, US banks had a much more powerful home funding market.

By the 1970s, 30 per cent of the banks' income came from international finance (Ramm, 2002). To keep ahead in global markets, however, German banks had to shift their focus from Luxemburg to London as the Eurodollar market centre (Dörry, 2014, p. 229). It was here that the new innovations were developing. Deutsche Bank set up its first representative office in 1972. The London office first served only as an extended arm of the Luxemburg subsidiary from where it raised Eurodeposits. Highlighting the initial tension with the club banks, this office was opened only a few months after Ulrich had claimed that their international strategy was with their club partnerships rather than on their own. To appease the EBIC partners, Deutsche agreed to deal with German clients only so that it would not rival the EBIC-owned London merchant bank (Pohl, 1998, p. 75).

Setting up a presence in London only complicated the need for USDs. Initially, acquiring customers was a problem. German companies were already dealing with UK banks and were not interested in Deutsche's outpost. To expand its business, Deutsche opened a new branch in 1976, the first under the name Deutsche Bank, to take deposits and do foreign exchange, celebrated as a new dawn in its global ambitions (Pohl 1998, p. 83). However, funding remained an issue. Restrictions on sterling lending at the time meant that it could only work with clients needing foreign currencies such as USD and DM. As swaps were also affected by tight government restrictions, it had to rely on its Eurodeposits for international clients and participating in lending syndicates to local corporations. While its triple-A rating made it a welcomed capital provider because British banks grew wary of the so-called secondary or cowboy banks that ran into huge troubles during the 1973–1974 crisis (Pohl, 1998, p. 87ff), Deutsche initially did not reach a lead position. Its London presence brought the lender closer to US innovations, but its traditional strengths in DM and corporate finance were only partially an advantage. It had to find new ways to participate in the Eurodollar markets, including learning the new financial innovations coming from the US.

That is why the European club banks also started to establish US subsidiaries in the 1970s when US regulation relaxed. Deutsche's EBIC consortium bank operated two subsidiaries. Their original goal was twofold: on the one hand, they aimed to provide services to internationalising European corporations (Drach, 2022); on the other hand, they aimed to provide consultancy to US businesses wanting to go to Europe (Büschgen, 1995, p. 755). In that sense, their objectives were modest: financing their traditional clients and attracting US companies with their 'European expertise'. To achieve that, they had to be creative because of their status as universal banks which Glass–Steagall prohibited. EBIC thus established two US institutions: The European American Bank and Trust (EABTC) took in deposits and held securities. To overcome the lending limits placed on such a bank, they established the European American Bank Corporation (EABC), which was not allowed to take deposits. This structure meant that EABTC could provide EABC with advances that it could lend to corporations at much higher rates. This structure at times even rivalled Chase and Citibank and was worth USD 1.7 billion in assets in 1973 (Kobrak, 2007, p. 313). In 1978, they were merged into European American Bank (EAB) but much of their business was targeting advisory services to the home firms of the partner banks.

Commerzbank was also engaged in London's Euromarket activities and, to its advantage, was not restricted by its banking club in expanding its own branch network in London (Ross, 1998, p. 364). However, because of its focus on cross-country strategies, Commerzbank channelled more resources into closer integrating with its European partners and less into London. Nonetheless, it kept up with the German banks in issuing Eurobonds, for example, partnering with Warburg for mixed-currency Eurobonds in GBP and DM (Burk, 1992; Singleton, 2009). In contrast to Deutsche, though, Commerzbank was mainly internationally involved in the Eurodollar markets as supporting bank. It co-led eleven out of eighty-seven emissions in 1978, lead-managing only one of them (Sattler, 2020, p. 355).

Commerzbank, too, moved to New York with its club partners. Europartners Securities Corporation was founded in New York in 1971 to attract more banks to join their club. This was successful because Banco di Roma, one of the most influential Italian merchant banks joined the club. Banco di Roma and Crédit Lyonnais were fully owned by the state. In contrast to EBIC, however, they branded themselves decisively European, with international business (Sattler, 2020, p. 321).

Supported by their joint ventures, German banks were crucially involved in the Eurodollar markets in London from the 1970s onwards.

It is difficult to get precise numbers for their Euromarket activities, and how much of it reached domestic markets. The extent of their Eurodollar practices was smaller compared to their German credit and compared to US and British merchant banks. However, it was big enough so that the Bundesbank was increasingly concerned about inflationary pressures (Germann, 2013; Rademacher, 2021; Story, 1996). They re-established their international networks and benefitted from the large loan demands of the MNCs and sovereign borrowers, which, throughout the 1970s, still sought syndicated – that is, more traditionally funded – loans (Stigum, 1990, p. 233). For sure, US banks captured the larger chunk, but the big German banks, including the public WestLB, at times rivalled some of the US banks (Battilossi, 2002, p. 18) with Deutsche leading among the Europeans. While the lack of USD support of their domestic system showed cracks in the otherwise tightly knitted networks of Germany Inc. ('*Deutschland AG*'), German banks were able to partially recover their corporate financial relations by going to the Eurodollar markets, and expanded beyond that into the US.

This initial success, however, was short-lived. While according to *The Economist* in 1976, the Consortium banks were 'the most important banking development for a generation' (quoted in Roberts, 2001, p. 38), the increasing sophistication of US and also British merchant banks meant the European club banks seemed comparatively cumbersome in issuing Eurobonds. By 1976, the clubs were in fact already 'dinosaurs' given the innovations coming from the US (Ross, 1998, p. 354). Within a decade, these initiatives had declined in importance. While the difficulties of coordinating among several international banks with competing interests cannot be downplayed, it was a specific financial technology that reduced the effectiveness of club banks.

Essentially, US banks dominated the Euromarkets through their innovative mechanisms of funding (Stigum, 1990). They had pushed LM so far that consortium banks had lost their advantages. The increased sophistication of LM and growing US money markets meant that syndicates were replaced by increasingly smaller groups. Loans were progressively sold on to secondary markets for refinance, with some banks starting to act in the prime and secondary markets at the same time. US banks' LM through which they dynamically raised liabilities and started to engineer their assets to match the corresponding liquidity requirements was 'an innovative technique that marked the most important structural change in the recent history of banking' (Battilossi, 2000, p. 169). US banks increasingly leveraged on their own through innovations and new financial securities, supported by growing US money markets. By contrast, club banks leveraged with the help of pooling resources from several banks.

Europeans' access to the US was restricted, however. Until 1970s, European banks could not access USD directly and were even constrained from issuing securities on Wall Street (Abdelal, 2006). Eurobanks could tap Eurodollar markets but had to offer higher returns on USD time deposits to attract funds compared to US banks (Battilossi, 2010, p. 45). As a result, club banks drained valuable resources from the parent banks. Club banks struggled with particularly vulnerable balance sheets because they juggled various foreign currencies and maturity transformations to finance their USD, which rendered the 1970s USD fluctuations particularly difficult for them. Club banks had to fund themselves to 81% on expensive inter-banking currency markets in comparison to 46% for US banks (Ross, 1998, p. 183). The parent banks did not appreciate continuous capital injections because they, too, had to get USD on expensive Eurocurrency markets. Given advanced securitisation expertise was increasingly common in the US, it was more and more difficult to keep up with rival US banks. Club banks could not provide the same leverage that LM could engineer.

For example, Deutsche's joint venture EAB independently advanced in Eurodollar markets, and even managed to buy Franklin National Bank, a New York retail bank which ran into trouble during the 1973 oil crisis. This gave EAB access to cheap USD retail deposits and turned EAB into one of the twenty-five biggest banks in the US at the time. However, Deutsche Bank was unsatisfied with its on-going dependence on the parent bank. More importantly, EAB was not yet able to manage increasingly complex acquisitions and assets, leading to many write-downs and problem loans. Deutsche seemingly put in more resources into this endeavour than it benefitted from it (Kobrak, 2007, pp. 315–316).

The other important reason for the demise of the club banks is also related to funding but from the demand-for-credit side. US banks increasingly issued commercial papers (CPs) a short-term, non-collateralised IOUs so that corporations funded themselves directly on money markets. By the 1980s, corporations issued their own securities (Stigum, 1990, p. 233), managed by the US banks (Sissoko, 2017). And while German banks did well with the EuroDM as a niche product for global corporations, with US money markets maturing, by the 1980s, US banks had learnt how to do foreign currency themselves. Banks such as Goldman Sachs swapped USD CPs into local currency for US corporations (Stigum, 1990). MMFs, too, invested in foreign CPs (Baba et al., 2009). Demand for syndicated loans decreased significantly by the 1980s, and the core advantage of the business model of club banks had diminished. Their international strategies of club banking became largely overtaken by the new developments in US markets.

CONCLUSION

The Eurodollar markets were a key steppingstone in the process of extroversion of the German banks. I have argued that German banks went to the Euromarkets to regain control over their assets from the 1960s onwards. The institutional set up of German model meant that international funding was difficult to get in Germany and had to be obtained from the Eurodollar markets instead. In that way, financialisation is a process that was already integral to the (re-) making of German finance in the post-WWII decades. This was aggravated by the financial power of US banks that started to provide European corporate funding. To tackle this issue, German banks firstly engaged with European club banking. This meant that they had to start buying USD, which they mainly did from their subsidiaries in Luxemburg. German banks also aimed to enhance their capacity to access USD liabilities more systematically in London and, tentatively, in the US, predominantly in form of club banking but also increasingly on their own to improve their management of large-scale projects in offshore markets. While London became the hub of financialisation and the connection from Europe to the US, Luxemburg's role as funding hub produced a legacy: foreign affiliates of German banks provided their parent banks with just under €20 billion in lending (aggregate net borrowing in 2012), while London and US subsidiaries became net borrowers of their German parent banks during the GFC (Düwel, 2013, p. 35).

In important ways, this history was triggered by the rise of LM which allowed US banks to dominate global financial markets from the 1960s onwards. As the second feature of EF foregrounds, this created the imperative for other banks to get more USD if they wanted to compete. Even if the German banks had not yet started to transform themselves towards US financial logics, the German banks were deeply affected by the rise of US finance. Failing to produce effective European financial structures, they engaged with offshore finance early on – during the rise, rather than demise, of Germany's coordinated market economy. The different locations and practices of the Euromarkets were fundamental in German banks' attempts to address the challenges of financial and corporate globalisation.

And yet, even though the big German banks shifted their strategies to Luxemburg and then to London, capturing significant volumes of Eurodollars, the practices of LM were one step ahead of the Europeans. The Euromarkets were thus important not simply as an early sign of externally expanding global markets, but as the terrain in which particular financial innovations posed new challenges for financial agents. In other words, the transformative impact was not financial globalisation per se, but a new financial practice coming from the US.

The following chapters build on this history to rethink the US Americanisation of global finance. I show that the US challenge caused the German banks progressively uprooted themselves from their home markets to address the imperatives of LM. To continue competing in the Eurodollar markets, they had to buy British and US financial institutions with more US financial expertise, and, eventually, institutionalising themselves in the US where they could get USDs at their source. For this, as I will show, they increasingly needed to adopt the practices of LM to enhance their institutional connections to US money markets, marking the fundamental transformation of the nature of their banking models towards US forms of finance.

5

Grounding USDs

INTRODUCTION

The first part of this book has shown that German finance was much more internationally orientated and less rigid or coherent than commonly understood. The first part of the book has also revealed a more refined understanding of US finance and its initial global impact. Both highlight that we need to go beyond the marketisation hypothesis to appreciate the transformations of financialisation. Doing this is the task of this second part. I use the concept of EF to explain how LM triggered the turn to financialised banking and why global finance became tethered to US financial logics.

This chapter embeds the Eurodollar markets into their institutional foundations and the transformation of the US financial system. We often hear about offshore financial centres as key mechanisms to the wealthy elites' ability to hide money. What is often less appreciated is how offshore finance is central to banks' ability to create money (Binder, 2023). Even less appreciated are the institutional connections of the Eurodollar markets to US money markets. Recognising the links between New York and London, however, helps to appreciate a crucial aspect of the banks' power and the supremacy of LM over other banking practices. This is important to understand why the German banks ventured from the offshore Eurodollar markets to the onshore USD markets in the US.

After having embarked on the Eurodollar journey, it may seem counterintuitive for the banks to integrate yet again into unknown markets, particularly considering the strength of US banks. Why go to a financial environment that presents even more disadvantages as it was the home of your competitors? German banks were initially mystified about what was going on in New York.

This chapter assesses the destination of their extroverted strategies. I aim to shed light on the reasons why non-US banks had little choice but to go if they wanted to be successful in global finance. As became clear to international lenders in the 1970s, US money markets afforded US banks critical advantages for banking in Eurodollar markets and for providing financial services to the globalising European corporate sector. As I will show, these connections afforded US banks two key USD funding markets and they could arbitrage between them. More importantly, using LM, US banks could exploit the flexibility and growing depth of US money markets to advance their practices in the offshore. And in turn, Eurodollar funding also significantly enhanced their domestic credit creation.

What served as an advantage for US banks, represented a significant restriction for European financiers. Counter to common assumptions of a US liberal financial system, it was, in fact, highly regulated. The unprecedented power LM gave to banks emerged from a controlled, rather than laissez-faire, environment in which some financial agents could exploit the restrictions of others (Knafo, 2022). US banks could capitalise on these limits to leverage growing debt resources and use this to capture on and offshore USD business. By contrast, European banks were barred by heavy regulations against universal banking and foreign investment in the US. The banks partly circumvented those restrictions by building offshore USD funding structures. But their traditional banking practices proved ill-suited to the US financial environment so that they remained second-tier banks, sometimes supporting, rather than rivalling, the US banks' dealings. While they tried to integrate themselves into US finance, and regulatory barriers eventually eased off, the German banks could not overcome their practical restrictions to engineer attractive securities and successfully tap US money markets.

This chapter is divided into three sections. The first section highlights the institutional connections of the Eurodollar markets to US money markets to flesh out how the dollars were ultimately located in US banks' balance sheets. The second section examines how, in contrast to US banks, European banks were excluded from capitalising on these links. In the third section, I trace the extroverted strategies through which European banks tried to overcome these limits by building further financial channels in the Eurodollar markets.

THE EURODOLLAR MARKETS' CONNECTIONS TO NEW YORK

The Eurodollar operations were what Marcia Stigum calls a 'merry-go-round' (1990, p. 209), centred on Fed reserves. Even though London was the centre of the Eurodollar markets and the major European and other banks booked plenty of Eurodollars on their own balance sheets, USD had to be cleared in the US, on US banks' balance sheets. For example, petrodollars were invested by the oil-rich countries and recycled through London to debtor countries in the Global South. Petrodollars never seemingly set foot onto the United States, but it was US banks that shifted their deposits and reserves at the Fed to make these transactions possible.

Regulations in the US meant that USD had to pass through US banks. European banks were therefore required to work with a US correspondent bank, until the 1978 International Banking Act allowed foreign branches to hold their own reserves accounts with the Fed. However, the Fed applied tight restrictions on the volume of their reserve accounts. Thus, even when major European banks had branches in the US, they kept depositing with US banks because they could hold more USD that way. This meant that if a non-US bank moved USDs, it was its US correspondent bank who cleared the deposits with the US counterparty in the US.

Stigum (1990, p. 206)[1] has an illustrative example in her excellent book: if Deutsche Bank received a loan of USD 10, let us say from Chase London, Deutsche's partner in the US increased its deposit account by USD 10 and therefore had to hold USD 10 more in reserves with the Fed.[2] The partner US bank of the creditor, Chase New York, decreased the deposit account that Chase London held with it by USD 10 and therefore decreased its Fed reserves by USD 10. This was simply done by a transfer of reserves from Chase to Deutsche Bank's partner bank in New York. The clearing system was centred on Fed funds, the US interbank market (see Morris & Walter, 1998), which meant that US banks turned into key nodes within offshore markets which, in addition to having LM, allowed them several privileges over their European counterparts.

As a result, the Eurodollar markets were essentially an extension of the US money markets (Helleiner, 1994) and US banks easily arbitraged between both. US banks used their foreign branches and moved easily between on and offshore USD to exploit any differentials for their own benefits. For example, in 1963 and 1970, domestic open market rates rose above Feds interest ceilings on domestic CDs. Unable to provide

1 See Stigum (1990, p. 199ff) for a more detailed and illustrative account of the different lending and investment practices. She explains the corresponding mechanisms of the changes on US balance sheets for the interested reader.

2 In million would make this example more realistic but I stick with simplicity.

higher rates to attract funding, US banks turned to the Eurodollar markets. The US banks' access to Fed funds meant that banks created a tight bond between their international and domestic money management and their global brokerage of USD (Stigum, 1990, p. 254ff). Because US banks were involved in both ends of the system, they had preferential access to information that they could pass on between their onshore and offshore entities. US banks could talk to their branches overseas over the phone, whereas German banks read about price movements in next day's newspaper. While Eurodollar deposits and onshore deposits with US banks generally kept similar rates because of arbitrage (Goodfriend, 1998, p. 54), it was US banks that exploited the price differentials.

Technological innovations eventually allowed instant communication across continents, which would diminish these benefits. Beyond informational advantages, however, this global USD clearing system favoured US banks management of funding in several ways. While US banks could enhance or offset their risk in the Eurodollar markets, Eurodollars represented an additional funding and currency risk for European banks so that they operated costly USD standby lines with US banks to better manage the fluctuations. But if Eurodollars dried up, non-US banks could not rely on European central banks to replenish USD. European central banks' USD reserves were only a fraction of foreign Eurodollar holdings. In case of crisis, US banks only faced the price of additional Fed reserve costs, whereas European banks had difficulties accessing USD even in normal times (Stigum, 1990, p. 286f). This is reflected in central banks' increased worry over USD flows on their domestic banks' balance sheets (Schenk, 2002, 2005), which in the case of Bundesbank, triggered severe criticism of its banks.

By contrast, US authorities accommodated and supported Eurodollars, even if the Treasury and Fed were initially very sceptical of those international capital flows and attempted to curb them through policies and voluntary controls on capital outflows. US financial regulation was highly politicised in the 1960s. Tight restrictions on capital movements, however, did little to curb FDI outflows. While the Fed was concerned about the inflationary impact of the Eurodollar markets, its response to a BIS-organised questionnaire in 1972 was already less conclusive. The Fed stated that the Euro-currency markets even helped with achieving certain monetary objectives and would have an inflationary impact only if other central banks would place too many securities of their own in the Euro-currency market (Braun et al., 2021, p. 804). Being critical of others, the Fed itself conducted ample Eurodollar operations as early as the 1960s to support

US banks credit creation and domestic funding, using the BIS to avoid appearing as a direct offshore market actor (McCauley & Schenk, 2020).

By the 1980s, the Fed had discovered that the financial inflows would *not* translate into the 'real' economy and cause inflationary havoc but rather support domestic financial flows. Capital flow expansions stayed within financial markets, further fuelling the deep and liquid infrastructure needed for successful LM (Konings, 2008b). Similarly, the Nixon administration adopted an approach of 'benign neglect' in the late 1960s. Much to the delight of the Treasury, the Eurodollar markets seemed to help finance a growing trade and current account deficit, aligning state authorities' positive stance towards Eurodollar markets (Ibid.). By 1981, US banks were allowed to engage with Eurodollar market activities on US soil via international banking facilities, which consisted of separate entities, not subject to domestic banking regulation (Cibriani & Gouny, 2015).

Beyond institutional support and advantages of currency exchange, the significance of the Eurodollar connections to New York is that US money markets uniquely accommodated the liquidity requirements of LM. As Chapter 2 clarified, LM was organically developed to take positions in US money markets. The globalising offshore infrastructure allowed the world to trade in USD, but how well banks could trade them depended on the banks' ability to do LM. And US banks made ample use of that. They used their money market funding to provide ever-larger funding structures and started to re-engineer assets that could be issued and subsequently funded wherever better funding opportunities materialised. They complemented their funding and investment of domestic dollars with Eurodollars and vice versa (Morris & Walter, 1998).

Growing US money markets gave US banks a deep pool of funding for their financial activities at home and internationally. Eurodollars were thus not only cleared on US soil, they were also spurred by the growth of US money markets. Nourished by the wider US financial architecture in the US (see Chapter 2), financial practices started to connect different financial markets and banking became closer and closer integrated with financial markets (Beck & Knafo, 2020; Konings, 2009). US banks had a unique flexibility to exploit these networks by combining different short-term papers to sell according to their liquidity needs. US banks could mobilise institutional and political resources to engineer financial innovations that would expand financial markets (Knafo, 2022). Indeed, one of the most striking developments of US capitalism is how the role of debt and finance became a defining feature of socio-economic life (Hyman, 2013; Ott, 2014), often used to ease political pressures and contradictions (Krippner, 2011). Policies, laws, tax incentives, economic practice and norms supported the use of debt and finance in social welfare, such as housing (Roberts, 2013), pensions (van der Zwan, 2017), or personal consumption (Montgomerie, 2006), but also in corporate governance (Knafo & Dutta, 2016) or real estate (Schwartz, 2008), which consistently fuelled big institutional investors and financial transactions that contributed to the rise of US money markets. That way, US banks had plenty resources for LM and to generate new assets that could accommodate its needs.

US banks had a plethora of opportunities for international arbitrage and advancing in the Eurodollar markets. Some of these benefits resulted of course from preferential regulatory conditions on the Euromarkets as an offshore financial system that held few constraints for making money. But the difficulties of German banks to compete with US banks arose out of a very specific institutional set up that enabled US banks to extend their debt relations to a volume and complexity not possible before. While the ending of the gold standard in 1971 ended a crucial US anchor for global USDs, the fact that US money markets uniquely supported LM meant the link to US institutions remained intact. The Eurodollar markets were an institutional extension of US finance, organically linked to US practices and public support. While the European banks remained somewhat puzzled as to how financial power was generated, they knew they had to get closer to the source of these innovations. They needed to route themselves into US money markets if they wished to have a better chance to regain some financial leeway.

THE RESTRICTIONS OF NEW YORK

While US banks swarmed Europe, their own institutions were well protected by US state managers who allowed their own banks to cross borders, but prevented capital from coming in, at least initially (Konings, 2010). French and German banks complained that selling foreign securities on Wall Street was virtually impossible before the mid 1970s (Feiertag, 2005, p. 240) and getting closer to the source of US-led financialisation was initially limited. The 'benign neglect' towards global finance, however, was slowly institutionalised into a more open US capital border in the 1970s. The SEC removed many restrictions for investment and international banks in the US (Gindin & Panitch, 2012, p. 122). The International Banking Act in 1978 allowed foreign banks to seek federal licenses and to acquire national banks. By the 1980s, all major international banks had opened branches in New York (Stigum, 1990, p. 215).

Liberalising capital controls, however, did not mean the German banks would directly benefit. When German banks started to establish their subsidiaries, US rules would restrict what foreign banks could do, particularly as universal banks. German universal banks were in constant danger of violating regulations, and they started to innovate to raise funding and issue securities. While the process of integrating banking with US money markets was advanced in the US, Glass–Steagall still restricted combining investment and deposit banking, a core feature of the universal banks.

Take, for example, Fed funds, a crucial inter-banking market to clear and manage offshore USD as described earlier. While Eurodollars and fed funds are treated the same in terms of reserve requirements, fed funds can only be lent by depository institutions, government-sponsored enterprises and a few others – but not European banks. Another crucial source of funding was growing pension funds' investments. The SEC restricted who can act as brokers for pension funds under the Employee Retirement Income Securities Act (ERISA) in 1974, and the German banks were not part of it. Deutsche Bank was lucky to manage at all as a universal bank, receiving an exception to operate as a commercial *and* investment bank because it arrived in the US before Congress had passed a law subjecting foreign banks to the same rules as local banks. Nonetheless, perhaps foreboding the series of lawsuits after the GFC, Deutsche was under constant threat of violating US requirements in the 1970s and 1980s because of its corporate entanglements as a universal bank (Kobrak, 2007). As a Deutsche banker who lived in the US in the 1980s to oversee the US expansion told me,[3] Deutsche's goal was to sell Eurobonds. However, they had to be 'seasoned' and Deutsche could only trade them on secondary markets. Instead of originating the bonds and pocketing the fee, Deutsche had to buy them from US banks, leaving the more profitable business to them.

Despite these drawbacks, Deutsche and Commerzbank used their club banks and foreign subsidiaries to build a US base (Büschgen, 1995; Sattler, 2020). Attempting to finance exporting and internationalising German companies, as well as advising US corporations to come to Germany, they slowly worked through what to them seemed like a mysterious network of practices and regulations. While Deutsche became more aggressive later on, it did not show much courage initially and searched for security in joining other fledgling European banks. Next to its EAB alliance, which engaged in institutional wizardry to comply with US regulations

[3] Personal conversation with upper – middle manager.

as documented in Chapter 4, Deutsche bought into UBS Corporation in 1971 for USD 4 million to attempt to tackle the USD markets as UBS-DB Corporation (Büschgen, 1995, p. 846). Its caution lasted seven years, and in 1978 Deutsche bought out UBS to attract and service foreign capital on its own terms, renaming it Atlantic Capital Corporation, which operated as a subsidiary. It also had to open a branch to take in deposits (Kobrak, 2007, p. 317). The legal form of a subsidiary meant that Deutsche could operate as an investment bank, while the branch ensured its status as a commercial bank taking in cheaper USD deposits (Büschgen, 1995, p. 858). Both was needed to fund its increasingly costly international network. Deutsche continuously found new entities, for example, the Capital Management International GmbH (CMI) in 1983 as an independent asset and money manager to exploit the growing pool of pension funds to comply with the SEC ban on foreign banks to access ERISA funds.

Unexpectedly, Commerzbank was quicker than Deutsche, perhaps representing the dynamism of changing financial relations and practices during financialisation. Commerzbank, the smallest amongst the big German three, was the first German bank to create a US branch in 1971, which emerged from its representative office established as early as 1967. This was even before its EuroPartners group established the EuroPartners Securities Corporation to foster investment banking in 1972 (Ramm, 2002, p. 191). Commerzbank's US outposts were dealing with a wide range of products, doing foreign exchange, investment banking and corporate finance, and private and government finance (Commerzbank AG, 1994; Ramm, 2002, p. 191). Its New York subsidiary was a key focus for Commerzbank, overtaking the expansion of its domestic financial development in Germany in the early seventies; its overall growth of 11 per cent was almost exclusively due to its branches in New York and London (Sattler, 2020, p. 362). Commerzbank started off being relatively more focused on USD finance.

Next to regulatory hurdles, the imperative for change was the practical difference between US and German finance. US money markets operated on different patterns, speed and performance indicators which were difficult for German banks to adopt (Lütz, 2005a, p. 148). The big three's financial power and expertise rested on fundamentally different strategies than what was useful in the US. Patient capital had an almost opposing temporal and operational logic compared to CDs and CPs. German banks' extroverted strategies could not benefit from their 'cosy relationships' in Germany. To recall, the German banks had a stable source of DM deposits that ensured cheap and secure funding of their assets. As a result, they did not have to worry about them as much as dynamic US money market funding required. By contrast, USD funding was expensive and not well known to the German banks. German banks operated on 'insider trading', and cross-shareholdings and metrics of firms' finances were not published in a standardised way. Information about economic performance was discussed in a small circle of economic and financial elites instead of through open market metrics (Hassel, 2003). In the US, German banks were outsiders to US elite financial circles, lacked the operational systems to accommodate US money market funding, and were behind on securitising corporate loans or any other financial papers.

Ironically, the US banks envied German banks' corporate lending practices in Germany. Deutsche Bank, Commerzbank and Dresdner Bank were commonly seen as the 'three rich powerful banks [that] dominate the market', jealously admired for their near monopoly position and their large scale of investments into the German industry (Kobrak, 2007, pp. 290, 443). Their position within the German economy seems to have placed them at an unfair advantage in banking because they were able to sell securities, hold large corporate stakes and lending regulation incorporated only a few restrictions for the universal banks (Höpner & Krempel, 2004; Schmidt & Tyrell, 2004).

Not so in the US. The turn to US money markets to catch up to US banks and to fund their increasingly global business was fraught with obstacles. Not only had they difficulties attracting profitable US business, 'their' German corporate clients also preferred their US competitors, and US investors were not necessarily interested to invest in the German banks' shares. For example, Commerzbank shelved the plans to list at the New York Stock Exchange in the mid seventies because its shares were not attractive to institutional investors (Sattler, 2020, p. 342).

All this meant that German banks had to adopt new financial practices. The initial strategies of the 1970s and into the 1980s between US and European banks were striking in this regard. US banks adopting LM were shrinking their loan books because they securitised their corporate loans to reduce expensive capital on their balance sheets. European banks instead were chasing assets to gain business, having not yet adopted different cost calculations. European banks ended up in the second row. They bought, and thus funded, corporate loans from US banks (Stigum, 1990, p. 301). The European banks initially had to get what they could with their limited resources and connections in the US.

The fact that the German banks abandoned their 'safe haven' (Lütz, 2000) that afforded them useful resources can only be explained by looking at the specific challenges that their chase for USD posed for them. To the detriment of German banks, seeking a US base to compete against US banks (and other large European banks) was fraught with restrictions and problems. While these obstacles were a key prompt for innovations and new financial practices to advance their investment banking capacities, they constrained not only the access to US money markets but also how universal banks could raise USD deposits and yield their previous sources of power – in the US, their close corporate ties did not produce guaranteed money. The US affiliates were not yet independently sourcing their own USD and needed further funding from their parent banks. Given the constraints of US money markets, particularly during the early years, German banks busily built their Eurodollar funding structures as alternative USD resources.

THE MAKING OF AN OFFSHORE FUNDING MECHANISM

German banks yet again had to find better ways to find USD because their advance in the US was slow. One way to deal with this problem was to expand their global network of subsidiaries in different offshore locations, not as part of clubs but on their own. All major public and private banks did that. This section thus embeds their Eurodollar strategies not primarily within strategies to escape regulation, but as part of their attempts to gain USD to catch up to US banks and to develop the means to finance a globalising economy, at least initially. As we already saw in previous sections, the banks' attempts to finance a globalising corporate sector quickly aligned them with the wider financial developments that led to the fact that banks were participating in finance's quest to finance … finance (Sgambati, 2019). One initial aim in the Eurodollar markets was indeed to follow their German clients, and the increasing offshore possibilities also became apparent to smaller German banks, claiming to focus on SME finance as a priority. But as Ramm (2002), chief macroeconomist of Commerzbank at the time, argues, the monetary domain ceased to provide purely 'auxiliary functions' since the 1970s.[4] While German banks repeatedly claimed to go abroad to follow their German clients, their US-based branches quickly aligned themselves with the broader financial developments. German banks shifted from primarily extending corporate loans to engineering financial products on the Eurodollar markets.

[4] Sgambati (2019) has a brilliant historical account about how 'banking' was never really a 'helpful' intermediary that merely passed money from savers to investors.

Nonetheless, an important goal initially was refinancing the German banks' global financial activities, particularly aiding their Luxemburg centres. Deutsche founded various entities, such as Deutsche Bank Finance N. C. in Curaçao (Büschgen, 1995, p. 854) or in the Cayman Islands in 1983 (Oermann, 2013) to capitalise on short-term funding opportunities in the Euromarkets to refinance its original centres in Luxemburg. The goal was to have representatives in all major financial centres. Commerzbank equally built its network in the Euromarkets. Commerzbank was, in fact, one of the twenty top underwriting firms of Eurobonds in the late 1970s and early 1980s, ranging from rank seven to rank twenty (Levich, 1984, p. 30), highlighting its initial large-scale involvement with global finance. Commerzbank also went to Curaçao, but also used Amsterdam to build its global Eurodollar network. (Sattler, 2020, p. 411). These subsidiaries would also channel their Eurodollars to the subsidiary CISAL in Luxembourg. As a result, a significant volume of Eurodollars never showed up on its balance sheets (Sattler, 2020, p. 11). This possibly contributed to the fact that these international activities barely made inroads into conceptualisations about German banking but highlight how important it is to look beyond balance sheet analyses.

The banks thus gradually built their global offshore funding network to complement their activities in the US. This, however, presented new challenges. Exchange rate concerns, a problem in the tumultuous crises of the 1970s, became central in the 1980s because of their growing, complex global funding mechanisms. Higher volatility of the USD against the DM made large-scale foreign currency exposures increasingly difficult. Both banks built their capacities to do foreign exchange (FX) and other financial techniques to gain and manage more flexible funding (Büschgen, 1995, p. 767; Commerzbank AG, 1994; cf. Singleton, 2009). Thereby, FX practices for others were increasingly inseparable from FX positions for themselves (Büschgen, 1995, p. 768; Sattler, 2020, p. 397).

The 1980s was a decade where Deutsche Bank started to advance significantly stronger than Commerzbank with its Luxemburg subsidiary starting to take positions in the growing derivatives markets. At first, despite its FX expertise, Deutsche bought its first interest swaps from Morgan Guarantee in 1982 to transform its long-term USD bond issues into a variable London Inter-Bank Offer Rate position. It quickly learned however, and used interest and currency swaps to manage the volatilities of the 1980s, including the disasters following the Global South debt crisis and the Volcker Shock. The necessary coping tools to survive a tumultuous USD world – swaps and derivatives – swiftly turned into a crucial asset. It is no coincidence that derivatives would become a core business for Deutsche: FX was key for non-US banks to swap their Eurodollars into their own currencies and vice versa. Deutsche would eventually rise amongst the five-leading swap-banks in 1990. 99 per cent of its swap deals were traded on its own books, rather than arranged for third parties (Büschgen, 1995, pp. 767–768). Commerzbank, too, developed practices such as currency options and partnered up with Goldman Sachs and Morgan Guarantee to do its swap transactions (Sattler, 2020, p. 397). While its FX business experienced severe losses during the 1980s volatilities, it nonetheless expanded its interest-currency-swap business (ibid.).

And yet, despite these various adaptions, the lenders' attempts to institutionalise Eurodollar and USD funding remained of limited success. They increasingly relied on US wholesale markets but, in contrast to relying on its traditional DM deposits, it needed better technologies to manage these flows. While the global expansion of Deutsche's and Commerzbank's Eurodollar network went ahead in the 1980s, they struggled to implement the new technologies of LM needed to survive the rapid transformations in US finance. Compared to the flexibility of the US banks, Deutsche's asset manager CMI, for example, only acquired a few investors. CMI still used different performance measurements and found it difficult to innovate new mathematical models. It was rather shunned by investors operating on different metrics that were hard to manage from Frankfurt (Büschgen, 1995, p. 762; Kobrak, 2007, p. 299). It took until 1987, when Deutsche had its first own influential large syndicate project, where they managed to pass on parts of their loan exposure (Büschgen, 1995, p. 766).

Commerzbank, on its part, was severely affected by the large loan losses of the 1980s Global South debt crisis (Tagliabue, 1986) and by increased funding costs resulting from the Volcker shock. Beyond the losses on its FX business, its growing international and US network became much more expensive, which was not conducive to concentrating on expensive, large-scale expansion. While it pressed ahead in the 1970s, the 1980s triggered a rethinking of its US expansion (Paul et al., 2020), as I will show in Chapter 7.

The 1980s were a decade of general financial turmoil,[5] but the money markets in the US were a particularly hard nut to crack for the European banks. Beyond simply representing an escape from German regulation

[5] The Volcker shock caused many bank failures, a concentration wave of the industry, and a huge debt crisis in the Global South, which caused many defaulted, large-scale loans from the USD recycling practices in the 1970s.

and 'underdeveloped' financial markets, the Eurodollar practices emerged as an additional or complementary strategy to the German bank's attempt to bank in the US. Being largely excluded from tapping US money markets, they further expanded offshore to raise USD and to fund their growing US subsidiaries.

While the German banks' offshore networks allowed them a significant stake in global banking, they were consistently outcompeted by US banks. Despite close relations with German corporations, German customers preferred services from US banks, not the limited services of the German banks (Kobrak, 2007, p. 318). While Deutsche's international strength traditionally was trade financing, it lacked the capacity to structure corporate financing needs on US capital and money markets such as CPs, (Euro-) bond emission, trading and taking firms public. It was only slowly from the 1980s onwards that another subsidiary, Deutsche Bank Capital Corporation (DBCC), managed to become interesting for large German companies. However, while DBCC was leading amongst non-US banks, even Deutsche as the most advanced German bank was far behind US banks such as Goldman Sachs and Morgan Stanley (Büschgen, 1995, pp. 766, 846, 855). With the help of LM, US banks had already established better means to finance German banks' previous customers, including their growing capital market funding and everyone else's FX.

As Herrhausen, chairman of Deutsche from 1985 to 1989 put it, Deutsche Bank had to learn the 'Anglo-Saxon way of money management' (Kobrak, 2007, p. 307). If it was to have any chance of accessing US money market funds, it needed better ways to buy and sell USD securities. Simply expanding globally and in the US was not enough to compete against US banks. German banks had to transform more radically to adopt LM. How they did that will be the subject of the Chapters 6 and 7.

CONCLUSION

The impact of US finance is often traced from the US into Europe. Lütz (1998), for example, argues that it was the power of the Securities and Exchange Commission (SEC) and US institutional investors that were able to spread US financial interests globally, pushing for financial deregulation and US financial norms. Indeed, US finance is often seen as a vortex (Konings, 2011) that is able to suck in capital to fund its huge twin deficit of its trade and currency accounts (Norrlof, 2010). Appreciating US hegemonic power and its capacity to attract USD and sustain its extraordinary volume of debt, this chapter has nonetheless analysed this impact the other way around: German banks actively tried to enter the US to get USD out to empower themselves in global finance. While part of their motivation was to follow their internationalising German clients to the US, they had few other choices if they wanted to keep up with US banks.

Power is about the kinds of resources that can be mobilised to win competition (Knafo, 2022), and US banks had US money market funding to be competitive. Through this hunt for USD, the European banks also continued to pursue their Eurodollar market practices. These practices quickly aligned them with the broader financial developments that increasingly allowed finance to provide financing for itself, further moving away from offering 'supportive' functions to the economy (cf. Gibadullina, 2023; Knafo, 2022; Sgambati, 2019). While these offshore structures were integral to their power as global banks, actively pursued and with force, it is these USD funding structures that would later turn into the Achilles heel of European banks' power.

What makes the institutional connections between the Eurodollar markets and New York so important is that the rise of money markets caused European banks to build ever more complex onshore and offshore institutional capacity to participate in global finance. The competition against US banks caused closer integration into USD networks, for which they needed further innovations and expansions to sustain them. While the German banks increasingly managed to build their own individual empires, away from their European partnerships and at times rivalling US banks, their US subsidiaries and their Eurodollar funding channels were not enough to engage on a level playing field with US banks. Even their colleagues from Germany Inc. preferred the services of US banks. What the German lenders realised, however, was that simple expansion and adoption of new financial practices was not enough. To learn the 'Anglo-Saxon way of money management' they had to embark on a more radical transformation and go on a 'much-publicised shopping spree, buying investment banks and bankers in London and New York' (Deeg, 1997, p. 64).

6

Liability Management and the Transformation of Deutsche Bank

INTRODUCTION

The key argument of the book is that German financialisation has been fabricated through the banks' extroverted strategies that forced them to significantly uproot from their home markets and to institutionalise into US financial markets. They embarked on this path to address the implications of LM. Deutsche Bank represents an ideal-typical bank of EF and in this chapter, I show how, why and when Deutsche Bank adopted US-style finance, but how it nonetheless never truly became a US bank.

Chapter 5 showed that key to US banks' power was not only LM, through which they conquered the Eurodollar markets, but also the advantages they drew from being connected to US money markets, which allowed them to fuel the practices of LM in unique ways. If other banks wanted to compete – and most large European banks did – they not only had to expand to the offshore USD markets, but they also had to go to the US. By 2002, 10% of banking assets of the core Euro area (5% of the South) were held in London and New York (Bayoumi, 2017, p. 36), and many major European banks had bought US or British financial institutions. But as I will show via the example of Deutsche, and Commerzbank in Chapter 7, going to the US was not that simple. Banking in US money markets needed a larger transformation than any of the German banks had anticipated. Despite attempting to grow organically, Deutsche eventually realised that it could not advance any further without embarking on a more radical transformation. The bank had to uproot its central operations beyond simply expanding through subsidiaries and branches, a shift that would eventually impact the very core of its banking nature. While all three major German banks had to do a 'qualitative leap' (Deeg, 2001, p. 30), Deutsche was amongst the major European banks that pushed this transformation furthest.[1]

It is important to note that Deutsche's thorough adoption of LM – and the following radical transformation – was not a foregone conclusion. When Deutsche first bought British Merchant Bank Morgan Grenfell in 1989, the lender aimed to keep Morgan Grenfell separate and independent as Deutsche Morgan Grenfell (DMG) so that it would not interfere with the rest of its German way of banking. In line with this effort, Deutsche resisted the introduction of money market funds (MMFs) in Germany, precisely because they would pose competitive challenges in Germany (Tanega & Baklanova, 2018). This is somewhat ironic, given its attempts to integrate into the flourishing New York money markets. As Ellen Schneider-Lenné, the only woman ever in Deutsche's board in the 1980s (serving from 1988 to 1996), stated, 'the bank has, [...], no intention of transferring British financing techniques wholesale to Germany' (quoted in Schenk, 2020, p. 482). Kopper, chairman at Deutsche in the 1990s made the same claim about adopting US conglomerate Bankers Trust practices (Fallon, 1994) – four years before the German lender acquired that very same bank.

As Chapter 2 has outlined, a key indicator of the financialisation of banks' is often read through the marketisation of banks' balance sheets. Banks started to sell their corporate loans and bought financial securities instead of relying on deposits for funding (see Figure 6.1) for Deutsche Bank, a shift in banking models from originate-to-hold to originate-to-distribute. Many consider this shift as riskier because customer deposits typically fluctuate little, and banks' would traditionally hold loans to maturity. And to recall, in Germany, this was coupled with the breakdown of Germany Inc. and its cross-border shareholdings that allowed German banks to monitor their clients and to resume a powerful position in the centre of the German economy. While I confirm here that German banks reduced their loan portfolios and ramped up their trading capacities, this chapter embeds that transition within the overall strategies of extroversion through which the banks' were forced to adjust to the institutional specificities of US finance.[2]

1 Dresdner Bank, for example, acquired Kleinwort Benson and outsourced all its investment banking into this British institution. Swiss Bank Corporation bought the wounded S. G. Warburg in 1995, which ultimately became part of UBS. ABN Amro, by contrast, expanded into London but in 1995, directly bought The Chicago Corporation, a US securities and commodities trading and clearing institution, to expand its US network that had started with LaSalle Bank Corp in 1979.

2 This chapter draws partially from my previous work on Deutsche Bank in which I already suggested that Deutsche's rise and fall are crucially connected to extroverted

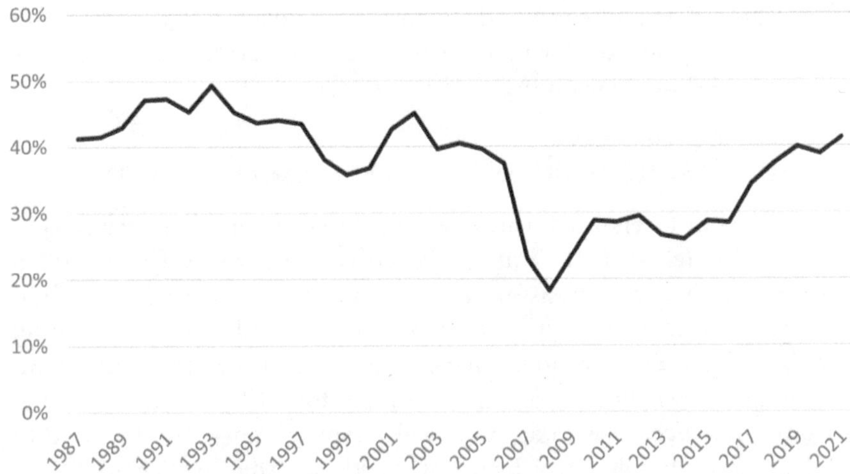

Figure 6.1 Deutsche Bank's customer deposits as share of total liabilities. Author's own calculation, source: Compustat Global (cf. Beck, 2022b, p. 8).

This chapter thus addresses the third feature of EF: the imperatives of US money markets, the markets at the centre of contemporary leverage and debt relations. From this perspective, it was US money markets that mattered, rather than markets per se. From this perspective, the banks' fundamental adjustments of their loan portfolios appear not as a sign of weakness vis-à-vis markets or corporations that turned away from their banks. Instead, the big sell out of Germany Inc. was part of a process of empowerment in a financialised world where assets ideally catch US money market funding. Banks increasingly engineered market-based assets in a way that allowed them to tap financial markets for further funding (so that they could go on to engineer more securities to fetch more funding and so forth). Market-based assets were thus needed to address the implications of LM. As I will show, it was these strategies that allowed Deutsche to ride the financial bubble in the 2000s to such heights.

This chapter has two sections. I firstly flesh out how Deutsche attempted to get a stronger foot into US and offshore markets with the help of DMG, which started the relocation of Deutsche's central operations to London. This, so I show, prompted a partial transformation

financialisation through which Deutsche ended up having two opposing logics within its business model (Beck, 2022b).

of its Eurodollar strategies and its corporate governance. The second section details the transformation caused by Bankers Trust, Deutsche's most radical shot at becoming a US investment bank.

DEUTSCHE MORGAN GRENFELL: LM IN LONDON

The first major foreign acquisition was the London-based merchant bank Morgan Grenfell so that Deutsche could gain a better grip on the US innovations that were transforming the Eurodollar markets in London and capturing USD deposits. As Chapter 5 explained, simply expanding into the US and the Eurodollar markets has been successful to an extent, but Deutsche was not yet a serious competitor to US banks. Realising it would not succeed with an organically grown transition, it started to think about a suitable US or British institution. Catherine Schenk (2020, p. 462 ff) shows in illuminating detail that Deutsche embarked on a long and controversially discussed search throughout the 1980s to find an institution that could not only advance its ambitions but one that it could actually afford. As she shows, not everyone at Deutsche was entirely enthusiastic about the prospects of Morgan Grenfell. Deutsche, however, settled on the British contender, as there were only a few options that could meet those criteria.

Morgan Grenfell was a traditional merchant bank founded in 1838 and a leading player in corporate and advisory finance. Morgan Grenfell was at the forefront of mergers and acquisitions business in the 1980s and was involved in securities trading since 1984. Deutsche Bank became one of the new shareholders of just under 5 per cent financing the expansion of this business. The merchant bank was also a top manager for international assets of US pension funds. It was closely related to the J. P. Morgan empire, but US regulatory constraints on operating as an investment bank while holding stakes in a commercial bank forced Morgan Grenfell to divest from 1933 onwards. Its last shares were sold in 1982 (Burk, 1989). Morgan Grenfell promised not only Eurodollar market funding and a stronger position in London as the leading European financial centre, but also close relations to the US. Morgan Grenfell could go a long way to overcome the practical and regulatory barriers highlighted in Chapter 5.

The takeover was itself an outcome of the dynamics unleashed by LM. Being a traditional UK merchant bank, Morgan Grenfell nonetheless struggled under the advance of US banks and the fundamental changes during the 1980s, culminating in the City's big bang. As Sahil Dutta (2018) aptly argues, the city experienced a profound transformation when US conglomerates entered en masse and, beyond their dominance on the Eurodollar markets, bought up British financial institutions. The city was previously characterised by smaller and traditional niche financial institutions, each with their own sectoral business, such as brokers or jobbers. Equipped with the powers of LM, US banks raised the capital needed to buy these institutions and captured more generally the growing mergers and acquisition business, a process often conceptualised as the death of gentlemanly capitalism. On top of that, the 1987 financial market crash caused heavy losses for Morgan Grenfell, including revealing a scandal over insider trading (Burk, 1989). Deutsche Bank taking over Morgan Grenfell is an interesting lens into the dynamics of US-led financialisation, where leading agents were often quick to fall at the next instance (cf. Knafo, 2022).

Deutsche Bank bought Morgan Grenfell for USD 1.48 billion as part of what both banks termed a 'friendly takeover' (Prokesch, 1989). Deutsche Bank represented a temporary solution for Morgan Grenfell because Deutsche's large balance sheet provided protection and possibilities to expand. Most importantly, Deutsche promised to keep Morgan Grenfell independent, a key demand of the British bankers, allowing it to continue its Eurodollar practices and investment banking. Deutsche appreciated this agreement because, it wanted to tackle US investment banking using Morgan Grenfell's distinctive approach, but, as Schneider-Lenné suggested, Deutsche also planned to continue its traditional way of lending to keep its German and European customers. Notwithstanding this goal, as we will see, by inviting the imperatives of LM into its own institution, Deutsche set in motion a path of fundamental change.

Buying Morgan Grenfell is often seen as a strategy to advance as the leading financial player in Europe and to seize the new opportunities of the developing European Economic Community and its common market. Corporate IPOs, widespread privatisations, interest-rate volatility and expanding bond markets provided profitable prospects for investment banking (Schenk, 2020, p. 463). Barclays, Crédit Lyonnais and Deutsche vied for the top position amongst the European banks in the 1980s (Drach, 2019), and having a strong position in London was a crucial condition for that endeavour. However, it was not predominantly European integration and expanding European branch networks that concerned the big European lenders. The dynamics of global markets and the rising offshore financial centres presented both bigger challenges as well as more lucrative business (Drach, 2020). As such, I argue that the Morgan Grenfell acquisition is deeply ingrained in the challenges that the rise of US finance presented to Europe.

Deutsche relied on Morgan Grenfell as a central outpost to access Eurodollars and to manage their increasingly complex internal distribution. Deutsche reorganised its banking subsidiaries under one holding that managed the entire US banking with a balance volume of 14 billion USD in 1992 (Büschgen, 1995, p. 859). It transferred its whole investment banking division to Morgan Grenfell to be managed from London, including newly hired people with experience on US money markets. Deutsche's hands-off approach was fundamentally different from UBS, its main European competitor, where the head office in Zurich decided almost all deals at the time (Celarier, 1996). Deutsche opted for a rapid makeover at this time, demonstrated by McClelland's claim that it will take Deutsche Bank five years to turn itself around into an investment bank. McClelland came from Morgan Stanley and became CEO of Deutsche's US securities business. This is an ambitious goal, as J. P. Morgan, previously a prime US commercial bank, took ten years for that transition, similar to Bankers Trust (Celarier, 1996).

Money market trading 'had leapt in importance' throughout the 1980s and 1990s (Burk, 1998, p. 136), and Deutsche could now participate in this process. Morgan Grenfell's money market practices, however, presented a significant change in the operations of Deutsche. But because the Hausbank and Morgan Grenfell systems did not match up, Deutsche managers feared that Morgan Grenfell could impact negatively on the rest of the bank so that they kept the merchant bank largely separate. As a result, Morgan Grenfell had large autonomy from Frankfurt, a freedom they much appreciated and exploited for their activities in the US. However, Deutsche realised quickly that by keeping Morgan Grenfell independent, it could not actually learn how to do US finance. In 1994, after the guaranteed period of four years of separation, its investment banking business was fully integrated into Deutsche's global operations, now called DMG (Burk, 1998, p. 136).

With the help of DMG, Deutsche made quick advances in the 1990s. DMG had a stake in the investment firm CJ Lawrence that traded with securities and brought in new experts from other banks (Kobrak, 2007, p. 329), including the securitisation team and software systems. At that time, Deutsche was wary of employing a 'star' trader such as Andy Stone, the head figure of the mortgage-backed securities (MBS), which contrasted too much with Deutsche's stodgy business culture (Kantrow, 1994), an approach it would soon have to abandon as well. Deutsche was also accepted as a primary dealer by the Federal Reserve Bank of New York (Kantrow, 1994). This allowed Deutsche to deal with SEC restrictions and increase the profit volumes that CJ Lawrence as a Section 20 subsidiary could make: The volume of government securities made sure that the 10 per cent revenue limit of Section 20 subsidiaries allowed for high absolute numbers.

More importantly, this signified Deutsche's growing power as a market maker or broker/dealer. US Treasuries have a uniquely important position within the game of leverage and within power struggles of banks. Primary dealers sell and buy government securities, and thereby commit to providing liquidity to public debt. Deutsche became a 'trusted' bank to generate enough liquidity with a capacity to bridge any squeezes in the market, so that the US government could reliably refinance its growing mountain of debt. This is a privileged position because government securities are sought after, particularly as 'safe' collateral in the growing repo markets (see more below), and primary dealers increasingly leveraged this position for themselves (Gabor & Ban, 2016). Government debt, as a safe asset, became a key security for money market funding. Becoming a primary dealer is therefore a key step into playing the game of US finance: that is, acquiring the means to get US money market funding more easily and growing the capacity of USD leverage. Deutsche thus advanced steadily the institutionalisation of LM supported by US money market funding.

DMG and the Redirection of Eurodollar Flows

DMG was important to fuse Deutsche's Eurodollar funding structures with its US ambitions. The building of a US position required changes in Deutsche's global USD funding strategies and to support its US subsidiaries and to buy new institutions, large volumes of USD were needed. Therefore, Deutsche rerouted its Eurodollar funds from London to the US. These strategies are representative of a general dynamic in the Eurodollar markets and the growing presence of European banks in the US. While German elites have made generous use of offshore finance to foster their German plans (Binder, 2023), the Eurodollar market increasingly turned into a supporting structure for the banks' extroverted strategies in the US.

In the 1980s, much of the Eurodollars (and EuroDM) were channelled into the European inter-banking markets, reflecting strategies of banks to gain USD for the global operations of the parent banks. What changed in the 1990s was that Eurodollar banks in London increasingly channelled their Eurodollars towards non-bank financial institutions in the US. The interbank market received relatively fewer capital flows from the

Eurobanks than the non-bank sector so that the share of funds available to the London banks dropped (McGuire, 2004, p. 70). By mid 2002, the share of interbank lending dropped to 50 per cent from roughly two-thirds in the 1970s and 1980s.

Part of this change resulted from the processes of European integration. The introduction of the Euro decreased FX trading, which was a crucial business for the European banks. FX trading relied on USD which had increased inter-banking transactions and Eurodollar volumes, but now USD business fell 15 per cent from 1998 to 2001, according to BIS numbers (McGuire, 2004, p. 73).[3] In addition, the consolidation process of the European banks (cf. Bayoumi, 2017) resulted in a reduction of the interbank transactions, which implied an increase in the share of dealings with non-bank financial institutions (McGuire, 2004).

The concentration of Eurodollar flows towards the US, and non-bank financial institutions, however, was needed to finance Deutsche's growing network in the US. The New York office oversaw more than 700 legal entities, including special purpose corporations, branches, joint ventures, offshore entities, etc. (Kobrak, 2007, p. 361). By 2002, one-fourth of its assets and revenue came from the US (Kobrak, 2007, p. 14). To accommodate these various acquisitions, large banks restructured themselves in a way that had one crucial branch in a financial centre that centralises all the operations of the bank, including the deposits collected by the branches within other countries (McGuire, 2004, p. 75f). These funds were then mostly passed on to non-bank institutions in the US, amounting to almost two-thirds of all funds to non-bank financials. These non-bank borrowers are mostly securities houses, hedge funds and other non-bank financials that take positions in fixed-income positions. The shift has been mainly orchestrated by the UK, German and Swiss banks, the leading banks that were rivalling for the top position within Europe, but more importantly, that aimed to keep up with US banks.

The third feature of extroverted financialisation emphasises the need for banks to establish themselves in US money markets. The advance of non-US banks in the US with the help of non-bank acquisitions and the increasing use of funds to finance other financial institutions – the financing of finance – is reflected in their use of the Eurodollars. The Euromarkets thus continue to be a supporting extroverted strategy for Deutsche Bank, but they also required the redirection of its global

[3] This shows how the introduction of the euro decreased this aspect of USD dependency. However, the dramatic rise in USD trading in the 2000s will dwarf this brief moment.

business into London – the partial uprooting of important operations had started. The next section will show how this required further changes that came to affect the rest of the bank.

LM and Corporate Governance

The dissolution of Germany Inc. by the early 2000s, the close network of German corporations based on interlocking directorates and cross-shareholdings, was one of the most crucial and widely debated transformations in German political economy (Streeck & Höpner, 2003).[4] This section embeds this shift within Deutsche's process of adopting LM. Using DMG to develop Deutsche's investment banking had far-reaching implications for the rest of Deutsche's operations as it affected Deutsche's internal capital management and its asset-based strategies.

These new strategies included new ways to assess risk and costs. A traditional risk management approach evaluated an asset (bank loan) according to the economic performance of the borrower – an assessment that was previously made by holding shares in their corporate borrowers and by taking positions in supervisory boards to get preferential information. As I showed in Chapter 2, the new integrated approach that made funding a central strategy of the overall bank evaluated an asset by accounting for the costs of capital, ease of selling the loan and cluster risk. Deutsche thus made an astonishing discovery in the 1990s: Deutsche's corporate investment portfolio comprised of only 8% of risk weighted assets but it held 21% of Deutsche's average shareholders' equity. Considering it as a cluster risk (Nolmans, 2006), its previous close relationships with the German economic network provided a big threat to the bank (Janssen, 2009, p. 110). In 1998, Deutsche created a separate subsidiary, DB Investor, to manage its corporate holdings much more dynamically (Deeg, 2001, p. 28), which for the first time made the extent of its industrial holdings visible: 45 per cent of its market value

4 The dissolution of its large equity holdings is often associated with the abolishment of the capital gains tax by SPD Finance Minister Hans Eichel in 2000 (effective in 2002) that allowed corporations to sell their holdings easily without paying large amounts of taxes (Beyer & Höpner, 2003; Lütz, 2005a, p. 147). The tax stood at 50%. Their share of ownership in publicly traded companies decreased from 12% in 1998 to 9% in 2003 (Vitols, 2005, p. 391). However, the ending of the tax only represented a final straw in a longer-term process (Höpner & Krempel, 2004; Lane, 2003, p. 92). The big banks attempted to get rid of their holdings since 1979 because they represented too much risk exposure (Deeg, 2001, p. 28). Using the tax law to explain the sale of equity holdings leaves unanswered why it took the banks twenty years to wait for a tax law change.

(Nolmans, 2006, p. 157). The pressures of banking on wholesale markets would make long-term holdings of low-yielding securities unbearable (Wieandt & Moral y Santiago, 2006, p. 91). Deutsche not only had to bolster its balance sheet with the selling of the 'family silver' (Janssen, 2009, p. 219; Schenk, 2020, p. 587), it needed the money to pay expensive traders and pay for its US acquisitions.

Before selling its shareholdings, Deutsche started to significantly reduce its corporate loans in the 1990s. This is partly a result of corporations seeking fewer loans because of their own internal funding capacities and capital market securities (Braun & Deeg, 2019), and partly because Deutsche changed its corporate relationships, structuring securities for firm finance. As I showed elsewhere (Beck, 2022b), adopting new accounting system such as RAROC, Deutsche found that a significant share of its corporate loans were loss-making. To recall briefly from Chapter 2, Bankers Trust pioneered RAROC to price and measure the performance of traditional lending practices by considering the risk of the individual positions to evaluate whether it was an efficient use of the bank's capital. That way, it could start measuring the risk and costs of holding a loan in the portfolio, exposing the costs traditionally ignored. RAROC uncovered a fundamental insight into lending that changed everything: corporate loans were, in fact, quite risky and expensive. If things go wrong, getting rid of a loan is usually much more difficult than selling a security. Deutsche started to question the viability of patient capital – holding long-term loans on its own books. If costs of capital were taken into account, patient capital was value destroying (Schenk, 2020, p. 591). A new strategy took hold at Deutsche: reducing capital-intensive business. While Deutsche thus tackled the nature of its traditional business (lending), Deutsche needed significant amounts of capital to adopt new practices and systems to build alternatives to its previous bread and butter business.

Ronaldo Schmitz, head of North American Capital Operations, came to the rescue. He started to transform Deutsche's approach to structuring its loan portfolio. Previously CFO at BASF, and therefore one of the few non-bankers at Deutsche, he claimed that: 'The bank had its traditional competence as a lender, but for more sophisticated products I found that my American colleagues turned to American banks' (Schmitz quoted in New York Times, Quint, 1992; cf. Lee, 1998). He started to turn around the New York branch and to develop Deutsche's expertise to offer securities for firm finance. Planning a listing on the New York Stock Exchange in 1992 and contemplating the acquisition of a major US bank or securities firm, he recognised the limits of Deutsche's capacity to compete in the US market, even with DMG spearheading investment banking. His role models were Bankers Trust and J. P. Morgan (Quint, 1992).

John Rolls was another new employee who, in contrast to most German bankers, was eager to push for money market activities. Previously CFO of Monsanto Europe, Rolls was hired to restructure Deutsche's US activities under the umbrella of the Deutsche Bank North America Holding (DBNA) (Kobrak, 2007, p. 32). Rolls struck a fee-sharing deal with investment bank Gleacher & Co., focusing on mergers and acquisition, and buying experience of the 1980s leveraged buyouts, aiming to jointly build another junk-bond business (Kantrow, 1994). The junk bond business was pioneering the practices of innovative debt financing through leverage, mobilising very limited but specific resources to exploit money markets, which gave corporations unprecedented funding power to take over potentially much larger firms (Knafo & Dutta, 2020). In equities, a disappointing weakness of DMG (Fallon, 1994, p. 34), Michael Phillipp, who came with Ed Mitchell to DMG, bought NatWest's equity derivatives group in 1997. This team, initially recruited from Morgan Stanley by NatWest, brought along systems that enabled Deutsche to treble its daily trading volume and catapulted it to a state-of-the-art trading firm on the New York Stock Exchange (Lee, 1998).

Deutsche's integration into US finance resulted in a radical cut of its loans as share of its assets from about 60% in 1993 to 20% in 2003 (Janssen, 2009, p. 108). With the rise of LM, banks generally started to sell off their loans to go on underwriting more, as I outlined in Chapter 2. Secondary markets became a key part of the global plumbing of finance. There were no official figures in 1993, according to *The Economist* (The Economist, 1993), but the market for loans was growing. To further this development, Citicorp developed a loan index in 1993 so that banks and investors could assess their loans more precisely. The aim was to get pension funds involved to draw more liquidity into the market. Since the mid 1980s, pioneered by Bankers Trust, the securitisation of loans had increased exponentially (ibid. 1993, p. 30).

DMG bought US securities houses to replace its previous banking strategies. Turning into a wholesale bank meant that corporate loans had to go, shaking the foundations of its traditional finance approach. Regardless of its ambitions to keep banking strategies separate, the implications of LM crept across the institution. Having uprooted its investment banking operation into London and with DMG, its loan portfolio lost out. This, however, caused new challenges, and most annoyingly to Deutsche, had not yet provided the key expertise and practices to challenge the top-notch US banks.

One key problem with securitising corporate loans was that banks had difficulties selling the high-risk assets (The Economist, 1993), and problem loans did not decline proportionally to overall loan portfolio so that average risk became higher. All universal German banks suffered increasingly from non-performing loans (NPLs), loans that are in default because borrowers missed repayments. While many NPLs were connected to the 2001 dotcom crisis and the failure of *Neuer Markt* (New Economy, a brief attempt to establish a German stock exchange for tech companies (Vitols & Engelhardt, 2005)), German banks experienced a wider crisis of banking in the 1990s (Hackethal, 2004, p. 101). Income from interest reduced from 60% in 1993 to 27% in 2003 (Janssen, 2009, p. 96) but was still relatively high in German banking. However, net income (interest minus costs) decreased dramatically and went negative in 2000 for the big universal banks, often used as an excuse for Deutsche's reduction of branches and corporate loans (Hackethal, 2004, p. 101; Pauli, 1999).

The profitability crisis of the 1990s was foremost related to the high costs of investment banking (Vitols, 2009). One important factor of Deutsche's NPL problems was that when it switched to US accounting standards in 2001, its NPLs weighed stronger on its balance sheet (Janssen, 2009, p. 106). Breuer, head of Deutsche Bank 1997–2002, was dismayed at the 76% cost to income ratio. Notwithstanding his promise to reduce it, it stood at 86% in 2002 (Janssen, 2009, p. 86). New institutions and US traders were expensive. And despite all that investment, corporations financing on international capital markets were often sidelining the big German three (Lanchner, 1998).

Worse yet, US banks kept innovating and threatened to make renewed inroads into the German markets. Goldman Sachs, for example, developed close links with the German government to capture the privatisation business of the 1990s. US banks were able to secure significant parts of the privatisations that swept over Europe in the 1990s (Gindin & Panitch, 2012). Foreign competitors beat German banks to bringing German companies to the new stock market *Neuer Markt*, and Deutsche had to pass on a USD 2 billion stock issue for Bayrische Vereinsbank[5] because J.P. Morgan was able to sell a higher volume of money (Lanchner, 1998). While the German banks struggled with declining interest income, the biggest US

[5] Bayerische Vereinsbank was the fifth largest bank after Deutsche Bank, Dresdner Bank, WestLB, and Commerzbank. In 1998, it merged with Bavarian-based Hypo-Bank to become Germany's second biggest bank but was already acquired by the Italy based UniCredit group in 2005.

banks were leaving that problem behind, securitising, selling and generating fee-based income (Gibadullina, 2023). They were making full use of LM. By contrast, DMG ran a loss of USD 55 million in investment banking and equities trading in 1997 (Lanchner, 1998). John Craven from Morgan Grenfell complained that primary debt and equity were still separated from secondary market activity (Schenk, 2020), making an integrated approach to managing funding rather difficult. Kopper recognised that 'international merchant banking thinks, speaks and acts Anglo-Saxon. We must accept this "culture" for ourselves, integrated as a multinational element, allow it to develop and make use of it' (quoted in Schenk, 2020, p. 478).

THE ROAD TO US MONEY MARKETS: BANKERS TRUST

The acquisition of Bankers Trust in 1998 signals Deutsche's most radical step in its extroverted process. It cemented its institutionalisation into US money markets, which marked its ascent as a top investment bank. This time round, Deutsche made no pretence that it would keep its original raison d'etre as a German house bank. Deutsche would have to leave behind its cherished position at the top of the German corporate club. During the 1980s and the 1990s, the board of Deutsche Bank still explored the possibilities of *expansion* in contrast to *transformation*. With the purchase of Bankers Trust, Deutsche made clear that it had opted for the latter, and that it was not looking back (Euromoney, 1999).

Bankers Trust was bought by Deutsche for USD 9.7 billion. The acquisition seemed to be orchestrated by Edson Mitchell, who came from Merrill Lynch, heading Deutsche's global market division and representing the 'trader star' that Deutsche tried to avoid in the early nineties.[6] The merger made Deutsche Bank the biggest bank in assets in the world, surpassing Citibank and UBS A.G. (Andrews, 1998) and the 4th largest asset manager (Janssen, 2009). Deutsche Bank became a mega bank of 1.3 trillion DM. Investment banking leapt from 28% to over half of its operating income before tax, 56%. Having pioneered practices of LM, the irony is that Bankers Trust, a 100-year-old US institution, was swallowed by a bank as part of its strategies to belatedly adjust to LM's rise. This represents the peculiar dynamics of financialisation in which the most dominant financial player

[6] Confirmed in a personal conversation with a former Deutsche banker. Schenk (2020, p. 517) claims it was Ronaldo Schmitz. Both were convinced about the need for a strong transformation towards US finance, so they probably both had an important input into this merger.

can easily fall at the next hurdle (Knafo, 2022). Having mis-speculated and being fined for derivative scandals in the early 1990s, Bankers Trust became a more financially viable target for Deutsche, even if many criticised that the acquisition price was still too high.

The deal with Bankers Trust addressed the gaps in Deutsche's business model in several ways. Firstly, it provided the operational capacities such as new IT technologies and expertise in risk management and high-speed trading. Secondly, it provided the expertise and connections to either buy assets that carry higher yields to finance Deutsche's expensive global funding mechanism, or to structure assets in a way that would allow Deutsche to sell them off quickly to reduce capital requirements for them. Bankers Trust was one of the leading banks that pushed over-the-counter (OTC) trading, particularly with currency options (Partnoy, 2009, p. 87). While Deutsche had started proprietary trading on the Euromarkets and through derivatives, Bankers Trust was state of the art. It made huge profits from cashing in on hidden upfront fees, beyond what was normal at the time (Partnoy, 2009, p. 53). With Bankers' help, Deutsche developed a dark pool that was rivalling those of J. P. Morgan and Goldman Sachs (Mattli, 2019). Dark pools were useful hidden exchanges through which those banks started to undermine public exchanges, including the New York Stock Exchange (Sissoko, 2017), so that Deutsche acquired yet again the ability for non-transparent and insider trading after its cross-shareholdings in Germany declined. After the merger, Deutsche developed into the 'best derivative house of the year' in 2003, according to the Risk Magazine, which made Deutsche enemy number one for US bank JPMorgan (Tett, 2012, p. 109; cf. Partnoy, 2009, p. 92). Finally, in 2005, Deutsche Bank acquired a global market share of over 14% (Schenk, 2020, p. 599)[7] and exceeded the (in)famous 25% pre-tax return on equity in 2006.

Securitisation and US Mortgage Finance

Proprietary trading, particularly during the mortgage boom in the 2000s, was key to Deutsche's advance (see Figure 6.2). No longer a German bank, Deutsche joined in the phenomenal production of the MBS industry. DMG started the MBS business with mortgage originators, buying and restructuring to an extent that in 1998 the central management was briefly concerned about its exposure (Schenk, 2020, p. 583).

[7] See Beck (2022b) and Schenk (2020, p. 590) for further acquisitions and internal changes to integrate US financial logics into the bank.

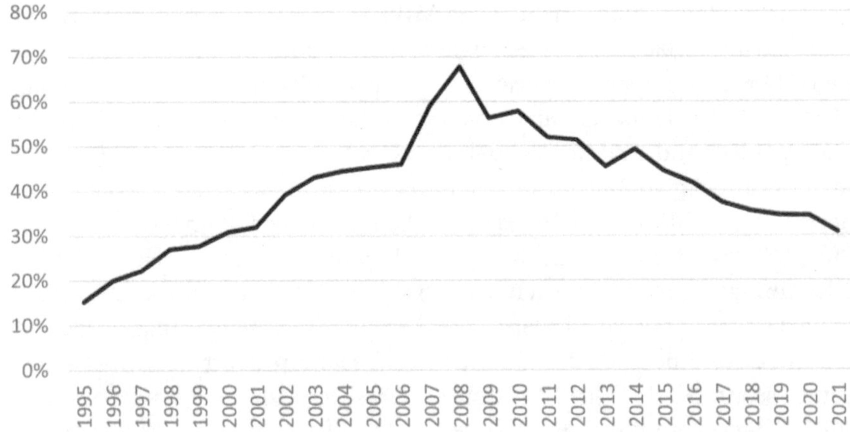

Figure 6.2 Deutsche's trading and dealing account as share of total assets. Author's own calculation, source: Compustat Global (cf. Beck, 2022b, p. 7).

Being saddled with sub-prime mortgages, US mortgage borrowers were systematically exploited by excessive interest rates and upfront fees. Mortgage originators sold those loans to mortgage banks and the savings and loans, which passed them on in bulk to global investment banks that repacked them, secured triple A ratings and sold them to other investors (Dymski et al., 2013; Hudson, 2010; Roberts, 2013). According to Fligstein (2021), practices related to MBS were endemic in the US banking community at the time. Banks transformed their business models so radically that they were involved in all steps of the mortgage pipeline at the cost of doing little else.[8] While US banks excelled in the production of this chain, European banks wanted their share as well (Bayoumi, 2017; Schwartz, 2010). In fact, European banks were amongst the key funder of the mortgage bubble (McCauley, 2018). As a result, while some European countries also experienced a mortgage crisis, the mortgage finance industry in the US was uniquely large, connected, transformative and when things went wrong, it was exceptionally devastating. This section shows that the funding of the bubble was an outcome of the extroverted strategies of European banks in significant ways.

8 For comparison, the financial sector in the US produced almost 40% of all the profits in the entire economy in 2003 with about 10% of GDP. The mortgage market was at USD 4 trillion in 2003, its peak. It fell to USD 3 trillion in 2007 (Fligstein, 2021, p. 7). In the middle of the mortgage asset boom, commercial banks' assets comprised of 54% real estate, compared to 32% in 1986 (Fligstein, 2021, p. 18).

From 2001 to 2004, the rise of MBS as global assets worked rather well. European banks invested huge sums, tapping US money markets to fund their MBS, a strong period for the earnings of the European banks (Tooze, 2018). Deutsche Bank was one of the more dominant banks, originating MBS and building global assets, rather than simply buying it as many European (public and private) banks did. DBNA had tried to engineer ABS and MBS in the 1990s but lacked its own personnel to do that. In the 2000s, Deutsche bought RoPro US Holding Inc., abbreviated RREEF, a leading real investment manager (holding company) in the US, which made Deutsche the world's largest real estate investment manager in 2002, a number one position in combined real estate property and real estate equity securities. In 2004, it acquired Berkshire Mortgage Finance and in 2005, Chapel Funding, which some would call a sub-prime mortgage corporation, others a predatory lender. It was now immersed in every step of the mortgage pipeline through originating, structuring, securitising and trading. Deutsche ranked first in the US in high-yield and second in asset-backed securities and third in US debt, fourth in USD clearing services (Wieandt & Moral y Santiago, 2006, pp. 89–94).

Deutsche had turned itself into a major broker-dealer, being involved in every step of the securitisation pipeline. This involved not only predatory lending but also further manufacturing-related securities such as collateral debt obligations (CDOs), including synthetic CDOs,[9] that were predominantly conducted offshore with the help of special purpose vehicles. Deutsche Bank Securities Inc. (DBSI) structured forty-seven different CDOs, worth about USD 32.2 billion (Schenk, 2020, p. 579), and was a major market maker in synthetic CDOs. Deutsche was finally part of all major aspects of the mortgage business, just when the industry could no longer hide signs of systematic tensions (Hudson, 2010), but more on that below.

In 2005, 71% of Deutsche's revenues came from abroad, slightly ahead of the Swiss contenders UBS (70%) and Credit Suisse (65%) but significantly ahead of the French banks Société Générale and BNP Paribas, which had less than half of foreign revenues (Schenk, 2020). Deutsche forcefully advanced to become the most global of the major banks, and its large US network allowed it to be one step ahead over other European banks within the US MBS business.[10] Despite European's major investment into these

[9] A product that relies on mortgage indexes rather than 'actual' mortgages.

[10] Credit Suisse and HSBC, for example, also aggressively built their mortgage departments, servicing CDO ABS (Tooze, 2018a, p. 75).

products, US banks were originating them and thereby reaping most of the profits (Lysandrou & Shabani, 2018), even if everyone made handsome sums of money. European banks also sourced fewer mortgages, the raw material of global MBS, which left European banks with synthetic CDOs. As I have argued in joint work with Samuel Knafo and Stefano Sgambati, the spectacular European investments in the 2000s CDO bubble were a sign of the round-about strategies the Europeans had to do to participate in US finance, investing in the most risky type of assets but leaving the biggest profits to US banks (Beck et al., 2023). Key to benefiting from the mortgage securitisation boom was to source, and thus engineer, the assets and sell it to others willing to pay the higher price, rather than simply investing in what others have generated. After building its funding capacity in the US and in Eurodollar markets, Deutsche had now successfully turned around its asset side, competing with dominant US banks in the MBS industry.

Already from the mid 2000s, however, just when Deutsche bought its sub-prime lender, the MBS industry already showed signs of tensions (Hudson, 2010). Deutsche realised some of the problems, but Greg Lippmann,[11] who famously shorted the sub-prime mortgage industry[12] confirms Fligstein's assessment that it was difficult to get out:

> In 05 for a time, we sold EVERY SINGLE one [AAA CDO] to AIG. They stepped out of the market in march of 06 after speaking with me and our research people (and I don't doubt other dealers). Since then it has been more hit and miss for us. Sometimes we sell to European banks but often (and for the last three deals) we are forced to put it into our commercial paper conduit. [...] Why have we done this? It is not without reluctance and we are looking for ways to get out of this risk, but for now the view has been, we like the fees and the league table credit (and dammit we have a budget to make) (quoted in Schenk, 2020, p. 606).

To Deutsche's luck, the investors' reluctance to buy Lippmans' innovations gave Deutsche room to pause, and then sell some of its risky positions during the crisis summer of 2007 already, which limited some of its initial losses (Schenk, 2020, p. 608). Nonetheless, the GFC proved devastating to the German lender, similar to all European banks.

While Bankers Trust finally triggered a wholesale transformation of Deutsche Bank, allowing it to co-construct the MBS industry alongside

[11] Deutsche's global head of ABS and CDO trading: his shorting strategy of the housing market in the early 2000s was made famous by the film The Big Short based on Michael Lewi's book with the same name about the build-up of the housing bubble in the 2000s.

[12] Shorting a financial product means to bet on a fall in price so that you win money if prices do fall, but lose if they rise.

US banks ahead of many other European contenders, its funding strategy resembled its previous funding strategies from its London centre, alongside other European banks. CDOs were important assets in this endeavour. European banks bought them, and at times, engineered them themselves, to build special conduits which sold asset-backed commercial papers (ABCPs) to US MMFs. While the ABCP market developed in the US, and was dominated by US banks initially, European banks discovered it as a useful USD funding channel and it turned into a key funding market of the ABS industry (Thiemann, 2018). This is a prime example of how the sourcing of assets was integrally linked to raising USD funds and thus their extroverted strategies. These conduits were a key vehicle for the USD 'round-tripping' the European banks conducted in the 2000s, fetching USD from the US to invest them back into US MBS (McCauley, 2018; Tooze, 2018).

When some CDOs started to fail, however, US MMFs stopped buying them across the whole market. The Fed's Term Auction Facility stepped in to stabilise the ABCP market (Sissoko, 2015b). Contra Deutsche's claims that it did not receive any public help during the crisis (Wilson, 2012), this liquidity injection cushioned the deleveraging process of foreign assets for the German banks (Buch et al., 2011; Ewerhart & Valla, 2008, p. 141). And after the Fed supported deflation of this market, however, MMFs shifted their sources elsewhere, and this market ceased to be of importance, alongside its CDO assets (Fligstein, 2021).

The fact that this market has declined so rapidly and not recovered since is evidence to the precarity of the funding structures that the European banks' have built. The ABCP market was a key source of US money market funding to sustain the European's extraordinary leverage in the 2000s but had become their Achilles heel during the crisis. To the banks' benefit, their practices had already constructed such an elaborate and interconnected financial architecture that it was in the Fed's interest to bail (most of) them out. And yet, Chapter 8 will show how they have not yet recovered since.

Repo, Reverse Repo and Leverage

Next to the ABCP market, repos were the second most important channel of funding for the MBS industry (Pozsar et al., 2010) and continue to be a crucial source of MMFs (Gabor, 2016b; Wansleben, 2020). Repo represent contracts in which the seller of a security agrees to repurchase it from the buyer for a higher price on a given date, effectively receiving an overnight cash loan. The higher price counts as the interest.[13] Repo started out as a niche market because it was used to substitute temporary liquidity constraints of government bond dealers (Sissoko, 2019). The 1990s, however, saw it grow tremendously as a convenient way for European banks to access US money market funding. Particularly after the Russian debt crisis in 1998, the use of collateralised lending increased after banks grew wary of unsecured interbank markets so that the Fed extended the spectrum of what counted as 'safe' assets and what was therefore eligible as collateral for repo funding. As a result, MBS got 'safe harbor exemption' alongside Treasury bonds (Gabor, 2016b). Deutsche's role in the MBS industry and as primary dealer ensured useful assets for funding in the repo markets. As a repo dealer, Deutsche took at a prime position within the growing connections between banks, money markets and the Fed (cf. Sissoko, 2015a).

The shift of the European banks towards acquiring securities houses in the US is associated with the increase in the US repo markets, which accelerated significantly at the turn of the century (McGuire, 2004, p. 76). Similar to ABCP, the repo market played a crucial role for non-US banks whose US-based foreign offices and London-based centres have had limited capacity to raise US deposits (Baklanova et al., 2015). German banks used them as a core source to finance their foreign subsidiaries. Their repo funding has increased from 7% in 2002 to about 17% of total funding in 2007, which amounted to 15% and to just under 30% of total short-term wholesale funding (calculated based on monthly reports to Deutsche Bundesbank, Düwel, 2013, p. 30).

DMG, rather than Bankers, was important to develop this strategy. In the 2000s, it was, in fact, easier to fetch repo-cash in London compared to the US. In the US, repeated repo collateralisation (multiple use of the underlying collateral for different repo transactions) was restricted to 140% of the original collateral. In the UK, practices by both European and US banks, there were no such restrictions, and the volume reached up to 400% adding USD 4.5 trillion in funding (Tooze, 2018, p. 82). This provided banks with a platform for leveraging that was not possible in the US. The most aggressive European banks, Deutsche Bank, UBS and Barclays, had a leverage ratios in excess of 40:1 whereas their US competitors had 20:1 (Tooze, 2018, p. 88). While high leverage sounds impressive, European banks needed more volume because

[13] See Gabor (2016b) for an analysis of the repo markets and Baklanova et al. (2015) for an overview of the US repo markets.

their individual transactions were less profitable due to the reasons outlined above. Repos were not only a convenient funding tool because they were a highly responsive mechanism to increase and manage short-term liquidity but also because it was a useful way for the European banks to attract US money market funding.

Repos are usually matched by a reverse repo (Gorton & Metrick, 2012). A reverse repo is a financial practice on the asset side of the banks' balance sheet (if it was actually recorded). Banks purchase a security from the capital markets, for example, a hedge fund, with a promise to reverse the trade at a later date. The bank then sells this collateral to US MMF, but also others, to get overnight cash from the money markets. While repos are mainly overnight loans backed up by Treasuries, and before the GFC by CDOs, reverse repos have longer maturity dates and fixed interest rates. Another key difference is that reverse repos are traded OTC, which means that banks directly trade with money managers, often in dark pools (see above). Reverse repos were another key link in how global banks, through proprietary trading, contributed to the growing CDO bubble in the run up to the GFC (Sgambati, 2019).

Repos and reverse repos are representative of how banks have increasingly used their assets as a means in themselves to raise the funds necessary to hold or buy them (Knafo, 2022; Sgambati, 2019). Deutsche increasingly engineered its assets not only in a way that would reduce the amount of balance sheet capital to reduce reserve costs and risks but also to be able to fetch more funds. LM centres on a dynamic management of securitised funding and the growing connections between assets and liabilities. The argument here is that beyond marketising Deutsche's balance sheet – the selling and trading of assets and liabilities –banks fundamentally changed assets to be able to tap growing debt markets and to attract funds before others hover them up. For Knafo (2022), this is a key factor that has led to widespread predatory lending because banks had to find ever more innovative ways to make assets more attractive so that they could offer better returns to other financial investors. This pressure potentially contributed to Deutsche Bank being involved in an increasing number of financial scandals over the past two decades, not least in relation to its MBS practices and its dark pool (cf. Enrich, 2020; MacKenzie, 2015).

While repo funding declined during the crisis, it has become even more important after the GFC (Baklanova et al., 2015). For contemporary repos, however, T-bills are necessary, reducing the flexibility of European banks to source CDOs and others for repo funding. Instead, they are now bound to T-bills after the MBS markets declined. The story of repo funding is another instance of the processes of EF. While the rise of repos has several origins, for European banks, they held a uniquely useful potential to attract US money market funding from abroad, and they made ample use of them. Repo, and the ABCP market, allowed European banks to participate in US financial innovations, and to leverage to the extreme. This confirms the on-going centrality of the City of London, and thus Eurodollar markets, within the extroverted strategies of European banks. While Deutsche was able to lead on some of these developments, when easy access to US money markets was restricted, the unevenness of US financial markets reappeared. With the deflation of these markets, European banks struggle to support their US expansion (Noonan, 2020). Chapter 8 will elaborate on this point and highlight how the process of EF resulted in deep contradictions for the German banks' business models. Before that, Chapter 7 will examine how Commerzbank conducted its own extroverted strategies.

CONCLUSION

This chapter traced the transformation of Deutsche Bank, through which it sought to establish itself in US money markets. EF foregrounds the institutional specificity of US money markets, and Deutsche tried to adopt the practices of LM to be able to tap US money markets. In pursuing this goal, Deutsche realised it could not progress organically and had to make a more profound transformation if it wanted to keep up with US banks. While it aimed to stick to its German way of banking initially, the purchase of DMG and more profoundly, the acquisition of Bankers meant that Deutsche had to abandon that goal. It relocated central resources first to London and then to the US, away from its previous financial practices. Deutsche built its on- and offshore scope to gain US money market funding, ramping up its leverage and predation capacity, which was in turn needed to attract yet more debt in the new financialised world. In that way, the sale of corporate loans and shares – the break up of Germany Inc – were connected to the integration of new practices that replaced Deutsche's traditional way of finance.

The need to connect with US money markets to survive global finance meant that Deutsche Bank entrenched these US financial logics into its own business model. As such, this transformation was an active pursuit but constrained by the imperatives of LM. Given US banks funding power, Deutsche Bank had few options but to try to emulate them in US home markets and to adjust to its short-term nature. This was a central imperative for producing the kinds of assets that it did – they attracted US MMFs. This continues to highlight the peripheral position from which Deutsche started, as the institutional differences of US and German financial markets put Deutsche at a disadvantage. However, this shows that the immersion into 'markets' is not best conceptualised as a sign of weakness (cf. Hardie and Howarth, 2013), even if corporations reduced the amount of bank loans they relied on. Instead, Deutsche's innovations actively transformed the lender as attempts of empowerment so that Deutsche did not have to rely on loss-making long-term loans within a world of LM. This relocation was part of the longer-term extroverted strategies through which the bank tried to cope – and succeeded in the 2000s – with the rise of LM from the 1960s onwards.

Chapter 7 will trace Commerzbank's strategies to show that it faced similar imperatives but turned a different way. As a result, while initially frontrunning US integration as Chapter 5 documented, Commerzbank advanced a more European investment banking strategy at the expense of an institutional network in the US. As a result, when it tried again to advance into US money and MBS markets in the 2000s, it quickly failed. But as I will show, Commerzbank, too, did not escape US exposure and the dynamics of LM, which came to haunt the banks until today.

7

Commerzbank

Attempting a Half-Transformation

INTRODUCTION

Commerzbank, too, experienced the growing tensions that the rise of US money markets posed for internationally active banks. Albeit adopting a more cautious approach to US finance and mostly claiming a 'European' label for itself, Commerzbank's experience on global markets is an important illustration that Deutsche's extroverted strategies are more than an outlier. Commerzbank was the smallest bank amongst the three big universal German banks until it bought Dresdner Bank in 2008. The German universal banks are often grouped – justifiably – as German universal banks, including by me. Comparing asset values of Deutsche and Commerzbank (see Figure 7.1), they indeed follow a similar trajectory. Commerzbank did not experience the 2008 GFC dip because it added Dresdner's assets just at the time when everything plummeted. The banks' advances into US money markets, however, differ to an extent that we cannot easily deduce from variations in size alone. Compared to Commerzbank, Deutsche's growth in the early 2000s is all the more striking.

Commerzbank assumed a rather erratic approach to global markets. While the 1970s saw Commerzbank as very active in the Eurodollar markets and the US, Deutsche's and Commerzbank's strategies significantly differed from the 1980s onwards. Commerzbank decided to withdraw during the Global South debt crisis instead of doubling up its London- and US-based strategies. Another key difference from other large European banks was that Commerzbank did not buy a major US investment bank. Commerzbank's smaller balance sheet size meant that it had less capacity to buy foreign institutions, like Deutsche did, and it spent fewer resources in US wholesale markets (Behr & Schmidt, 2015; Hardie & Howarth, 2009,

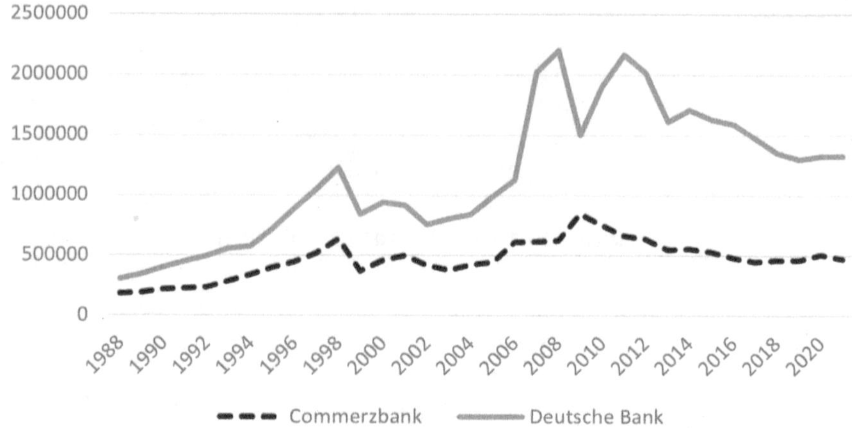

Figure 7.1 Deutsche and Commerzbank's asset values. Author's own calculations, source: Compustat Global.

p. 1023; Wixforth, 2010). Commerzbank tried to grow and adapt to US finance organically without relocating central resources and management into London or the US.

It did renew its efforts to transform towards US logics in the 1990s, for example, by adopting RAROC in 1994, the new risk management tool that Bankers Trust had pioneered. Nonetheless, Commerzbank might have missed the implications of prioritising liabilities as a key strategy and neglected to include the costs of funds in its calculations. Going against the trend, Commerzbank expanded its loan portfolio in the mid 1990s while other European banks reduced them. As I will show in this chapter, this had serious implications. When Commerzbank renewed its advance to conquer Wall Street in the 2000s, it expanded into US asset management. Alas, having missed the restructuring of funding that Deutsche underwent, it lacked institutional grounding in the US and the new endeavour fell flat as quickly as it had started.

Commerzbank's swift failure in the US around the turn of the millennium highlights how difficult it is to source US-based assets profitably without the capacity of US money market funding. And when Commerzbank bought Dresdner Bank during the GFC, it had no chance to cope with Dresdner's MBS exposure and had to be bailed out by the German state. Commerzbank's history demonstrates the need of foreign banks to integrate themselves into US money markets to sustain high leverage and trading with speculative assets, making LM one of the central banking practices of financialisation. But while the rise of LM posed similar imperatives to the German banks, their responses, and thus their transformations towards US finance, differed.

This chapter is divided into four sections. The next section examines Commerzbank's 1980s Eurodollar practices to show how it reversed its early foray into the offshore during this difficult period. In section two, I show how Commerzbank's alternative path was still international but represented a more organic transition, relatively focused on European SMEs and competing against German banks, rather than fostering any US money market integration. The third section shows how its renewed attempt at doing US finance missed important implications of LM, and the fourth section examines why Commerzbank, despite its 'European' focus, cannot escape the implications of US money market funding.

TROUBLED EURODOLLARS: WITHDRAWING FROM THE EARLY ADVANCES

To recall from Chapter 5, Commerzbank was initially successful in expanding on the Eurodollar markets, despite its smaller size. While it did not quite lead manage large syndicate loans, it substantially expanded its Eurodollar activities. In 1973, it issued thirty-nine international bonds worth DM 3.7 billion, while in 1978, the number grew to ninety-eight with a volume of DM 12 billion. In 1978, Commerzbank issued eighty-seven bonds in foreign currencies worth USD 4.4 billion but lead managed only one of them (Sattler, 2020, pp. 354–355). This is in line with the European banks' role of capital providers without being able to capture the most profitable part of the business. With its US foreign office in 1971, Commerzbank was a pioneer in the US amongst the German banks.

Its Eurodollar network developed to fund Commerzbank's US activities and the bank's capacity to do foreign exchange and other financial techniques (Commerzbank AG, 1994; cf. Singleton, 2009). Reflecting the general trend amongst European banks, Commerzbank held high USD positions (Bayoumi, 2017; Sattler, 2020, p. 396). While initially, Commerzbank used Goldman Sachs or Morgan Guarantee to engineer its swap transactions, it increased the volumes of those transactions throughout the 1980s and started to offer those practices, including futures and options, to its own clients and increasingly traded on its own accounts (Paul et al., 2020, p. 398). However, its London-based subsidiary, the key European connection to US financial innovations, was not particularly profitable in the first half of the 1980s (Sattler, 2020, p. 398), while Commerzbank's Luxemburg subsidiary, CISAL's wealth management, fared better in the latter half of the 1980s, increasing its balance sheet size from DM 16.97 billion (1986) to 18.79 billion (1989), and profits from 25 to 100 million (Sattler, 2020, p. 399).

While Deutsche Bank was looking for a major acquisition with US expertise in the 1980s, Commerzbank's US advance was more limited, even if it continued to develop its Eurodollar network. It used the newly developing International Banking Facilities (IBFs) in the US, rather than transforming towards US financial systems directly or buying a US institution. In 1981, the Fed allowed foreign banks to use IBFs to book Eurodollar liabilities in the US without having to park reserves at the Fed (Cibriani & Gouny, 2015). This provided a convenient way for Commerzbank to increase its USDs without adjusting its practices. In 1984, Commerzbank started to trade in the CP market using Commerzbank US Finance Inc. in Delaware, but with the help of US banks such as Goldman Sachs as dealers and hesitating to allow securities beyond USD 300 million (Sattler, 2020, p. 401). It structured CPs for corporations but also for itself, and these funds were used to expand its New York subsidiary (Sattler, 2020, p. 400), but setting such a limit signifies its more cautious approach in which Frankfurt, rather than London, keeps the reins.

Commerzbank's offshore network made good strides in expanding its international business, particularly in the US. By 1986, 60 per cent of the overall business volume of the New York branch was generated by US customers. While 20 per cent came from German clients, the remaining 20 per cent from international transactions (Ramm, 2002, p. 192). It also bought out its Euro partner club banks in 1988 and renamed the previously joint venture Commerzbank Capital Markets Corporation (CCMC). CCMC managed to underwrite US shares and bonds, including for institutional investors and states (Ramm, 2002). Rather than strictly representing intermediaries to the German industrial sector, Commerzbank had interests of its own that cannot easily be deduced from their relations to Germany Inc. As we will see, Commerzbank in fact started as the first German bank to reduce its corporate empire.

Commerzbank's history exhibits interesting pioneering initiatives only to fall back into 'traditional' German ways of banking. The 1980s also posed a decade of troubles for its global advances (Ahrens & Wixforth, 2010). This started with the Volcker shock already. Commerzbank had significantly expanded its long-term public bonds throughout the 1970s, and Volcker's hike in interest rates shot up its USD funding costs, which ate up all interest income so that Commerzbank had zero retained earnings in 1980 (Sattler, 2020, p. 370) and struggled to make much profit the following years. By contrast, Deutsche's net income in 1985 rose to a record of 536.3 million, well ahead of Dresdner and Commerzbank (Tagliabue, 1986).[1] In response, Walter Seipp, incoming chairman in 1981, pushed for an integrated asset and liability approach to manage funding of the bank. In an uncommon approach compared to the other German banks, Seipp planned to decrease Eurodollar liabilities in favour of customer deposits and bonds as a source of funding (Sattler, 2020, p. 376).

The 1980s sovereign debt crisis following the Volcker shock also affected Commerzbank's lenders. Having expanded forcefully into the Eurodollar markets, Commerzbank, alongside Dresdner Bank, had to write down sovereign and other foreign loans (Tagliabue, 1986). Commerzbank lobbied heavily against a global restructuring of Latin American debt that would securitise non-performing debt and involve significant write-offs (Sattler, 2020, pp. 380, 385). By contrast, Herrhausen of Deutsche Bank was a key advocate for the securitisation of Latin American debt (Büschgen, 1995).

To compensate for the losses, Commerzbank started to sell parts of its German industrial shareholdings from the 1980s onwards (Sattler, 2020, p. 380). By 1993, Commerzbank had reduced its integration to DM 5.7 billion worth of equity capital (Janssen, 2009, p. 131).[2] Its strong foray into the Eurodollar markets had already resulted into an important casualty, breaking up parts of Commerzbank's corporate finance infrastructure. But rather than pouring more resources into improving its USD funding channels to cope with higher costs and vulnerability of global markets, such as Deutsche, Commerzbank went the other way. The 1980s experienced Commerzbank's first attempt to escape the imperatives of LM to foster more home-grown financial relations in Germany and Europe. The bank restructured its lending towards medium- and short-term loans to avoid being caught again between long-term low-yielding loans and rising short-term funding costs. Commerzbank also made the explicit plan to recentre German SMEs as primary customers, and it bought a German *Pfandbrief* bank (see Chapter 3).

1 Part of this record high was a deal for the Flick corporation in Germany. However, a few years later, it became apparent how Flick was involved in a large scandal and could not actually pay back his debts (Binder, 2023; Schwarz, 2003).

2 It reduced them further around the turn of the century, similarly to the other big German banks.

Commerzbank's smallish size became more vulnerable with diminishing protective cross-shareholdings (Tagliabue, 1986), which meant that it was repeatedly subject to hostile takeover threats throughout the eighties and nineties (Wixforth, 2010, p. 117). This was not conducive to competing with US banks in a financial environment that rapidly developed the means for firms to take over their competitors, and for banks to reap high fees from those operations. Rather than improving its capacities to access dynamic funding possibilities in the US, Commerzbank was busy fighting off attacks. Commerzbank's smaller size is obviously a key problem in a period of growing conglomerates. But size is not the problem per se; the rise of junk bonds and leveraged buyouts in the 1980s have meant that smaller firms have often bought much bigger ones, if they were able to mobilise enough external funding (Knafo & Dutta, 2020). Commerzbank was not.

These strategies to deal with the growing Eurodollar markets and exposure to US finance represent crucial differences between Deutsche and Commerzbank because they shaped how the banks competed in USD markets. Commerzbank's gaze refocused on rivalling German banks rather than US banks. And when Commerzbank contemplated purchasing a UK institution in the early 1990s to keep on top of the fast-developing Eurodollar markets, it was beaten by Merrill Lynch in a race for UK securities firm Smith New Court (Euroweek, 1995). Its hesitant approach certainly contributed to the fact that Commerzbank was not able to renew its Eurodollar expansion, despite ambitions. While Deutsche started to relocate its strategies to DMG, I show in the next section how Commerzbank instead built its European investment banking.[3]

EUROPEAN INVESTMENT BANKING

Commerzbank had its strategic focus on Europe, whereas Deutsche Bank saw Europe as one part of its global strategy. Commerzbank significantly advanced its European strategies throughout the 1990s: by 1999 its wholesale and investment banking ranked 4th in capital allocation among European universal banks (Hackethal, 2004, p. 77). Europe's periphery and Germany's east were a strategic focus for all large German banks, and they were quick to benefit from expanding capitalist relations (Mertens, 2017,

[3] It is important to note that Deutsche also expanded its European branch and corporate finance network. Deutsche's European practices received less attention because Deutsche's primary focus was the US. While the expansion of its branch network in Europe wasimportant and added to its balance sheet size, it was not transformative.

p. 12). Commerzbank in particular saw its chance to rival its counterparts, acquiring equity stakes in Eastern European institutions (Janssen, 2009, p. 133f).[4] Commerzbank made 24% of its total revenues in Europe, which is the majority of its 30% international share of total revenues (Ramm, 2002).

Commerzbank's investment banking activities consisted of bond underwriting and equity, particularly for SMEs (Janssen, 2009, p. 142f). Commerzbank focused more on European capital markets and needed fewer new innovations, as it had a long history on European capital markets (Commerzbank AG, 1994). To recall, market-based banking is nothing new in Germany. The universal banks' peculiar strength traditionally combined securities trading with deposit banking (Fohlin, 2007), and *Pfandbriefe* attest that asset-backed securities have German origins (see Chapter 3). To tackle the growing challenges of market expansion, Commerzbank maintained its work with European partner banks (Wixforth, 2010), exploring tighter cooperation with Crédit Lyonnais in the form of a share swap to jointly tackle European integration, but Crédit Lyonnais eventually shelved the plans to continue on its own (Sattler, 2020, p. 463).

The focus on European investment banking had two implications for Commerzbank's extroverted strategies: Firstly, Commerzbank did not majorly change its funding strategies. Expanding its branch networks in Europe was relatively more important, compared to Deutsche, and was a viable strategy for Commerzbank's expansion of its non-US investment banking activities. Commerzbank was less integrated in USD markets and therefore less reliant on a short-term financing scheme that would necessitate transforming its business model towards the practices of LM. The bank, for example, founded subsidiary Commerz Financial Products to build up its derivative business in 1994, but Commerzbank hired Antoine Paille and his group from rival French bank Société Générale to build the entire system (Sattler, 2020, p. 483), rather than gaining US or British bankers. While the decline in customer deposits relative to total liability and equity was a general trend in Germany, Commerzbank compensated for the loss primarily by financing through bank deposits (Janssen, 2009, p. 142).

Money market funding increased in the 1980s and 1990s through Commerzbank's Eurodollar networks and US subsidiaries, but USD

[4] For example, a stake of up to 72 per cent in the former state-owned Polish export development bank (Janssen, 2009, p. 133f).

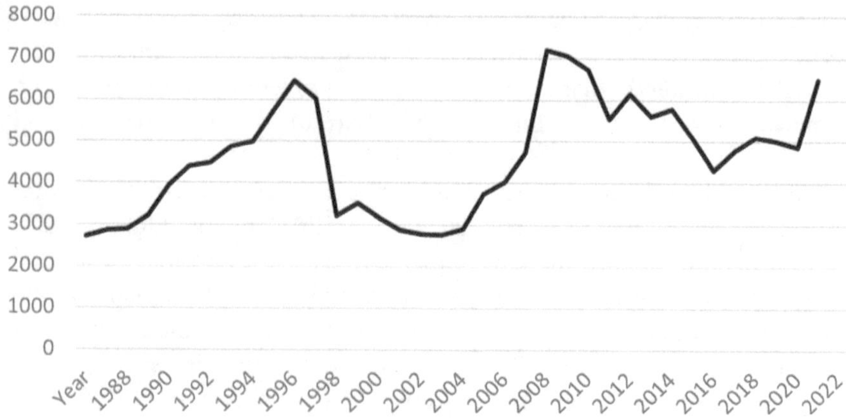

Figure 7.2 Commerzbank's net interest income. Author's own calculations, source: Compustat Global.

funding was limited. Commerzbank also adopted RAROC, similarly to Deutsche Bank; but the crucial difference was that it did not integrate it systematically (Janssen, 2009, p. 141). Commerzbank somehow neglected to focus on the costs of capital as a key organising principle for its investment and funding decisions, one of the core features of the 'risk management revolution' (Sanford, 1996) pioneered by Bankers Trust. Given European money markets and customer deposits work on less short-term and less-expensive funding practices, compared to US money markets, Commerzbank pushed limited changes in liability management. As a result, Commerzbank focused on expanding its asset side, disregarding the approach to the management of liabilities more dynamically.

As a result, a second striking difference to Deutsche's strategies was Commerzbank's management of its assets. Contrary to common trends, Commerzbank's loan portfolio increased during the 1990s (Euroweek, 1995) with an average of 15 per cent from 1993 to 2000 (Janssen, 2009, p. 142; Euroweek, 1995). Along with that went a steady increase in interest and related net income until 1996 (see Figure 7.2).

The latter half of the 1990s, however, put a pause to Commerzbank's tactics. Net interest income fell sharply. As mentioned in Chapter 6, the German financial sector struggled with rising firm bankruptcies resulting from a stagnating economy (The Banker, 2001) and the failures of dotcom and *Neuer Markt*, which led to higher loan loss provisions reducing overall income (Vitols, 2009, p. 143). Despite Commerzbank's partial withdrawal from the Eurodollar problems of the 1980s, it was

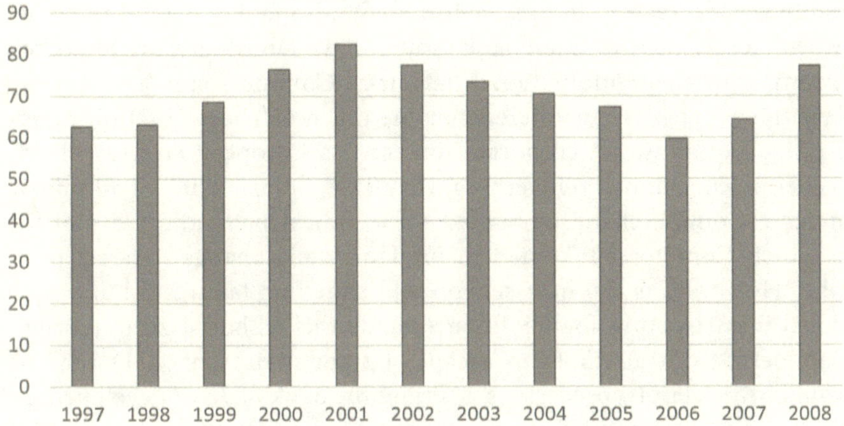

Figure 7.3 Commerzbank's cost-to-income ratio. Author's own calculations, source: Annual statements.

costs, not income, that were increasing steadily during the 1990s, with the domestic branch network having a cost-to-income ratio of 73.6% compared to 63% for the overall bank in 1998 (annual statement, compare with Figure 7.3).

While the number of subsidiaries and participations in other countries tripled from 1987 to 1995 (Sattler, 2020, p. 463), its income did not. Advancing European financial integration and harmonisation added growing external pressures that, in fact, started to necessitate changes in banking business models. While it was mostly large European corporations that had shifted to self-finance and securities (rather than loans) (Deeg, 2009), and Commerzbank had strategically shifted to SME finance, the general trend was disintermediation (Schmidt et al., 1999). Moreover, SME finance in Germany was very competitive because it was populated with the public savings banks and cooperatives that operated strong local branch networks. The rise of securitisation meant that the traditional corporate clients of the universal banks were financing more and more on capital markets (Deeg, 1999), leaving fewer and fewer candidates for Commerzbank's loan portfolio.

Commerzbank's interest income fell behind Deutsche Bank and Dresdner Bank in the 1980s while its costs rose (Sattler, 2020, p. 438).[5] The lack of higher-yielding assets and fee income meant that return on

[5] One reason here was in no doubt the lack of European economic growth that Commerzbank's loan portfolio depends on.

equity was decreasing in this environment, also falling behind the other two banks. While Commerzbank did not have Dresdner's or Deutsche's expenses for their international networks, Commerzbank also did not have their higher fee or interest income nor much securitisation expertise that could attract corporate finance. Its European strategy clearly needed a 'continuous reinvention' (Erturk & Solari, 2007). To improve income, Commerzbank embarked on a radical path into US markets in which Commerzbank tried to fundamentally change its asset portfolio. However, as the next section will show, its failure to build up a global infrastructure for US finance made this a short-lasting journey. Commerzbank's attempts to escape the constraints of USD funding would bring about a precarious position: the bank had not developed the capacity to cope with US money market funding when the logics of US assets started to bite.

A SHORT-LIVED REINVENTION? US ASSET MANAGEMENT

From the mid 1990s onwards, Commerzbank attempted to catch up to Deutsche, Dresdner Bank, and other European banks by significantly reducing its loan portfolio, hiring new financial traders with experience in London and the US, and engaging in new asset management practices. As such, Commerzbank joined the frenzy into US markets of the late 1990s and 2000s (cf. Bayoumi, 2017; Hardie & Howarth, 2013b), but without having undergone the fundamental transformation towards US money market funding that we have seen with Deutsche. As a result, Commerzbank's account of securities trading and dealing rose to almost 30 per cent as share of overall assets in 2002 (see Figure 7.4) but has since seen a rather rollercoaster approach. It has been steadily declining since 2014.

In the time of the 1990s booming equity markets, Commerzbank followed the general trend of buying foreign institutions, but it stayed in Europe. It bought London-based Jupiter Tyndall International in 1995 and Boston-based Martingale Asset Management. The corporations were worth GBP 45.3 million and USD 1.08 million (representing 60 per cent of the shares).[6] These are rather small sums compared to what Deutsche Bank acquired as its main foreign expansions (The Banker, 2001). This increased the share of international assets under management to 17 per cent of Commerzbank's total assets in 1995 (Sattler, 2020, p. 481).

[6] The price Commerzbank paid is unclear, according to Friederike Sattler.

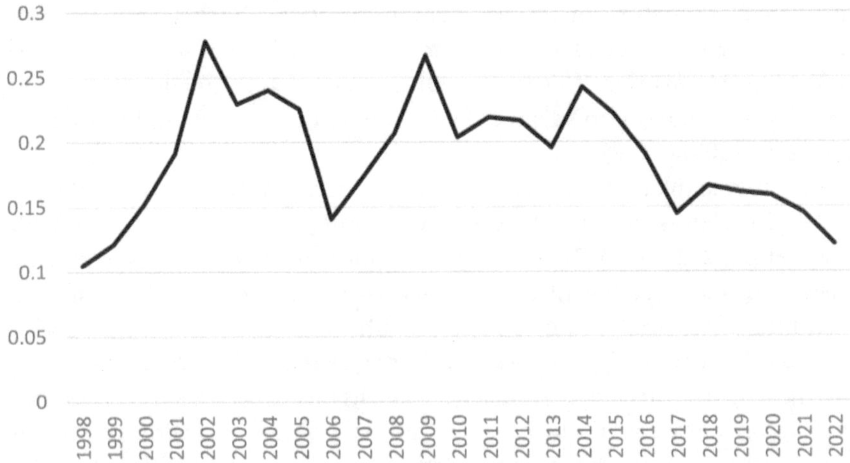

Figure 7.4 Commerzbank's trading and dealing account as share of total assets. Author's own calculations, source: Compustat Global.

Montgomery Asset Management completed this growth into asset management in 1997. This was a prestigious asset manager in San Francisco, a key step to breaking the 200 billion mark of assets under management in 2000.

Commerzbank even attempted to gain primary dealer status in the US in 1995 (Sattler, 2020, p. 482). The difference to Deutsche, however, was Commerzbank's concentration on asset management, without having substantially built up its (Euro-)dollar funding structures. Lacking these institutions, Commerzbank tried to steer this expansion from Frankfurt, growing organically, rather than handing over global investment banking to London (Bowley, 1997). However, despite aiming for organic growth, Commerzbank could not proceed without new expertise and hired Mehmet Dalman (who previously worked at Deutsche) to oversee the rise into global investment banking. He was the first non-German in Commerzbank's board and built up the global investment division almost from scratch (The Banker, 2001). He became head of investment banking in 1999, only two years after he joined, and member of the board after only four, exemplifying the speed of this transition. He combined corporate and investment banking in 2000, and he tried to gain access to the SME customers at Commerzbank, the biggest groups of clients, to integrate them into his division. To manage Commerzbank's funding more dynamically, Dalman also wanted to bring together equities and derivatives together (Janssen, 2009). To date, this represented the biggest effort to change the nature of the lender. During 2000–2003, Commerzbank fundamentally reduced its loan portfolio with the help of securitisation of risks. This means that it used derivatives as insurance for the underlying security, which frees up balance sheet capital but does not sell the security (Janssen, 2009, p. 142).

Commerzbank's shot at US-based asset management did not yield the hoped-for results. Return on equity was reduced to 22.1 per cent in 2000 (Paul et al., 2020, p. 487). These new acquisitions and changes increased costs even more, and with the asset management department boasting a near match between income and costs with a cost-to-income ratio of 97.4 (Annual Report 2002, compared to 77 per cent for the overall bank, see Figure 7.3). By this time, Deutsche was engineering MBS pipelines and had significantly transformed its operational systems and adopted LM. In comparison, Commerzbank struggled to stay alive in the US. When the euphoria on the equities markets stopped, Commerzbank had not built a US distribution network. Its asset managers lost in equity with little chance of gaining new capital or shifting to other options. Jupiter International declined by 2 billion within the first few years from USD 9.5 to 7.5 billion in 2001 (Janssen, 2009, pp. 134–136). Commerzbank's securities business lost EUR 147 million in 2003 with additional restructuring costs of 132 million to scale it back, amounting to an expense ratio of 121 per cent and posing a USD liquidity crisis for Commerzbank (Sattler, 2020, p. 530).

When European banks geared up to increase their investments in the US in the early 2000s (see Chapter 6), Commerzbank had to size them down. By 2003, Commerzbank had sold its major stakes in the US. To compensate for the net losses of EUR 39 million in 2000 and EUR 165 million in 2001 for a portfolio of EUR 140 billion (loss of 1 per cent), Commerzbank sacked one-third of its investment staff (Janssen, 2009, pp. 134–136). Dalman left in 2004. The bank refocused its derivative business towards corporate finance, and German customers in particular (Sattler, 2020, p. 529), but it is hard to imagine that Commerzbank would not do proprietary trading. Trading in assets had a short-lived life at Commerzbank. Its trading account halved again by 2006 to just under 15 per cent of overall assets (see Figure 7.4). As we will see later, this did not deter it, of course, from trying its own luck again just three years later when acquiring Dresdner Bank and its large share of US-based MBS.

In sum, Commerzbank briefly relocated important resources into the US and towards its US securities dealings but otherwise kept its European and US investment banking strategies separate. Its US and Eurodollar expansions emerged at a similar time to Deutsche, but its engagement with LM was only temporary and seemingly haphazard. It was affected by the growing costs of its international expansions and the overall change of European and German finance towards the practices of LM, including securitisation, changing corporate – bank and investment banking relationships, but not from a driver's seat. And when it attempted to respond to these challenges, its journey into the US could not be sustained. Without fundamental transformations, it could not participate profitably in the growing securities business in the US.

The failures in US markets led Commerzbank to a renewed focus on the German *Mittelstand* (Deeg, 1999; Krahnen & Schmidt, 2004; Vitols, 1995), for example, planning to bring medium-sized firms onto European capital markets (Bowman, 2017). One of the more major new strategies was that Commerzbank bought Eurohypo in 2005. Eurohypo was founded in 2003 when the three German lenders combined their real estate lending operations into this bank, which had largely been non-performing, essentially an outsourcing strategy for their NPLs. The banks each held an equal share, and by 2005, Eurohypo had become the largest European *Pfandbrief* issuer and a key player in European real estate securitisation.

Tracing Commerzbank's strategy suggests that practices of European investment banking and US investment banking are critically connected. With the benefit of hindsight, we can see how Eurohypo would connect Commerzbank closer to US markets, rather than allowing it to turn away. While it was thought that its European investment banking strategies would also help to bring about success in the US (Janssen, 2009, p. 130), the focus on assets was not only limited in dealing with the cost increases and general impact of US finance on Europe, but they were equally limiting its US expansion as US money markets required different forms of strategies. Having failed to integrate these interconnections into its own business model more thoroughly, Commerzbank failed badly in the US finance. While this section already outlined the challenges of US money market funding for Commerzbank, the bank had so far resisted to integrate the practices of LM substantially. This is about to change when Commerzbank exposed itself more fully into the dynamics of US money market funding at the dawn of the GFC.

THE DRESDNER DEBACLE

Commerzbank was the only bank of the German big three that did not try to transfer its business model wholesale to US finance. While most of European finance was affected through the losses and funding squeezes in

2008 (Baba et al., 2009; Fender & McGuire, 2010), I refer here to the transformative impact of LM. Commerzbank nonetheless immersed itself into EF from the 1960s onwards, and was deeply affected as global competition slowly changed its coordinates, even if Commerzbank kept its more traditional banking features.

Commerzbank's deep exposure to US money markets came in form of one transaction. Similar to Eurohypo, it was through buying a German institution, rather than a US bank. In 2008, Commerzbank acquired Dresdner Bank and seems unable to reverse its misfortune since (Bowman, 2017; Wixforth, 2017). Dresdner was hugely invested into ABCP conduits that could not roll over their debt during the GFC. Commerzbank bought Dresdner without realising the extent of Dresdner's exposure to the US MBS industry, either because of lack of expertise, ignorance, or because it aimed to expand desperately to shield itself from potential takeover threats. It is unclear and German banks have been called stupid, but after all, it was US-based Lehman Brothers who became one of the biggest casualties.

Dresdner was exposed to assets financed by offshore ABCP vehicles amounting to 364 per cent of its own capital, according to Fitch Ratings (cited in Hüfner, 2010, p. 5). In comparison, Commerzbank's 85 per cent was significantly lower. It was Dresdner' Kleinwort Benson, previously a middle-sized but leading British merchant bank, bought in 1995, as well as US-Investment Bank Wasserstein Perella, bought in 2000, that had led Dresdner's transition and pushed the integration into US money markets. The failures of Dresdner's securities business meant that Commerzbank ranked eleventh (Deutsche sixth, Bank of America first) amongst the largest borrowers of the Federal Reserve (Thompson, 2016, p. 226). Beyond USD support, Commerzbank had to seek rescue with the German state. SoFFin (Sonderfonds Finanzmarktstabilisierung) was a German public fund from 2008 to 2015 that transferred public funds to the banks that could not sustain their own speculation. Commerzbank accessed Euro 18.2 billion in total. The state received a 25 per cent plus one share stake in Commerzbank. Without Deutsche's capacity to source assets and its vast global network of funding, Commerzbank had few options but to access the public bailout fund and handover some control, even if it did not last long. In 2013, this declined to 17.3 per cent which ended the government's veto power.

Since the GFC, Commerzbank tried again to scale down its structured financing products and its activities related to USD markets, an approach that has not been easy. After selling most of Dresdner's previous

US practices (Commerzbank AG, 2018), Commerzbank got out of the most profitable markets. It struggled to find value generating practices. As Michael Reuthers, member of the board of managing directors at Commerzbank, admits that the challenge for Commerzbank is 'to lay a stronger emphasis on increasing the profitability of risk-weighted assets that we are employing' (Bowman, 2017). Commerzbank might succeed at some point, but Chapter 8 will further emphasise the problems and contradictions of having adopted LM. Important to take away from this section is that Dresdner's acquisition meant that also Commerzbank, a bank rich in deposits and bank bonds, rather than money market papers, was caught up in the failures to roll over USD debt. Its European focus could not separate it from the rise of LM because, firstly, Commerzbank repeatedly tried to integrate into the US, and secondly, its German acquisitions themselves (Eurohypo and Dresdner) were already too much immersed into US financial logics.

CONCLUSION

Commerzbank represents an example of a bank that has been impacted by US finance early on, as its embrace of US and Eurodollar markets in the 1960s and 1970s evidence. As financialisation started to tie banks to New York, Commerzbank was amongst the first. In the 1980s, however, Commerzbank's international advance shifted to German and European markets. Its expansion into US finance rekindled only in the mid 1990s but this was a catastrophic, short-lived endeavour. Costs shot up, but the new acquisitions were not properly integrated and did not yield any return so that they could not be sustained. Commerzbank's takeover of Dresdner Bank in 2008 brought about another round of US securities' defaults. Thus, Commerzbank's draw to US finance was present throughout this history but to a lesser extent than Deutsche's and riddled with continuous difficulties.

The key argument of the book is that German financialisation is best understood as the banks' extroverted strategies that forced them to partially uproot themselves from their home markets and to institutionalise themselves into US financial markets to address the implications of LM. Commerzbank's case suggests that individual banks have responded differently to these challenges. Apart from the initial advance into US and Eurodollar markets, Commerzbank did not relocate away from Frankfurt to the same extent as Deutsche Bank. Its extroverted strategies turned to German and European innovations, rather than LM, which triggered fewer internal tensions with its traditional strategies.

Only in the mid 1990s did Commerzbank make renewed inroads into US finance. Failing to adopt LM, however, meant that it could not tap US money markets, which severely restrained any ambitions of sourcing US assets. Simply expanding into US asset management did not work, it lacked a larger distribution network of USD and a new approach to finance. Finally, it was the takeover of German institutions, particularly Dresdner Bank, that presented the biggest challenge of US money market funding and caused fundamental losses. Like at Deutsche, a half-transformation has not worked, even when putting more emphasis on its traditional banking cultures. Commerzbank's focus on European investment banking did not shield its traditional model from the rise – and tensions – of US finance. Commerzbank did not initially change the liabilities side of the balance sheet, and thus its central strategy of banking, but its participation in the US asset management business failed quickly as a result. And because of its on-going troubles to manage its US exposure, albeit now limited, it is still in danger of takeover (Storbeck & Morris, 2019).

Commerzbank's example highlights how the rise of US finance triggered a broader change in the nature of finance. To better control, source and fund their financial practices, German banks needed to improve their institutional connections to US money markets. Having mostly failed that, Commerzbank still had to cope with the dynamics that US-led financialisation unleashed. Interestingly, by attempting to introduce SME's to securities funding as part of its response, Commerzbank became itself a key agent of changing bank-firm relations away from corporate loans, which in turn necessitated further changes towards a more dynamic way of funding, including LM's potential for financial vulnerability, crisis and growing need for deep and liquid financial markets.

In Chapter 8, I drill further into the tensions of this transition. While I have outlined Commerzbank's troubles already, the final empirical chapter shows how even for Deutsche, the adoption of LM presented more fundamental problems than simply higher costs and complications of adjustment. EF has imbued fundamental contradictions into the global financial architecture because German banks had to uproot themselves and reorient some of their central strategies into US finance – a split they cannot easily overcome. By looking at contemporary banking more generally, Chapter 8 shows that the rise of US finance brought fundamental problems that cannot be addressed by going back to their German roots of banking nor by simply taming the banks so that they focus on productive investments again.

8

Financialised Banking and Its Discontents

'There will certainly be further challenges and shocks facing the global financial system in the months and years to come' says Klaas Knot, chair of the Basel-based Financial Stability Board (FSB) (cited in Noonan, 2023b), a rather modest portrayal of a crises-ridden system. Since the GFC, there have been many of these challenges and shocks, despite large-scale stabilisation and rescue programs. As Bell and Hindmoor (2018, p. 19) summarise, 'the Eurozone banks have, on average, the highest absolute levels of leverage; the highest levels of dependence upon wholesale borrowing; amongst the highest levels of dependence upon non-interest sources of income; and (relative to the American banks but not the British banks) the lowest levels of profit and returns on equity'. German banks in particular have been in crisis (Beck, 2022b). Deutsche (cf. Schenk, 2020) and Commerzbank (cf. Paul et al., 2020) have been struggling to align their traditional business models with their global investment banking ambitions.

Some argue that the banks' problems are related to tightened regulations that had finally put them on a leash and tamed their excessive speculatory activities. Banks have yet to find alternative profitable investments. This is in stark contrast to the pre-crisis years, where regulatory failure (Moschella & Tsingou, 2013) or lack of regulation (Bayoumi, 2017; Rixen, 2013) meant that financial markets had gone out of control. Since then, policymakers dutifully promised improvement and introduced many changes to make finance more stable and serve the 'real economy'. Demands and attempts of structural reforms, including improved capital reserve requirements, consumer protection, or climate-sensitive banking, have been extensive (Howarth & James, 2023). Banks have faced the 'louder politics' of bank reform as opposed to the quiet politics (Bell & Hindmoor, 2018; Culpepper, 2010) as public critique of their speculative and offshore banking activities grew more prominent (Baker & Wigan, 2017). The Basel III agreement in particular has increased regulatory burdens for the banks, and many commentators claim that they are now more stable and resilient, if less profitable.

Alas, it seems that regulatory efforts have not gone far enough. The financial system is as powerful as ever, capable of producing crisis after crisis only to resurge again (Braun & Koddenbrock, 2023; Cohen, 1996). The tighter regulatory environment is not necessarily the banks' problem. Banks are exceptionally well equipped to reinvent themselves to respond to new pressures (Erturk & Solari, 2007), and tight regulations for some only serve other financiers to take advantage of the restrictions (Knafo, 2022). There is ample research showing that despite these regulatory changes, banks still have potentially too much power to bend regulation in their favour. They have watered down the initial ambitions of the Basel III regulatory reforms (Howarth & Quaglia, 2013) European reforms to ring fence proprietary trading (Hardie & Macartney, 2016), or the financial transaction tax (Gabor, 2016a) that would have curbed unwanted activities.

From a macroeconomic perspective, scholars argue that part of the problem is that policymakers have discovered the potential of large globally active banks for their own geopolitical reach and power (Massoc, 2019, 2022), and states benefit from financial innovations such as repo finance for their own objectives (Braun, 2020; Gabor & Ban, 2016), giving banks a significant source of structural and infrastructural power. UBS is now 2½ times Swiss GDP. BNP Paribas, Barclays, Deutsche Bank, Groupe Crédit Agricole, ING, Santander, Société Générale, UBS and HSBC all make it to the Globally Systemically Important Banks (G-SIBs) list of the FSB and the Basel Committee on Banking Supervision (BCBS). Banks have the potential to wreak havoc in global as well as local markets with few strings attached because public finances bail them out. Banks gained too much (transnational) market (Culpeper, 2012; Pagliari & Young, 2015; Woll, 2014) or instrumental (Hardie & Macartney, 2016) power to resist more wide-reaching regulatory changes.

There is then a controversy in how we perceive of the power of European banks and what troubles them. On the one hand, they are huge and influential, on the other, they struggle with financialised banking. MBB highlights that while banks are indispensable to the global economy, it is banks' funding gap that creates considerable vulnerability and risk for them. To recall, the funding gap denotes the difference between their deposit base as stable and long-term funding sources and the value of their assets. The difference must be filled with market-based liabilities, which are short-term and subject banks to the fluctuations of markets and skiddy investors – the SVB and Credit Suisse crises are cases in point. From that perspective, European banks need to return to traditional ways of banking, such as deposit, corporate, and retail banking to regain their strength, and the regulatory changes should force or incentivise banks to do that. That way, we can ameliorate systemic risk, frequency of crises and provide much-needed funding for the real economy or efforts to respond to the climate crisis because they force banks to turn away from markets.

This would be nice, indeed. But the rise of LM produced more fundamental problems that are insufficiently addressed if we think of them as a market-based problem. I thus introduce the term 'financialised banking' to foreground that contemporary banking problems are related to LM, rather than markets per se. This chapter uses the fourth feature of EF to lead through the inherent contradictions of global finance and financial agents themselves, which go beyond the challenges of inadequate capital reserves, lack of deposits, and risky investments. As I show, these problems have been critically aligned with the German banks' paths of extroversion that saw them transforming towards a business model that they are not only ill-equipped to sustain but that has also made maintaining traditional ways of banking rather difficult.

From the perspective of EF, the funding gap is indeed a key vulnerability of finance. But while it is a problem for some, it is a lucrative source of power for others. Engineering market-based liabilities, US banks have managed to greatly leverage their balance sheets and thrive off the flexible management of their books. Meanwhile, European banks' struggles are perhaps more closely related to the USD funding gap, the gap between EUR and USD funding, instead of their bank-based deposits and market-based liabilities per se. This unevenness is important to keep in mind because US banks have juggled profitably unprecedented mismatches and funding gaps, whereas German banks have been stuck between their 'European' and US strategies, struggling to bridge the gaps between the two. Besides their large balance sheet sizes, they seem to have little to offer to sustain USD leverage and to cope with the turmoil of financialised banking.

This chapter is divided into three sections. The first section examines the various battles and tensions that arose against other banks and itself as Deutsche Bank transformed towards US-style finance. LM had an irresistible pull, despite the difficulties of uprooting and transforming itself. The third section delves into liquidity management of the balance sheet: I show how European banks struggle to sustain their USD debt while US bank on funding gaps and leverage. The final section documents the limited success of the European banks' response that has often been vetted to attempts of merging to grow out of the crisis.

CONTROLLING LM? GERMAN BANKERS VS. FINANCIALISED BANKING

In 1997, Ronaldo Schmitz[1] complained that 'it was not acceptable that North America should be run at a loss or be subsidised by the rest of the investment bank' (Schenk, 2020, p. 520). Deutsche's US investments often produced losses, and DMG had disappointed in US money market funding. Russian and Asian crises during those years did not help either. Deutsche had little faith in the prospects of enhancing profitability in Germany because of a stagnating German economy, and it seemed utopian to restructure German financial markets to adequately support global Deutsche's expansion with a strong German base. At that time, Deutsche contemplated exiting investment banking as some of the British competitors did (Lee, 1998).[2] While Chapters 6 and 7 already underlined that relocating to foreign markets was not easy, Deutsche's transformation was not a foregone conclusion even though it ended up pushing this transformation furthest amongst the German banks. It was problematic beyond initial adjustment costs of buying US and London-based institutions.

The increased costs of USD investment banking led to the fact that the German banks' profits declined in the 1990s (Janssen, 2009, pp. 105, 144; Vitols, 2009, p. 145). While the decline in profits partly resulted from the erosion of interest margins in corporate lending in the 1990s, the additional expensive US traders meant that profitability per employee declined as well (Janssen, 2009, pp. 105, 144). Despite repeated attempts and commitments to cutting costs, Deutsche has been failing to get its cost-to-income ratio below the 92 per cent mark, running huge year end losses at times (Schenk, 2020). Only in the 2000s period did Deutsche manage, briefly, to compensate its enormous increase in costs. The average increase in net income from 2002 to 2006 was 175 per cent (Wharton Campustat, author's own calculation).[3]

1 Member of the managing board and responsible for investment banking and the US/North American expansion, introduced in Chapter 7.

2 UBS and Credit Suisse, for example, similarly accepted huge losses of their US subsidiaries (Celarier, 1996).

3 Commerzbank made a net loss in 2002 and 2003 (ibid.).

According to German banker Staecker, who was sent to head the branch in New York (interviewed by Kobrak, 2007, p. 320), the board in Frankfurt did not understand LM, which was so crucial for banking in New York. German managers 'had little feeling for the American problems and facilities, which were beginning to emerge in the 1980s' (Kobrak, 2007, p. 320). So to improve its banking performance, Deutsche had to hire new people – something all German banks pursued (Deeg, 1999, p. 90) – to adopt US practices and to catch up quickly. The expenses of large US salaries were criticised because they exceeded what even the German management board received. As *The Economist* (1999) observes: 'It would be hard to find two financial-services firms with more different approaches: buzzy deal makers and traders at Bankers, stodgy commercial bankers at Deutsche. The German bank has a sorry record of trying to succeed in the racier field of investment banking; its prospects with Bankers look little better'.

Despite its quest to learn US finance, Deutsche tried to control its US traders from Frankfurt. The board attempted to set limits on the volume and speed of dealings and wanted to confirm larger transactions. This was impossible in the age of money market funding, where deals were agreed on in split seconds. The naivety of this approach, for example, is highlighted by the limit of USD 2 million that Deutsche's New York branch had. Rival New York bankers (quoted in Stigum, 1990, p. 303) regularly took out as much as USD 100 million of cash to hedge interest rate risks through Eurodollar futures. Deutsche's attempts to manage its US finance division meant that it was ill-equipped to play the game of (mis-) matching their books (Beck, 2022b).

But Deutsche's management loathed handing over too much control to its US operations, even though they tasked their foreign subsidiaries with finding USD and aimed to improve securities clearing, performance measurement, and accounting in the 1990s (Lee, 1998). The chaos of financialised banking was also visible in the structure of Deutsche's management of New York activities from the Frankfurt offices. According to Staecker (Kobrak, 2007, p. 323), adapting the trading system was a real nightmare. Deutsche hired IBM as early as the mid 1980s to come up with a system for the whole of Deutsche. In 1992, Staecker hired John Ross, Bank of New York's head of global asset and liability management, to advance New York systems for LM. However, to Ross' dismay, this misaligned the managerial and operational channels between New York and Frankfurt. With derivatives and futures becoming more and more crucial, New York bankers could not work through the chain of command in Frankfurt.

Ross had to restructure the operations in Frankfurt to adjust the systems between the continents so that New York bankers could (mis-) match the books. That way, the operations based on the liquidity needs of New York spread across the institution.

Deutsche originally thought it could keep its investment banking separated in London while the 'parent bank' would engage with commercial banking in Europe. But the requirements of LM made it very difficult to control US financial practices from Frankfurt when the bank operates on different systems. We have already seen the reduction of the loan portfolio because the move of firm finance to securities when corporate loans did not fetch enough profits to finance Deutsche's expansion. Updating the whole management and operational mechanisms at Deutsche started to influence the metrics of traditional lending practices and the business model at its core. Add to this changes in risk management (cf. Beck, 2022b) and new financial personnel, and Deutsche slowly became unrecognisable to many throughout the 1990s.

The transition produced power struggles between the bankers at Deutsche. Deutsche's US traders in the 1990s loathed Deutsche's attempts to curb their flexibility and independence in trading and structuring, despite wanting to advance into New York. US employees thought German bankers were stupid (Lewis, 2011) or – more generously termed – confused (Kobrak, 2007) about how US finance works. Financiers in New York complained that 'stodgy' (Tett, 2012) Deutsche did not let them do their business, which required speedy transactions in US money markets. US bankers in fact often quit after a short while at Deutsche (Deeg, 2001, p. 30).

German bankers, on their part, disagreed with this assessment of their intelligence. According to them, US banking culture was the problem: it was too speculative or, interestingly, too 'notoriously provincial' as a German newspaper claimed (Kobrak, 2007, p. 345) because it lacked the German universal aspect. Deutsche bankers wanted to continue the way they were used to and good at. The shift to US financial practices created 'psychic costs' and many internal disagreements (Deeg, 2001, p. 30). Previously, seniority and loyalty were highly valued in German companies and were preconditions to become CEO. Internal managers were favoured over external ones (Freye, 2015). But to implement the changes to accommodate the growing business in the US in the 1980s and 1990s, Deutsche Bank hired a lot of new and young traders, which also entered forcefully into the management ranks. Huge layoffs were particularly affecting corporate finance (Hackethal, 2004, p. 101). While more senior people had pushed for advancing into New York in the 1980s, once they saw that LM would imply more radical changes to the rest of the bank, they tried to stop the process. Older 'traditional' bankers did not necessarily see the benefits of changing their practices so radically, which might make them obsolete (Nolmans, 2006). More and more people started to speak out against the costs and difficulties of integrating Morgan Grenfell and Bankers Trust (Kobrak, 2007, p. 454), or the general trend of Deutsche towards US finance (Rodgers, 2016).

This transition, however, was needed to adjust the institutional and technological systems towards LM. Deutsche Bank had gaping shortcomings in US investment banking it had to overcome.[4] Despite all warnings against 'having lost its way', the 1990s saw Deutsche progressively transforming itself to meet the liquidity requirements of US money markets, despite the growing opposition. Deutsche's attempt to 'learn' the US-way of finance turned into a rerouting of core parts of its business model into US money markets. Because Deutsche needed to construct new ways of controlling its new financial environment the changes outweighed the resistance. Once started on the path to regain control in global finance, it was difficult to control where it went.

And despite all these efforts, Deutsche's years of glory were rather short-lived. This is a more general problem for European banks. While the progressive institutionalisation of LM allowed them to keep up with the changes in global finance, they never in fact, systematically caught up to the top US banks. This was already apparent in the run up to the crisis in how European banks' engineering of MBS fared compared to US banks (Beck et al., 2023). Banks such as Deutsche or Paribas were among the 'top ten banks in 2001 and managed to compete with Morgan Stanley and JP Morgan in arranging CDOs (Hart, 2002), but from an estimated USD 11 trillion ABS and USD 3 trillion CDOs outstanding in mid 2007, only 17 per cent were originated by European banks' (Lysandrou & Shabani, 2018). ABN Amro, for example, was a top European broker of CDOs, "the bank still [hadn't] run the books on any U.S. CDOs in almost five years, according to Asset-Backed Alert's ABS Database" (Anonymous, 2004)'. Despite all resources spent, it was US banks that produced the more profitable assets, while European banks remained their customers, and thus in a peripheral position to financial engineering.

4 Catherine Schenk (2020) has a brilliant, detailed history of the precise managerial discussions and strategic projects Deutsche attempted to implement in order to strengthen its investment banking, and their corresponding costs.

BANKING ON THE USD FUNDING GAP

LM was the engine of the advance into global finance but has turned into a bit of a nightmare for the German banks – and by extension for anyone else suffering the consequences of the global financial architecture. While German (and European) banks substantially deleveraged, reoriented their business models, and decreased US money market dependency, they do not seem to reverse their misery and vulnerability. In fact, they rather linger back and forth between trying to expand, improve, reduce, or decouple their US financial activities – none of which seems to work just yet.

German banks built their global funding networks when access to US money markets was relatively easy in the 2000s. Before the GFC, German foreign affiliates would supply Deutsche Bank with USD. As a Deutsche investor told Financial Times, describing the old model: 'we can fund cheaper than Goldman Sachs, leverage that and make a decent amount of money' (Morris et al., 2018). Prior to the GFC, subsidiaries in the US and the Eurodollar markets would supply the parent banks with USD. By the time of the Lehman collapse, this relationship changed. Foreign subsidiaries borrowed €50 billion, or 10 per cent of their total assets, from their German parent banks (Düwel, 2013, p. 9). A BIS study shows that US branches and subsidiaries of non-US banks have become net borrowers of their home headquarters (Aldasoro et al., 2018, p. 8), reducing flexibility and increasing costs for Deutsche. ABCP conduits – a key vehicle for European banks to participate in the 2000 US mortgage boom – have all but lost their funding importance (Sgambati, 2019).

Having transformed their systems[5] they must now sustain US money market access and the new forms of financial innovations that arose with the shift to LM. In a USD financial world but located in Germany, German banks must consistently find ways to leverage their limited USD resources. Having home markets in euros, rather than in USD, they must consistently bridge the gap (Aldasoro et al., 2019). German banks' assets are to a significant extent denominated in USD, and the better their USD base and internal USD distribution mechanisms, the better they can sustain USD funding and the better they can cope with sudden shortages (Abbassi & Bräuning, 2018). In 2022, 19% of Deutsche's investor base was located in the US (24% in Germany). In 2022, short-term unsecured wholesale

[5] Commerzbank took on substantial systems from Dresdner, but has of course, a more limited overall transformation than Deutsche.

funding and capital market issuance totalled EUR 135,980 million,[6] 55,792 million of which were in USD, that is, 41 per cent (Deutsche Bank Annual Report, 2022, p. 172).

The infrastructure needed to fund this and much higher levels during the 2000s has not only been costly to build up, but US money markets can dry up quickly. European banks were heavily exposed to the USD money markets (Shin, 2012; Tooze, 2018), which led to their bankruptcies when US money markets froze (Baba et al., 2009). The so-called run on repo during the GFC meant that European banks could not roll over their debt, which proved much more detrimental than their MBS losses. Failing to refinance their short-term USD debt, they would have collapsed if it were not for the public gift. Despite Deutsche's claims that it did not receive any public help during the crisis (Wilson, 2012), it received USD loans from the Fed as part of the Fed's Term Auction Facility (TAF) rescue program, which cushioned the deleveraging process of foreign assets for the German banks (Buch et al., 2011; Ewerhart & Valla, 2008, p. 141).

The 2008 disaster motivated the big European banks to shrink their investment banking activities (Bell & Hindmoor, 2018; Hardie & Howarth, 2013a). USD liabilities have shrunk from almost 10 trillion to about 6 trillion (Aldasoro & Ehlers, 2018, p. 18; IMF, 2018, p. 44). German banks have been reorienting their resources towards German and European retail banking (Hardie & Howarth, 2013a, p. 124; Paul et al., 2020; Schenk, 2020). Deutsche explicitly promised during the 2019 AGM that it would reduce its US investment division (Storbeck et al., 2019), and its current CEO, Christian Sewing is celebrated for his prudent German roots. Commerzbank, too, recollects its 'European' nature and closeness to SME funding (Paul et al., 2020). Both banks engage in one restructuring and cost-reducing programme after the other – to very little avail. Despite consistent attempts, Deutsche has not managed to reduce its cost-to-income ratio over the past decade and its troubled US investment division is still a central part of its business model (Schenk, 2020). By 2019, Deutsche was still losing 25 cents for every USD of its US business, according to an analysis by JPMorgan Chase (Storbeck et al., 2019).

The problem is that most USDs remain in the US and can only be accessed through cross-border transactions (Aldasoro & Ehlers, 2018). When MMFs reduce their funding, foreign banks need to find ways to make up for the loss (Aldasoro et al., 2017 Graph A1, left-hand panel). In part, this is a structural problem because demand for USD is higher

[6] Of which 16,389 were secured, all in EUR, and 119,591 were unsecured.

than for Euros, leaving European banks at a structural disadvantage in FX, swap and repo markets. While they attempt to row back towards 'European' ways of assets and banking, it is not that simple. US money market centrality means that the way German banks source their assets must meet the requirements of US MMFs. For example, during the European debt crisis, European banks had to engineer their assets in a way that invoked USD money market confidence (Thompson, 2015, 2016). As Helen Thompson describes, German and French financial authorities coordinated Greek rescue efforts for their banks in a way that would not harm US money market investors, lest their banks were cut off from USD. Thus, even if banks have reduced their USD liabilities, they cannot turn away from obtaining assets to tap US money markets. From the perspective of EF, then, the vulnerabilities associated with the German banks' funding gap are best read through the differences of USD and Euro funding resources, rather than the difference between deposits and market-based activities – *the USD funding gap*.

There are many opportunities for European banks to make money through USD leverage and they do. The difficulty with closing USD funding gaps, however, is that banks must not only constantly chase USD-denominated assets and liabilities to match their books – a problem European banks previously did not have. More broadly, financialised banking rests on an everyday game of matching books to ensure enough liquidity meets liability commitments on an everyday basis. Matching books, however, is a peculiar description of what global banks are involved in because books are rarely matched because assets and liabilities work on different time frames – important differences in transactions that exploit price movements of time frames of split seconds. Neither does a matched book mean that debts are settled or that things could not horribly go wrong.

The practice of matching books in the repo markets shows this well. Matching books refers to a strategy of a dealer bank that buys a security using a reverse repo (in exchange for an overnight cash loan) and then sells this security using a repo to another financier. This effectively finances the initial purchase and 'matches' the book because both transactions are cancelled out. The dealer bank pockets the difference in rates, successfully using its position in both markets to their benefit.[7] However, if asset prices

[7] Dealer banks also settle repo transactions for other parties in which they unwind the deals in the morning (that is, receive the cash and security from the other parties), but only officially settle the deals in the evening, giving them access to large pools of cash essentially for free.

fall, and banks cannot meet their margin calls, this results into an asset value downward spiral with widespread knock-on effects – the repo market is worth trillions. Given recent trends of rising interest rates and declining asset values (at the time of finishing writing this book), this practice becomes dodgier by the month.

The complication with funding gaps is that they have become an inherent feature of financialised banking, something to be exploited by banks on an everyday level for money-making. Matching or rather *un*matching the books is a complex game. US banks have mastered LM to go *beyond the limits of matching books*. As Stefano Sgambati explains: 'Banks routinely make loans that are not immediately matched by deposits – that is, they generate market liquidity that is *not* funded' (Sgambati, 2019, p. 18). Pozsar (quoted in Sgambati, 2019, p. 18) suggests in 2015 that 20% of global bank activities are unfunded, while Baklanova and colleagues estimate that nearly 40% of loans are not immediately financed (ibid.). While the 2018 IMF Global Financial Stability Report confirmed that regulatory changes since the GFC have forced banks to increase their capacity to reliably meet their short-term claims, the shift of banking towards shadow banking globally is well documented (Dafermos et al., 2022; Gabor, 2018; Wullweber, 2020) so that many of their short-term claims are unknown and moved off the balance sheet. It is unclear if the funding risks of global USD flows have increased or decreased since the GFC (Aldasoro & Ehlers, 2018). We rely on estimates to assess the extent of underfunding. Funding gaps are not necessarily a vulnerability from the perspective of banks that use it as a practice of leverage and profits. They have become part and parcel of financier's success in financialised markets.

This not only demonstrates the level of leverage and complexity of US money markets but also highlights that European banks are continuously bound to the US if they want to participate in this bonanza. Sgambati again: 'the problem of matching the books is the problem of making money via capital market lending and having it validated via money market funding' (Sgambati, 2019, p. 18). In part, banks can rest assured because the Fed has recognised this shift in money-making and stands ready to provide funding whenever there is a shortfall in the banks' liquidity needs through repo, FX and USD swaps markets,[8] allowing banks to systemically run on unmatched books (Sgambati, 2019). This courtesy has been extended to global offshore markets because non-US

[8] See Dafermos et al. (2022) for an analysis of how the differences in these practices show how the Fed reproduces the inequalities of the global financial architecture.

banks' funding squeezes have the potential to translate into domestic shortages of credit creation (Pape, 2022). Nonetheless, this is a complicated game and when banks fail, asset prices plummet quickly as repo buyers scramble to follow margin calls.

This has tremendously enhanced the power of *some* banks. The big US banks can make their loans without worrying too much – at least initially – about matched funding – be it market-based or otherwise. This dynamic asset and liability management generates a process in which the big broker-dealer banks can source their loans out of nothing, and at some point in the future, if ever, refinance on US money markets and reap tremendous profits along the way (Sgambati, 2019). German banks' challenge is not simply finding more profitable investments but having to engineer assets to participate in this game. Being able to run 'matched' books while finding ways to effectively underfund their books is a competitive pressure they have not yet found a way to turn into their own benefit yet.

Conceiving of the power of banks in this way means that the institutional embeddedness remains key to how banks can participate in global finance. Bridging mismatches of books is easier with better access to deep and liquid money markets, Fed funds, financial networks. Greater ability to manipulate, postpone and hide any mismatches through other means, including expertise in accounting, IT, financial models' wizardry and shifting them off balance sheets into dark pools or shadow banking entities also helps. Given Deutsche's multiple litigation fees, the bank has so far failed to sufficiently hide its practices.

It is here that the key differences of European and US banks' power becomes clear. US banks have much more institutional support and possibilities to manage the mismatch. While the Fed stabilises global USD flows, its concern is to benefit US rather than global financial markets (Dafermos et al., 2022; Pape, 2022). European capital markets remain poor sources for those assets, despite efforts to create more unified, liquid and deeper European financial markets. While more wholesale funding potentially leaves banks more prone to financial shocks compared to deposit funding (Howarth & James, 2023, p. 9), US banks have mastered using wholesale funding to increase their own profits and power within those markets (Knafo, 2022).

As a result, German banks go back and forth between trying to reduce their US investment banking activities or expanding it to make it profitable. As such, German banks find themselves between relatively high leverage because they must consistently overstretch their resources, but have lower profitability compared to the US banks because they are bad at it. Revenue at Deutsche still depends heavily on the investment banking division (Schenk, 2020, p. 637), but it has failed to reduce its high cost-to-income ratio and its high leverage for the past decade. In 2015, the bank had leverage of EUR 900 billion and wanted to reduce it to 650 by 2018 (ibid.). Commerzbank also seemingly fails to find new profitable business strategies (cf. Paul et al., 2020), particularly when it became apparent that its resources are insufficient to participate in US wholesale markets. According to financial commentators, it is a matter of when Commerzbank will be bought by a competitor, not if.

This is not to say that European banks cannot be successful in global markets, and they have certainly tried. But while European banks have had great leverage in the past, in their play of catch up, European banks are still far behind. In a world where financial agents run unfunded books, manipulating US money markets remains key to financial power, but this is unevenly distributed.

THE BIGGER THE BETTER? THE MYTH OF NATIONAL CHAMPIONS

While the big US dealer banks ride the debt bubble through leverage, German banks have a peripheral position to LM and to bind US MMFs to their own liability strategies. How, then, do German banks deal with US finance's risk, speed, unpredictability, and complexity? Often, they aim to compensate through balance sheet size, which should shield against markets and support their return to more retail and corporate banking. While the GFC and subsequent recession sparked 'a call for all manner of returns to previous states of existence, both real and imagined' (Adkins, 2012, p. 621), this nostalgia is particularly present in the imagination of German banking. The call for a return to 'boring' banking is widespread, including from financial watchdogs, politicians, and shareholders. German banks should stop speculating on US markets in favour of funding the 'real economy'. Deutsche's CEO himself invoked this imaginary, something for which he was widely applauded for (Schreiber & Willmroth, 2018).

European banks more generally have been supported in this endeavour by their own national governments, who want globally strong banks and functioning capital markets, not least to support their exports and have geopolitical reach (Massoc, 2022). As mentioned above, European universal banks are still huge and take a central position in national and European industrial strategy. One important strategy has been public support to merge banks, a tendency that contradicts the aim to contain too-big-to-fail banks that was prominent just after the GFC. Europe has an average concentration for the largest five banks to hold 46% of assets (Germany 31%). This section shows that mergers neither necessarily build market power for the European banks nor do they support industrial development or progressive social goals. Mergers are often an emergency rescue solution, such as during the GFC or the more recent example of Credit Suisse that was swallowed by UBS because banks failed to sustain their USD debt. But mergers also fuel the dynamics of financialisation, making further failings more likely in the boom-and-bust cycles of our leveraged world.

Building a *global* national champion to finance German companies was a brief but concentrated attempt by a large coalition in Germany to get the German banking sector back on its feet. In 2019, the German political and financial establishment attempted to merge Commerzbank and Deutsche into a mega bank that could rival US banks such as JP Morgan and regain financial independence (Morris et al., 2019; Storbeck, 2019). The merger would create a German giant that would manage EUR 1.8 trillion in assets (Massoudi et al., 2019). This attempt of merging failed after several weeks of negotiations between the two banks, despite strong state nudges as part of its wider industrial strategy. What the failed merger highlighted, however, is that the discourse surrounding this initiative remained trapped in an outdated understanding of what banks do and the imperatives they face.

Peter Altmaier, Federal Minister for Economic Affairs and Energy at the time, sums up the role he imagines for finance and Deutsche Bank in his industrial strategy: 'A country like Germany also has to lay claim to playing an international role in financial markets and banking' (cited in Schieritz & Nienhaus, 2019, own translation). Olaf Scholz, finance minister at the, time maintains that 'we will only be able to seize our global opportunities if we have an efficient financial sector' (cited in Storbeck, 2019). Aiming to rescue Germany's inefficient financial sector and ensuring better corporate finance again (Gammelin, 2019), Scholz strongly encouraged the merger, threatening to find another European buyer for Commerzbank if the merger fails.[9]

This merger plan was criticised for several reasons. Merging would entail huge restructuring costs that would require fresh cash to pay for

9 I could not establish how much this plan is aimed at protecting the government's stake of 15 per cent in Commerzbank.

it. The new bank would have higher capital requirements because of its higher systemic relevance (Storbeck & Morris, 2019). Various financial experts, such as Isabel Schnabel, member of the German Council of Economic Experts at the time, have pointed out that it would be very problematic if there was only one big private bank. It would practically enjoy a state guarantee (Schnabel, 2019). Such a guarantee is often taken as a license to neglect prudent financial conduct, leaving banks free to speculate too much, resulting in financial crises, which is a repeated critique against G-SIB and other huge conglomerates. The mega bank would be even more difficult to control, monitor and understand. It would be 'too big to fail', a feature of banks that represents their 'perverted power' and constitutes a 'threat to society as a whole' (Wixforth, 2017, p. 605).[10]

The history told in the preceding chapters suggests that these criticisms do not go far enough. Commerzbank and Deutsche already effectively enjoy a state guarantee anyway. The discourse and policy implications of the attempted merger reproduce overly simplified versions of financialisation, and consequently what might represent the banks' power and interest in navigating global financial markets. It is true that large global banks can navigate turmoil in financial markets more easily because they can source higher volumes of sovereign bonds and other 'safe' assets to use as collateral in repo markets to increase funding. They can also spend more money to set up offshore subsidiaries, shadow banking entities and buy financial institutions in the US, key EF strategies they have pursued in the past. As mentioned above, big balance sheets also help to navigate financial turmoil as they can easily hide or absorb non-performing loans. All this helps to gain flexibility of USD funding needed in global finance. However, focusing on market size, people underestimate how the logics of financialised banking question the effectiveness of national champions to navigate global financial markets and to provide financial support to German or European industrial, social or environmental projects. The most recent case in point would be the failure of Credit Suisse.

The debate surrounding the merger reflects a perspective that views US financial markets, rather than German banks, as the problem, resting on the popular conceptual binary of markets vs. banks. This perspective is steeped in an understanding of traditional German bank-based system as representing a more progressive 'social' market economy, in which banks act as the guardians of German industry, until US finance forced financial liberalisation in the 1990s. German banks' patient capital was

[10] Own translation.

heralded as allowing corporations to focus on long-term investment and high-quality production. This would ensure a form of corporate governance that is characterised by compromises between different stakeholders so that benefits are shared more consensually (cf. Heires & Nölke, 2014; Streeck, 2009). Consequently, Scholz would need to set the market conditions right for German banks to fulfil their inner, normatively better, purpose again. The bigger the banks are, apparently, the better they could keep at bay the troubles of US market-based finance. This misses how LM changed German banks towards a different nature of banking, which, as I highlighted in the previous section, makes a decoupling from US markets almost impossible. As their business models turned into a site of financialisation, they became inseparable from US financial markets. 'National' champion is a poor description of their financialised banking motivations and constraints.

The idea of the mega bank saviour thus replicates another popular myth in which banks are financial intermediaries serving the 'real economy', deriving what banks do from their ideal-typical relations with corporations. The wish for a return to traditional banking practices carries the delusion that banks would go back to acting as financial conduits, passing on liquidity to the industrial sector, if they only could. However, banks never acted as passive intermediaries of capital allocation. Looking at the paths of extroversion, the appearance of stability of the German financial sector and the 'harmonious' relationship between finance and industry was in many ways deceptive. Banks' principal interest in global finance was learning and doing US finance, which fundamentally reduced their ability in addition to their interest in providing loans.

Scholars and policymakers underappreciate how financialisation has not been brought about by a change of assets (reducing the corporate loan portfolio in exchange for securities) but a change in funding practices. As the GFC confirmed, a primary choking point for the functionality of banks was their ability to sustain their USD debts, rather than the value of their assets. The rise of LM rendered raising USD liabilities a central strategy of financialised banking, which subsequently forced banks to re-engineer their assets to suit LM. In other words, the imperative to shift their asset management was precipitated by a radical transformation of funding. What banks invest in or trade with cannot simply be reversed, as the assets of banks follow the requirements of LM. Too often, people think of risk-taking at the level of assets, rather than liabilities, which misguides what we need to fix in financial systems.

Focusing on balance sheet size runs the risk of missing the transformation of finance over the past decades. The rise of LM has elevated USD as the central currency for the everyday of global banking, also for non-US banks. Funding on US wholesale markets is inherently volatile and can provide a weak link to banks outside the US. As a result, global banks are neither 'efficient', nor would they be a German 'national' champion able to rival US banks such as JPMorgan Chase. While states pursue 'their' banks as geopolitical tools of statecraft (Massoc, 2022), this is possible only to a limited extent as financialisation has deeply ingrained a USD dependence that any efforts of 'economic patriotism' or 'sustainable finance' would have to consider.[11]

The problem of G-SIBs, their systemic risk and power, is not only market size or the resulting lack of competition per se. While these are crucial problems, such a critique underestimates how crisis, default and takeover have become a driving factor of processes of financialisation. As Knafo (2022) argues, the problem is more fundamentally a change in the nature of trading and banking that has allowed some banks to do well with LM while others suffer. From that perspective, the 'rescue' takeovers of the recent decade are an outcome of some banks maintaining huge levels of leverage while others fail. For example, while UBS bought Credit Suisse for a bargain, and including state guarantees, Deutsche and Barclays were interested in Credit Suisse's structured private credit business in the hope of capturing their (cheap) bits from the (profitable) wreckage (Wright, 2023). The constant failures serve in themselves to further fuel dynamics of financialisation because other, more powerful banks can buy up ruins cheaply to reengineer those assets for further funding and profits. In the case of Deutsche and Commerzbank, it remains to be seen when the banks themselves become the next victims of someone stronger[12].

CONCLUSION

If a member of the British economic policy establishment titles his co-authored book 'Radical Uncertainty' (Kay & King, 2020) and argues that we do not know what is going on in complex markets, we know that something has gone bad and financial authorities seemingly have little hope of improving it. In the book, Mervyn King, Governor of the Bank of England from 2003 to 2013, describes how policy makers such as central

[11] This is not an argument for the fact that we should pursue economic patriotism.

[12] As this book goes to print, UniCredit has made unwelcomed advances on Commerzbank.

bankers rely on problematic mathematical tools that give a false sense of precision and are hence ill equipped for decision making processes about global finance. King and Kay's discovery that our economy is complex, unforeseeable, and that neoclassical models are an impoverished version of reality is perhaps radical for economists. The accuracy of mathematical modeling in describing or discerning financial markets and rational decision-making has, however, always been questioned (Braun, 2016; Helgadóttir & Ban, 2021; Lave et al., 2010). In political economy, there is a long history of critical scholarship that exposes – beyond uncertainty and mathematical models – inherent problems of power and inequality in financial markets.

What then can a focus on EF add to this long list of problems in financial markets? Beyond seeing the problem in the short-termist markets, EF exposes much larger structural problems connected to LM and US dependency. On the one hand, LM is needed to sustain banking in US wholesale markets and to take advantage from the deep and liquid money markets. On the other hand, LM had several systemic and operational requirements that are incompatible with European banks' traditional practices and financial relationships. The means to empower themselves as global banks are a primary cause for the problems that European banks are experiencing vis-à-vis their own institutional financial environment. Financialised banking has become an inherently contradictory state of affairs, even for some of the more powerful players driving its development.

More broadly, while market risk, regulatory capture and funding gaps are crucial issues, these concepts miss how banks' financial practices are concerned with the imperatives and constraints of meeting the liquidity requirements of LM, and the corresponding changes in assets and loans. From that perspective, financial power is not market size per se but the borrower's ability to manipulate US assets and liabilities to mismatch the books. This has certainly driven the transformation of European banks. US banks' power to use LM to mobilise unprecedented amounts of USD, to participate in new trading strategies, and to manipulate financial markets as new sources of leverage is what German banks tried but mostly failed to become successful at. Reading financialisation in this way, market instability is not only produced because markets or banks are big. The instability results from the fact that non-US banks continue to be dependent on USD leverage to compete on global markets but their peripheral position makes this difficult to achieve.

The fourth feature of EF – the contradictions of financialised banking – thus conceptualises contemporary problems of finance as deeply ingrained in the US Americanisation of global finance. The history of this book has shown how these practices – and particularly LM – have been deeply institutionalised into an uneven global financial architecture. So far, attempts to overcome this unevenness have only further fueled US-led financialisation.

As the banks have deeply transformed their own modus operandi, how might we respond to this mess? One way to think about a more radical transformation is to tackle the question of how we democratically govern debt, and who benefits from that. And by debt, I mean USD. I will return to this question in the conclusion.

9

Conclusion

This book has analysed the US Americanisation of global financial markets. I have argued that the financialisation of German finance is best understood as the banks' attempts to catch up to US banks, which forced the German banks to build off- and onshore USD funding structures and to adopt the practices of LM. This dynamic triggered the German institutions to uproot themselves from their home markets to institutionalise into US money markets, which caused a transformation of their business models.

German banks' path to financialisation have thus been driven by their strategies of internationalisation. In the 1960s, it was the Eurodollar markets that shaped the banks' strategies as they were part of European syndicates and club banks to pool resources and jointly issue loans and bonds, which distributed the burden of raising USD and the risk of the unknown Euromarkets. In the 1970s, German banks established their own subsidiaries first in Luxemburg and then in London. Luxemburg was a Eurocurrency hub in which the banks developed FX and mix-currency loans. In London, by contrast, German banks engaged more directly with new US practices connected to more complicated structures of Eurodollar securities. Deutsche and Commerzbank not only helped to establish the EuroDM market as the second reserve currency, but their activities made the Euromarkets an integral part of post-war German political economy.

The next phase of internationalisation started in the late 1970s as German banks established foreign subsidiaries in the US and pushed their Eurodollar structures. Alongside other European banks, the two German lenders set up their own foreign affiliates targeting new money market practices such as CPs to enhance and manage USD debt in an increasingly turbulent world. This phase was characterised by strong attempts to establish themselves within US markets and to use Eurodollar networks to fund their activities, such as complex corporate projects but also increasingly proprietary trading. Deutsche and Commerzbank resembled less and less the myth of financial intermediaries passing savings on for industrial investment, though the question remains if they ever did.

From the 1980s onwards, the international strategies of Deutsche and Commerzbank diverged. Deutsche concentrated its strategies towards the US. Two foreign mergers were crucial in Deutsche's transformation, Morgan Grenfell in 1989 and Bankers Trust in 1999. With Morgan Grenfell, Deutsche adopted more systematically US practices such as money market papers and became a primary dealer of Treasury bonds. But to make that work, Deutsche relocated its investment operations in London and changed its corporate governance, significantly reducing its loan portfolio and its corporate cross-shareholdings. With Bankers Trust, Deutsche not only started to trade with ABS on a large scale, but also to originate new assets and build repo networks to enhance US money market funding. This marked its period of huge returns prior to the GFC, a phase during which many thought of Deutsche as a US investment bank.

Commerzbank, on the other hand, did not engage systematically with US wholesale markets after its initial advance. Implementing LM only partially, and lacking a similar global USD funding network, Commerzbank could not sustain high leverage with high-yielding assets in the 2000s. While it tried to establish itself in the US through several smaller acquisitions, it largely failed to sustain its US wholesale presence over a longer period. Largely defeated, it focused instead on expanding its European investment banking and European deposits. In contrast to general trends, Commerzbank increased its loan portfolio in the 1990s and 2000s, rather than selling it off. Nonetheless, Commerzbank did not escape the dynamics of US money market funding. It was first affected by the large losses of its *Pfandbrief* bank Eurohypo in the course of the 2008 financial crisis, its large European player in the real estate industry, and then, spectacularly, by Dresdner's US MBS business, forcing Commerzbank into public rescue arms.

I revealed that Deutsche's advance was in fact not straightforward, despite initially looking glorious at the balance sheet level. Its transition to US-style finance was largely characterised by internal struggles and resistance against new financial practices. Uprooting Deutsche's investment banking from Frankfurt to London and then New York meant that certain German bankers, if not the banks themselves, became obsolete in favour of US traders, a situation they were not very happy with. Since the GFC, Deutsche battles on but without any profit boosts from its US business. German banks more generally have been in crisis since. They seem to run losses, narrowly escaping crises, and seem to struggle to escape their misery or to disconnect their US practices. This is not for the lack of trying, as various programmes for substantial overhauls attest. They have tried common solutions, such as merging or 'derisking' their asset investments, but have so far failed. How then should we account for this transformative trajectory and the fact that German banks have tried but not quite achieved to become US banks?

Many accounts use the notion of marketisation to foreground the expansionary nature of financial markets as key driver of this transition. From this perspective, the transformation of German banking is depicted as a US imposition since the 1990s in which German banks succumbed to the profit imperative which made traditional long-term loans impossible to sustain. Banks are profit-seeking, so much is obvious. Yet the history in this book suggests that the profit imperative and the ideal types that underlie it might hide as much as they reveal. Instead, relying on the *Pfandbrief*, I started from concrete financial practices to show that German political economy was *more* marketized than the US in the nineteenth century. This is an interesting point in itself but this also highlights that not all market-based practices lead to financialisation. Rewriting German finance in this way, I have also shown that German banks' practices in USD markets have not necessarily been very profitable. Tapping US money markets, however, was needed to compete against US banks, which were posing challenges to their European strategies. The competitive pressure came from the funding power of US banks, rather than markets per se. As such, the notion of marketisation partly mischaracterises power relations during processes of financialisation. We do not have a dynamic in which banks fight against markets but instead compete against each other to use USD debt for their own ends.

To account for these uneven power relations during processes of financialisation, I have developed the concept of extroverted financialisation. I argued that key to German financialisation has been the banks' extroverted strategies that forced them to leave their home markets behind and to institutionalise significant parts of their operations into US financial markets. EF aims to capture the problems and practices of financial agents and highlights that non-US banks oriented their international strategies towards Euro- and US-dollar markets since the 1960s because US banks were outcompeting them. With EF, I propose four features that represent four distinct imperatives that can account for why European banks have taken their specific paths towards US finance and why they build extensive but often precarious USD funding structures abroad. It is this relocation that has blurred the boundaries between financial systems, and that has triggered their financial transformation.

The first feature accounts for a new nature of finance that emerged in the process of financialisation. EF starts from a radical transformation in the way US banks have funded themselves on the US money markets. LM developed out of pragmatic responses to the crisis of funding in 1960 New York and represents a new strategy that actors use to finance themselves much more dynamically by buying and selling short-term securities in money markets. While powerful, this new strategy imposed novel pressures on banks. To manage higher costs and volatility of funding, banks started to invest in higher-yielding assets with more risk and they sought new ways to sell securities quickly to reduce capital trapped on the balance sheet. As a result, banks started to centralise funding as key strategy, rather than prioritising asset investment without taking costs of funds into account. This reversed what banks did: Banks started to engineer new securities (their assets) that sold in US money and Eurodollar markets to attract more funding. This caused a huge rise in financial transactions, and US banks were uniquely able to exploit that transition.

The second feature emphasises that the rise of LM caused non-US banks to seek USDs. They needed USDs to compete against the growing funding power of US banks in Eurodollar markets. While non-US banks had always used USD to a small extent, tapping USD markets – rather than any other currency – became the central part of their international ambitions. This was a key imperative to which they responded innovatively by developing large-scale offshore funding structures in Luxemburg, London and, amongst others, the Caymen Islands. This helps to explain why German banks have actively engaged with the Eurodollar markets since the 1960s and why Eurodollar markets have become such an integral part of financialised banking. They provided an opportunity to find USD funding to compete with US banks. Importantly, this feature not merely foregrounds the additional effort of exchanging or swapping, say, EUR into USD. Feature two highlights that the need for USD caused the initial step of extroversion to respond to the rise of LM.

Third, EF foregrounds the institutional specificity of US money markets. LM developed organically alongside US money markets. This provided US banks with a unique ability to exploit rising US money markets, a skill everyone else had to learn from afar, and an institutional embeddedness few foreign banks have reached today. The money markets gave US banks an additional funding source for their Eurodollar practices, arbitraging between both markets, and a useful infrastructure to exploit. At the same time, the institutional specificity of US money markets constrained the range of available strategies non-US banks could employ. European money markets were small and only complementary rather than primary funding sources. As a result, German banks had to uproot themselves and transform to fit the logics of US money markets. For that to work, they had to build new connections to the US and to adopt the practices of LM. This imperative is key to help explain why Commerzbank failed to sustain its US investments in the 2000s, and why Deutsche embarked on its phenomenal rise.

Fourthly, the concept draws attention to the contradictions of financialised banking and the global financial architecture to which EF gave rise. While a lot of money has been made, adopting LM and rerouting strategies to a different geographical location has been fragile, expensive and riddled with problems. Besides bridging the USD currency mismatch, non-US banks have to overcome the differences in practices and managerial strategies. The financialised strategies are ill supported, and in conflict with European strategies. EF has not only created a global USD bottleneck that only the Fed can temporarily solve; this also means that German banks' find it difficult to develop their strategies outside the logics of US money market funding. As a result, their efforts to rescale their US practices or to outgrow their USD dependence have so far not found a way to disentangle themselves from or manage profitably their USD funding gaps. Instead, they seem to only further fuel the dynamics of uneven and US-led financialisation.

The methodological benefits of EF are, I believe, threefold. First, it incorporates the history of the changing nature of US finance by foregrounding the specific imperatives this posed for banking since the 1960s (cf. Beck & Knafo 2020; Dutta 2020; Knafo 2022). This has enabled me to develop insights into a global financial transformation from its very origins, that is, from the financial practices that played a core role in starting the process in the first place. As such, the making of a USD financial architecture is itself an outcome of competitive problems that US banks tried to solve. If important processes of financialisation were started by a financial practice, hopefully this provides some motivation to delve deeper into financial practices and let go of the myths of markets. Second, the concept permits a careful historicisation of financialisation outside the US because it provides the conceptual tools to trace how the practices of LM travel to new places, and to what extent. This allowed me to demonstrate why a change in US finance would affect global banking practices in such a transformative way. Relying on distinct imperatives and constraints can highlight different kinds of challenges for various financial agents. This includes other European banks, for example, French banks (Beck and Massoc forthcoming; Massoc, 2022) but perhaps also financial agents from emerging economies even if they face distinct challenges of their own during financialisation (Bonizzi & Karwowski, 2023). Financial agents can also include corporations that have increasingly used financial securities as funding (cf. Braun and Deeg, 2019) and enlisted financial markets for their own ends (Knafo & Dutta, 2020).

Third, EF suggests that banks are best understood in their own terms, rather than as financial intermediaries. We cannot simply deduct banks' nature or their activities from their relationships to corporations or national financial frameworks. This shifts the attention to banking practices as attempts of empowerment, that is, of gaining control over US money market funding, Eurodollar markets and the competition against US banks. This allowed me to portray non-US banks as active participants in the making of offshore, global and US financial infrastructures, if from a peripheral perspective (Beck, 2022a). This points to a research agenda that connects the 'micro' and 'macro' more closely (Beck, 2022b) and pays more attention to financial agents themselves as sites and drivers of financialisation.

WHAT IS NEXT FOR PROGRESSIVE POLITICS?

How do we respond to the problems of global finance? Since the GFC, calls have come forward that we need a deep change in what constitutes a bank and what their purpose might be (Rethel & Sinclair, 2012). As a first step, I argue that we need to take the banks seriously as global gatekeepers and producers of USD. This sounds perhaps obvious, but like the academic debate examined in this book, practitioners and expert commentators too often sideline banks in their diagnoses of the problems of finance. This is a hangover from traditional myths of banks as passive intermediaries merely responsible for passing on other people's money. While few would deny that something is wrong with global banking, the crux of the issue is – paradoxically – too often located in the regulatory sphere or with investors, rather than with the nature of banking. This problem was recently replicated during the Silicon Valley Bank and Credit Suisse crises, when European banking regulators blamed US policymakers, US and European authorities criticised Swiss authorities, and everyone else blamed 'the regulators' as having failed to prevent banks from behaving unruly.

There is of course, much to gain from discussing regulation, skiddy investors, and the failures of monetary authorities. Looking at the frequency of banking crises since the late 1990s, one cannot help but wonder what monetary authorities were thinking of when they claimed to have stabilised the financial system. I do not argue that they are not to blame. Equally, long-term deposits might at times be more useful to banks than short-term deposits. However, if we continue to sidestep the business model of the banks themselves, we will continue to miss the underlying cause of why banks behave the way they do. Unruly is a description that can only be a euphemism for the banks' reckless and destructive behaviour. As such, my first way into this section is to highlight the discursive and epistemological obstacles to a more wider discussion with respect to a fundamental change in banking and finance.

As I outlined in the introduction, the sidestepping of banks has a long history in policy discussions. When financial agents are blamed for driving financial flows in dangerous directions, it is often investors, institutional or otherwise, that are held responsible. In 2005, Franz Müntefering, head of the German Social Democrats, accused private equity of causing Germany's troubles of the early 2000s, calling them locusts for bleeding out German companies without considering resulting losses of employment. He did not point a finger at the extroverted strategies of banks that have integrated German finance into US financial practices much more thoroughly than any US private equity firm ever did.

Fed banker Ben Bernanke was lauded with the alternative Nobel Prize in economics for his diagnosis of financial crises and their remedies. During his reign at the head of the Fed, his analysis suggested that global current account imbalances were a driving factor of crisis. Capital surplus in Asian countries, notably China, enabled Asian institutional investors to invest too much capital into US markets prior to the GFC. As a result, too much money drove down interest rates, motivating investors to search ever more risky investments to compensate for yields, which ultimately led to the mortgage bubble (Bernanke, 2005; cf. Beck et al., 2023). This was an oversight on the part of the Asian money managers, who should rebalance Chinese financial in- and outflows, a claim he repeated during his prize speech.

While we know since the GFC that economists do not necessarily have the tools to understand global financial markets and their impact on the economy, this outside-problem view of banking is reflected in heterodox economics debates that foreground banks as key drivers of the GFC. For scholars working at the IMF or the BIS, followers of the banking glut argument (Bayoumi, 2017; McCauley, 2018), it was not institutional investors who had too many savings and therefore unbalanced financial markets. Instead, it was the banks that raised and invested too much capital in the US, which induced too much risk into financial systems. According to this perspective, European banks engaged in 'round-tripping' taking USD out of US money markets to invest back into US capital markets via RMBS and related derivatives. Nonetheless, if searching for remedies within this reasoning, one is guided to the problem of regulation. European banks were permitted to engage in excessive leverage and invest in the riskiest financial securities, while US banks had stricter rules and therefore engaged in less excessive leverage (also cf. Tooze, 2018). European regulators failed to tame the banks which apparently forgot what they should naturally do: to provide long-term loans to corporate investors.

The problem in these debates is a misunderstanding of the driving factors of banks' strategies. The history presented in this book suggests that we need to analyse the micro-processes of business models much more closely to understand the nature of banking. Taking EF into account reveals that it was not the lure of higher profits per se, but instead the imperatives of LM that first and subsequently drove the banks' transformation towards speculative assets. We cannot simply 'tame' banks' risky investments because they followed, rather than preceded, the banks' short-term funding needs and are deeply connected. If we restrict further banks' asset strategies, as has happened since the GFC, we inhibit their ability to tap US money markets and raise USD. In a financial world dependent on USD, this would only cause further problems to European banks. In fact, this would only exacerbate what I have argued is a key driving factor of financialisation. Further restrictions to US money markets would increase the uneven power relations between US and European banks, potentially tempting European banks to even more reckless behaviour to overcome the difference. This has not turned out well in the past.

What then does an analysis that incorporates EF suggest we should do? Instead of 'taming' the banks, we might be better off by changing the banks' funding strategies, which is nothing less than changing the nature of their banking. Furthermore, looking at the nature of financialisation, US money market dependency emerges as a key issue more widely. Chapter 8 showed, this produces deeply uneven power relations, vulnerability, and crises, which are difficult to untangle and reverse because this unevenness produces an important feedback loop which further fuels dynamics of financialisation. For example, Eurodollar and other international markets are important for funding conditions in the US itself and therefore supported by the Fed, which intervenes to ensure continuous support for US banks without considering the inequality this reproduces

(Dafermos et al., 2022; Pape, 2022). In fact, the Fed and US authorities arguably embrace the resulting differentiated monetary power (Konings, 2008b). This in turn helps US domination of global finance, further fuelling a concentration in power.

If we cannot get out of this, maybe we must start thinking about a more fundamental transformation of global finance and debt. Anything at this scale can only be speculative at this point, but the institutionalisation of speculation is an underlying theme of the book. We could start thinking about how we take away the base for LM, which means tackling how banks can fund themselves. Given how large repo markets are, and how deeply ingrained they are not only within banking but also for sovereign debt management (Gabor, 2016b), global monetary policy and crisis management of the Fed and other financial agents, it is difficult to imagine a useful starting point that could alter this complex web of interconnected funding structures without producing a huge crisis once we shrink those markets.

A starting point could be a redistribution of who can use the monetary infrastructure and who reaps the gains of leverage power – so crucial for the relentless increase in money and financial transactions (see Dutta, 2023). This would start sharing the benefits, rather than simply the costs, of our global financial architecture. From that perspective, we admit that financialisation is here to stay but we aim at a democratic participation in the practices of LM. After all, we have big tasks at hand, including the energy transition, stopping global warming and wars and they need powerful funding sources.

In a complementary manner, we can start to distribute the power of money creation. From that perspective, we would need to introduce global democratic structures that govern US money markets, Eurodollar markets and the Fed so that they start to serve a wider spectrum of people, rather than US financiers and other global financial elites in their shadows. One way in this spirit is to put money creation in the service of fiscal and environmental ends. As such, financial governance moves away from technocrats towards direct democratic decision-making. More importantly, the USD must be set into a global democratic setting as the implications of EF mean that we cannot think of financial agents and funding from the perspective of a national jurisdiction. This is admittedly a vague proposal, and neither of these proposals is an immediate possibility. However, the history presented in this book suggests that smaller, incremental changes will not have a chance of reversing many of these trends. As such, we are well served if we start to contemplate more radical solutions.

WHAT IS NEXT FOR GLOBAL FINANCE?

Given a radical democratic restructuring of USD debt might not be on the immediate horizon, how might global finance continue? I could speculate about where global banking might go next. The true answer is: I do not know. I suspect that nobody knows because global finance is exceptionally complex, much is hidden by design and predictions of the future have proved impossible in easier scenarios. It is safe to predict another global crisis looming, but whether that will originate in the European, US or perhaps the Japanese financial sector, I am unsure. Given the state of the European sector, we would not be wrong to expect another big bank to default soon. Larger financial crisis, however, have so far been contained because of the elasticity of the US and European central banks' balance sheets. The Fed has progressively expanded its rescue services to new regions that need USDs and that would cause larger problems if they do not have them. The Fed might continue to do that.

It may therefore be more productive to reflect upon possible avenues for future research that could help us continue to trace transformations of global banking and finance. We certainly need more conceptual innovations that allow us to ponder more recent banking and financial transformations since the GFC. While Chapter 8 revealed my reflections and research about contemporary problems of financialised banking, the question remains where US finance has been heading and how others are restructuring and responding from their peripheral positions. While the rise of LM has made it a key practice of financialisation, its transactional logic has also introduced a dynamism into finance that was unprecedented and remains a key logic of global markets. As the history of EF suggests, LM triggered a transformation that went from a liquidity crisis to finding ever new ways of sourcing assets for the sake of tapping US money markets. If you can do LM successfully, this transformation has mostly eradicated the problems of scarcity of funds. The question of how, and if, European banks manage to tap into those dynamics and thereby change their own business models and global finance remains crucial.

One of the European banks' strategies to get back on their feet is wealth and asset management. Deutsche Bank's investment manager DWS is making renewed attempts to target the super wealthy and family offices in the areas of real estate and private credit[1] (Benitez & Stupples, 2023).

[1] Private credit or private lending, includes a variety of debt issues extended to a company that are not publicly traded (for example, a bond). It has been steadily increasing since 2009 and yielded consistent returns.

Private credit has become popular in recent years as bank loans are becoming more expensive with rising rates, a 'golden moment' for private equity according to Blackstone president Jonathan Gray (Wigglesworth, 2023) as both US and European banks increasingly struggle during their recent liquidity crises. This represents a renewed attempt for Deutsche to hike up its fee income and find new business areas. While it consistently searched for strategies to become a number one bank again – either in Europe or the US – it was only during the Credit Suisse crisis that it saw a chance to use the turmoil to increase its asset management business. This did follow its recent lingering approach. It closed its equity business in 2019 as part of a larger restructuring programme to cut costs, but it is now trying to gain a share of the fee generating activities again. In what seems like a déjà vue, Deutsche expands again into London with a new acquisition, a large broker and investment bank, Numis, that advises almost a fifth of companies in the FTSE 350 index on everything from equity raisings to acquisitions. And yet, Numis' profits plummeted 70 per cent last year at a time when initial public offerings and equity raisings were declining (Levingston et al., 2023). Is Deutsche following a cooked up dream again where some, that is US-based, financial actors make millions in equity and asset management while European finance stays behind?

Equity and asset management are larger trends in global finance. Andy Haldane, chief economist at the Bank of England at the time, heralded the age of asset management as a new period since the 2000s in which banks have turned themselves into asset managers (Haldane, 2014) away from trading. Indeed, beyond representing a financial sector or a niche investment strategy for the rich, recent scholarship has argued that we live in an asset economy that has inflated asset values hugely over the past decades (Adkins et al., 2020). This has been in part fabricated by financial institutions (ibid.), encoded by legal frameworks (Pistor, 2020) and socio-economic organisation of society (Adkins, 2018; Bryant et al., 2022). Those trends have made asset relations a key organising principle of socio-economic life and social stratification as wages have been stagnating and asset wealth rising. If assets continue to inflate, which they arguably will despite small dips in housing prices at the time of finishing this conclusion, European banks will have a growing asset sector to get their teeth into, for example, as various types of housing are increasingly turned into new asset classes (Gabor & Kohl, 2022; Montgomerie & Büdenbender, 2015; Wijburg et al., 2018).

Asset manager capitalism (Braun, 2021) or asset manager society (Christophers, 2023) are other conceptual frameworks to foreground the centrality of assets in contemporary capitalism. Large US corporations, often private equity firms such as Blackstone (Christophers, 2021), buy assets and private equity-owned companies cheaply and reconstruct them in a way that allows them to attract external funding and to generate extensive income flows, much higher returns than you could reasonably expect from the asset in question. Importantly, US private equity firms have found new ways of investing directly into homes, often the ones whose occupiers had to default during the sub-prime crisis (Fields, 2018), road tolls, libraries, water or any other public infrastructure you can think of (Bayliss et al., 2021; Christophers, 2023). This type of financial engineering is not dissimilar to the packaging of sub-prime mortgages in the 2000s. It also sources assets in a way that allows asset managers to liquify parts of it to collect fees upfront, this time from two types of asset users: from the financial investors who invest in private equity funds and from the actual users of these assets (tenants, water users, road users, etc.).

This means that – potentially – more and more European public infrastructure is available for asset management by European banks. European private credit– through which Europeans currently try to join the asset management frenzy and make up for losing loan business – is, however, only a small percentage of global private credit, totalling USD 221bn compared to 1.5tn (Louch & Mourselas, 2023). Alas, for the banks, recent regulatory efforts curbed the European banks' capacity to lend to highly leveraged private equity-owned businesses, giving private equity firms and other asset managers chances to pounce (Lee, 2023). More importantly, US banks seem to, yet again, be better at this game. While the US managers and private equity firms often team up with European banks such as Barclays and Société Générale, it remains to be seen if and how European banks cope in these new developments of US-based equity and asset management.

For the sake of the rest of us, we can only hope that the 2008 financial crisis will not be repeated. This would mean stopping to build ever larger asset markets and refraining from turning more housing or public infrastructure into financial assets. Leaving the financing of those to the banks has historically not been a good idea. In this sense, I hope there will not be another round of European banks providing funding for US-engineered financial assets. Alas, European banks certainly liked financing (highly leveraged subprime) housing markets in the past.

References

Abbassi, P., & Bräuning, F. (2018). *The pricing of FX forward contracts: Micro evidence from banks' dollar hedging* (Discussion Paper Deutsche Bundesbank 42). Deutsche Bundesbank.

Abelshauser, W. (2016). Deutsche Wirtschaftspolitik zwischen europäischer Integration und Weltmarktorientierung. In W. Abelshauser (Ed.), *Das Bundeswirtschaftsministerium in der Ära der Sozialen Marktwirtschaft: Wirtschaftspolitik in Deutschland, 1917–1990, Volume IV* (pp. 482–581). De Gruyter.

Abdelal, R. (2006). Writing the rules of global finance: France, Europe, and capital liberalization. *Review of International Political Economy, 13*(1), 1–27. https://doi.org/10.1080/09692290500396602

Abelshauser, W. (1983). *Wirtschaftsgeschichte der Bundesrepublik Deutschland (1945–1980)*. Suhrkamp.

Adkins, L. (2012). Out of work or out of time? Rethinking labor after the financial crisis. *South Atlantic Quarterly, 111*(4), 621–641.

Adkins, L. (2018). *The time of money*. Stanford University Press.

Adkins, L., Konings, M., & Cooper, M. (2020). *The asset economy: Property ownership and the new logic of inequality*. Polity Press.

Aglietta, M. (2000). Shareholder value and corporate governance: Some tricky questions. *Economy and Society, 29*(1), 146–159.

Ahrens, R. (2010). Identitätsmenagement und Kontrolle: Die Reformen der Dresdner Bank um 1970. In R. Ahrens & H. Wixforth (Eds.), *Strukturwandel und Internationalisierung im Bankwesen seit den 1950er Jahren* (pp. 71–95). Steiner.

Ahrens, R., Gehlen, B., & Reckendrees, A. (Eds.). (2013). *Die 'Deutschland AG': Historische Annäherungen an den bundesdeutschen Kapitalismus* (1. Auflage). Klartext.

Ahrens, R., & Wixforth, H. (Eds.). (2010). *Strukturwandel und Internationalisierung im Bankwesen seit den 1950er Jahren*. Steiner.

Aldasoro, I., & Ehlers, T. (2018). The geography of dollar funding of non-US banks. *BIS Quarterly Review*, December, 15–26.

Aldasoro, I., Ehlers, T., & Eren, E. (2018). Business models and dollar funding of global banks. *BIS Working Paper, 708*, 48.

Aldasoro, I., Ehlers, T., & Eren, E. (2019). Global banks, dollar funding, and regulation. *SSRN Electronic Journal.*

Aldasoro, I., Ehlers, T., Eren, E., & McCauley, R. N. (2017). Non-US banks' global dollar funding grows despite US money market reform. *BIS Quarterly Review*, March, 22–23.

Altamura, C. E. (2016). *European banks and the rise of international finance: The post-Bretton Woods era* (1st ed.). Routledge.

Altvater, E., & Hübner, K. (1988). Das Geld einer mittleren Hegemonialmacht – Ein kleiner Streifzug durch die ökonomische Geschichte der BRD. *PROKLA: Zeitschrift für kritische Sozialwissenschaft*, *18*(73), 6–36.

Amato, M., & Fantacci, L. (2012). *The end of finance*. Polity Press.

Andrews, E. L. (1998, December 1). Bank Giant: Deutsche Gets Bankers Trust for $10 Billion. *The New York Times*. www.nytimes.com/1998/12/01/business/bank-giant-the-overview-deutsche-gets-bankers-trust-for-10-billion.html

Anonymous. (2004). ABN overhauls CDO leadership. *Asset – Backed Alert*, 3.

Baba, N., McCauley, R. N., & Ramaswamy, S. (2009). US dollar money market funds and non-US banks. *BIS Quarterly Review*, March, 65–81.

Baccaro, L., & Höpner, M. (2022). The political-economic foundations of export-led growth: An analysis of the German case. In M. Blyth, J. Pontusson, & L. Baccaro (Eds.), *Diminishing returns: The new politics of growth and stagnation* (pp. 238–267). Oxford University Press.

Baccaro, L., & Pontusson, J. (2016). Rethinking comparative political economy: The growth model perspective. *Politics & Society*, *44*(2), 175–207.

Baines, J., & Hager, S. B. (2021). The great debt divergence and its implications for the Covid-19 crisis: Mapping corporate leverage as power. *New Political Economy*, *26*(5), 885–901.

Baker, A., & Wigan, D. (2017). Constructing and contesting city of London power: NGOs and the emergence of noisier financial politics. *Economy and Society*, *46*(2), 185–210.

Baker, M., & Collins, M. (2005). London as an international banking center, 1950–1980. In Y. Cassis & E. Bussière (Eds.), *London and Paris as international financial centres in the twentieth century* (pp. 247–263). Oxford University Press.

Baklanova, V., Copeland, A., & McCaughrin, R. (2015). *Reference guide to U.S. repo and securities lending markets (staff reports 740)*. Federal Reserve Bank of New York. www.newyorkfed.org/research/staff_reports/sr740.html

Baklanova, V., & Tanega, J. (Eds.). (2014). *Money market funds in the EU and the US: Regulation and practice* (1st ed.). Oxford University Press.

Balaban, I. A. (2022). Banking and Eurodollars in Italy in the 1950s. *Enterprise & Society*, 1–25.

Ban, C., & Gabor, D. (2016). The political economy of shadow banking. *Review of International Political Economy*, *23*(6), 901–914.

Battilossi, S. (2000). Financial innovation and the golden ages of international banking: 1890–1931 and 1958–81. *Financial History Review*, *7*(2).

Battilossi, S. (2002). Banking with multinationals: British clearing banks and the Euromarkets' challenge, 1958–1976. In S. Battilossi & Y. Cassis (Eds.), *European banks and the American challenge: Competition and cooperation in international banking under Bretton Woods* (pp. 103–134). Oxford University Press.

Battilossi, S. (2010). The Eurodollar revolution in financial technology: Deregulation, innovation and structural change in Western banking. In A.-A. Kyrtsis (Ed.), *Financial markets and organizational technologies* (pp. 29–63). Palgrave Macmillan.

Battilossi, S., & Cassis, Y. (Eds.). (2002). *European banks and the American challenge: Competition and cooperation in international banking under Bretton Woods*. Oxford University Press.

Bayliss, K., Mattioli, G., & Steinberger, J. (2021). Inequality, poverty and the privatization of essential services: A 'systems of provision' study of water, energy and local buses in the UK. *Competition & Change, 25*(3–4), 478–500.

Bayoumi, T. (2017). *Unfinished business: The unexplored causes of the financial crisis and the lessons yet to be learned*. Yale University Press.

Beck, M. (2022a). Extroverted financialization: How US finance shapes European banking. *Review of International Political Economy, 29*(5), 1723–1745.

Beck, M. (2022b). The managerial contradictions of extroverted financialization: The rise and fall of Deutsche Bank. *Socio-Economic Review*, mwac050.

Beck, M., & Knafo, S. (2020). Financialisation and the uses of history. In D. Mertens, P. Mader, & N. van der Zwan (Eds.), *Handbook of financialisation* (pp. 136–146). Routledge, Taylor & Francis Group.

Beck, M., Knafo, S., & Sgambati, S. (2023). Leveraging financial claims: Transatlantic bank struggles and the power of US finance. In B. Braun & K. Koddenbrock (Eds.), *Capital claims: Power and global finance* (pp. 33–49). Routledge.

Behr, P., & Schmidt, R. H. (2015). *The German banking system: Characteristics and challenges* (SAFE White Paper Series 32). Goethe University Frankfurt, Research Center SAFE – Sustainable Architecture for Finance in Europe.

Bell, S., & Hindmoor, A. (2015). Masters of the universe but slaves of the market: Bankers and the great financial meltdown. *The British Journal of Politics and International Relations, 17*(1), 1–22.

Bell, S., & Hindmoor, A. (2018). Are the major global banks now safer? Structural continuities and change in banking and finance since the 2008 crisis. *Review of International Political Economy, 25*(1), 1–27.

Benitez, L., & Stupples, B. (2023, August 10). Deutsche bank's asset manager targets 'Holy Grail' of world's ultra rich. Bloomberg.Com. www.bloomberg.com/news/articles/2023-08-10/deutsche-bank-s-asset-manager-targets-holy-grail-of-world-s-ultra-rich

Berghahn, V. R., & Vitols, S. (2006). *Gibt es einen deutschen Kapitalismus?: Tradition und globale Perspektiven der sozialen Marktwirtschaft. Mit einer Einleitung von Jürgen Kocka*. Campus Verlag.

Bernanke, B. S. (2005). *The global saving glut and the U.S. current account deficit* [Sandridge Lecture, Virginia Association of Economists]. www.federalreserve.gov/boarddocs/speeches/2005/200503102/

Beyer, J. (2003). Deutschland AG a.D.: Deutsche Bank, Allianz und das Verflechtungszentrum des deutschen Kapitalismus. In W. Streeck (Ed.), *Alle Macht dem Markt?: Fallstudien zur Abwicklung der Deutschland AG* (pp. 118–146). Campus Verlag.

Beyer, J., & Hassel, A. (2002). The effects of convergence: Internationalization and the changing distribution of net value added in large German firms. *Economy and Society, 31*(3), 309–332.

Beyer, J., & Höpner, M. (2003). The disintegration of organised capitalism: German corporate governance in the 1990s. *West European Politics*, 26(4), 179–198. https://doi.org/10.1080/01402380312331280738

Binder, A. (2023). *Offshore finance and state power*. Oxford University Press.

Bonizzi, B., Kaltenbrunner, A., & Powell, J. (2019). *Subordinate financialization in emerging capitalist economies (Working Paper GPERC69).* Greenwich Political Economy Research Centre.

Bonizzi, B., & Karwowski, E. (2023). Commonality without convergence: An analytical framework accounting for variegated financialisation in emerging economies. *Competition & Change*, 10245294231209276.

Borio, C. E. V., & Disyatat, P. (2011). Global imbalances and the financial crisis: Link or no link? *BIS Working Paper No. 346, 346.*

Borio, C. E. V., McCauley, R. N., & McGuire, P. (2017). FX swaps and forwards: Missing global debt? *BIS Quarterly Review*, September, 37–54.

Bowley, G. (1997, May 26). Commerzbank boosts investment side (London edition). *Financial Times*, 24.

Bowman, L. (2017, April). Commerzbank: This time they hope it's different. *Euromoney; London.*

Braun, B. (2016). Speaking to the people? Money, trust, and central bank legitimacy in the age of quantitative easing. *Review of International Political Economy, 23*(6), 1064–1092.

Braun, B. (2020). Central banking and the infrastructural power of finance: The case of ECB support for repo and securitization markets. *Socio-Economic Review, 18*(2), 395–418.

Braun, B. (2021). Asset manager capitalism as a corporate governance regime. In J. S. Hacker, A. Hertel-Fernandez, P. Pierson, & K. A. Thelen (Eds.), *The American political economy: Politics, markets, and power.* Cambridge University Press.

Braun, B., & Deeg, R. (2019). Strong firms, weak banks: The financial consequences of Germany's export-led growth model. *German Politics, 29*(3), 358–381.

Braun, B., & Koddenbrock, K. (Eds.). (2023). *Capital claims: Power and global finance.* Routledge.

Braun, B., Krampf, A., & Murau, S. (2021). Financial globalization as positive integration: Monetary technocrats and the Eurodollar market in the 1970s. *Review of International Political Economy, 28*(4), 794–819.

Bryan, D., Rafferty, M., & Wigan, D. (2016). Politics, time and space in the era of shadow banking. *Review of International Political Economy, 23*(6), 941–966.

Bryant, G., Spies-Butcher, B., & Stebbing, A. (2022). Comparing asset-based welfare capitalism: Wealth inequality, housing finance and household risk. *Housing Studies, 0*(0), 1–22.

Buch, C. M., Koch, C., & Koetter, M. (2011). *Crises, rescues, and policy transmission through international banks* (Deutsche Bundesbank Discussion Paper 1). Social Science Research Network.

Burk, K. (1989). *Morgan Grenfell, 1838–1988: The biography of a merchant bank.* Oxford University Press.

Burk, K. (1992). Witness seminar on the origins and early development of the Eurobond market. *Contemporary European History, 1*(1), 65–87.

Burk, K. (1998). Eine kurze Geschichte des Bankhauses Morgan Grenfell 1938–1998: Leben, Tod und Wiedergeburt. In M. Pohl & K. Burk (Eds.), *Die Deutsche Bank in London: 1873–1998* (pp. 113–156). Piper.

Burn, G. (1999). The state, the city and the Euromarkets. *Review of International Political Economy, 6*(2), 225–261. JSTOR.

Büschgen, H. E. (1995). Die Deutsche Bank von 1957 bis zur Gegenwart: Aufstieg zum internationalen Finanzdiestleistungskonzern. In L. Gall, G. D. Feldmann, H. James, C.-L. Holtfrerich, & H. E. Büschgen (Eds.), *Die Deutsche Bank, 1870–1995*. C.H. Beck.

Bussière, E. (2005). French banks and the Eurobonds issue market during the 1960s. In Y. Cassis & E. Bussière (Eds.), *London and Paris as international financial centres in the twentieth century* (pp. 265–281). Oxford University Press.

Cafruny, A. W., & Ryner, M. (2007). *Europe at bay: In the shadow of US hegemony*. Lynne Rienner Publishers.

Callaghan, H. (2018). *Contestants, profiteers, and the political dynamics of marketization: How shareholders gained control rights in Britain, Germany, and France*. Oxford University Press.

Carlin, W. (1996). West German growth and institutions, 1945–90. In N. F. R. Crafts & G. Toniolo (Eds.), *Economic growth in Europe since 1945* (pp. 455–497). Cambridge University Press.

Celarier, M. (1996, November). Battle of the bulge. *Euromoney*, *331*, 38–42.

Cerpa Vielma, N., Cömert, H., D'Avino, C., Dymski, G., Kaltenbrunner, A., Petratou, E., & Shabani, M. (2019). Too big to manage: US megabanks' competition by innovation and the microfoundations of financialization. *Cambridge Journal of Economics*, *43*(4), 1103–1121.

Christophers, B. (2021). Mind the rent gap: Blackstone, housing investment and the reordering of urban rent surfaces. *Urban Studies*, 59(4), 698–716.

Christophers, B. (2023). *Our lives in their portfolios: Why asset managers own the world*. Verso.

Cibriani, M., & Gouny, J. (2015, May 27). The Eurodollar Market in the United States. *Liberty Street Economics*. Federal Reserve Bank of New York. https://libertystreeteconomics.newyorkfed.org/2015/05/the-eurodollar-market-in-the-united-states/

Cohen, B. J. (1996). Phoenix risen: The resurrection of global finance. *World Politics*, *48*(2), 268.

Commerzbank, A. G. (1994). *Die Bank – Dienstleister im Wandel. 125 Jahre Commerzbank 1870–1995*. Knapp.

Commerzbank, A. G. (2018). *Commerzbank AG Annual Report*. www.commerzbank.com/en/hauptnavigation/aktionaere/publikationen_und_veranstaltungen/unternehmensberichterstattung_1/index.html

Cooper, M. (2017). *Family values: Between neoliberalism and the new social conservatism*. Zone Books.

Culpeper, R. (2012). Financial sector policy and development in the wake of the global crisis: The role of national development banks. *Third World Quarterly*, *33*(3).

Culpepper, P. D. (2010). *Quiet politics and business power: Corporate control in Europe and Japan*. Cambridge University Press.

Dafe, F., Hager, S. B., Naqvi, N., & Wansleben, L. (2022). Introduction: The structural power of finance meets financialization. *Politics & Society*, *50*(4), 523–542.

Dafermos, Y., Gabor, D., & Michell, J. (2022). FX swaps, shadow banks and the global dollar footprint. *Environment and Planning A: Economy and Space*, 0308518X221128302.

Danielson, A. G. (2016). *International banking: America's rising role*. SDP Publishing Solutions.

de Goede, M. (2004). Repoliticizing financial risk. *Economy and Society*, *33*(2), 197–217.

Deeg, R. (1997). Banks and industrial finance in the 1990s. *Industry and Innovation*, *4*(1), 53–73.

Deeg, R. (1999). *Finance capitalism unveiled: Banks and the German political economy*. University of Michigan Press.

Deeg, R. (2001). Institutional change and the uses and limits of path dependency: The case of German finance. *MPIfG Discussion Paper*, *01/6*, 39.

Deeg, R. (2005). Change from within: German and Italian finance in the 1990s. In W. Streeck & K. Thelen (Eds.), *Beyond continuity: Institutional change in advanced political economies* (pp. 169–202). Oxford University Press.

Deeg, R. (2009). The rise of internal capitalist diversity? Changing patterns of finance and corporate governance in Europe. *Economy and Society*, *38*(4), 552–579.

Deeg, R. (2010a). Industry and finance in Germany since unification. *German Politics and Society*, *28*(2), 116–129.

Deeg, R. (2010b). Institutional change in financial systems. In G. Morgan, J. L. Campbell, C. Crouch, O. K. Pedersen, & R. Whitley (Eds.), *The Oxford handbook of comparative institutional analysis* (pp. 469–505). Oxford University Press.

Deeg, R. (2012). Financialisation and models of capitalism: A comparison of the UK and Germany. In G. Wood & C. Lane (Eds.), *Capitalist diversity and diversity within capitalism* (pp. 121–149). Routledge.

Deeg, R., & Hardie, I. (2016). What is patient capital and who supplies it? *Socio-Economic Review*, *14*(4), 627–645.

Deeg, R., & Lütz, S. (2000). Internationalization and financial federalism: The United States and Germany at the crossroads? *Comparative Political Studies*, *33*(3), 374–405.

Deutsche Bank AG. (2022). *Deutsche Bank Annual Report 2022*. https://investor-relations.db.com/files/documents/annual-reports/2023/Annual-Report-2022.pdf

Deutsche Bundesbank. (2006). *New legal and regulatory framework for the German securitisation and Pfandbrief market* (Monthly Report March). www.bundesbank.de/Redaktion/EN/Downloads/Publications/Monthly_Report_Articles/2006/2006_03_regulatory_framework.pdf?__blob=publicationFile

Dörry, S. (2014). Global production networks in finance: The example of Luxembourg's investment fund industry. *Espace géographique*, *43*(3), 227.

Dörry, S. (2016). The role of elites in the co-evolution of international financial markets and financial centres: The case of Luxembourg. *Competition & Change*, *20*(1), 21–36.

Drach, A. (2019). A globalization laboratory: European banking regulation and global capitalism in the 1970s and early 1980s. *European Review of History: Revue Européenne d'histoire*, *26*(4), 658–678.

Drach, A. (2020). Reluctant Europeans? British and French commercial banks and the common market in banking (1977–1992). *Enterprise & Society*, *21*(3), 768–798.

Drach, A. (2022). An early form of European champions? Banking clubs between European integration and global banking (1960s–1990s). *Business History*, 1–24.

Dutta, S. J. (2018). Sovereign debt management and the globalization of finance: Recasting the City of London's 'Big Bang'. *Competition & Change*, *22*(1), 3–22.

Dutta, S. J. (2020). Sovereign debt management and the transformation from Keynesian to Neoliberal monetary governance in Britain. *New Political Economy*, *25*(4), 1–16.

Dutta, S. J. (2023). Countering financial claims: On the political economy of definancialisation. In B. Braun & K. Koddenbrock (Eds.), *Capital claims: Power and global finance*. Routledge.

Düwel, C. (2013). *Repo funding and internal capital markets in the financial crisis (SSRN Scholarly Paper ID 2796912)*. Social Science Research Network.

Dymski, G., Hernandez, J., & Mohanty, L. (2013). Race, gender, power, and the US subprime mortgage and foreclosure crisis: A meso analysis. *Feminist Economics, 19*(3), 124–151.

Einzig, P. (1969). *The Euro-Bond market*. Palgrave Macmillan.

Enrich, D. (2020). *Dark towers: Deutsche Bank, Donald Trump, and an epic trail of destruction* (1st ed.). Custom House.

Epstein, G. A. (2005). *Financialization and the world economy*. Edward Elgar Publishing.

Erturk, I., & Solari, S. (2007). Banks as continuous reinvention. *New Political Economy, 12*(3), 369–388.

Euromoney. (1999, September). Deutsche Bank – Exclusive interview: Rolf Breuer on Bankers Trust. *Euromoney*; London.

Euroweek. (1995). Commerzbank joins growing German line-up of international equity issuers. Euroweek; London, *418*, 5.

Ewerhart, C., & Valla, N. (2008). Financial market liquidity and the lender of last resort. *Financial Stability Review*, Banque de France, 11, 133–148.

Fallon, P. (1994, January). The battle plans of Hilmar Kopper. Euromoney; London, *297*, 28.

Feiertag, O. (2005). The international opening-up the Paris Bourse: Overdraft-economy curbs and market dynamics. In Y. Cassis & E. Bussière (Eds.), *London and Paris as international financial centres in the twentieth century* (pp. 229–243). Oxford University Press.

Fender, I., & McGuire, P. (2010). European Banks' US Dollar funding pressures. *BIS Quarterly Review*, June.

Fields, D. (2018). Constructing a new asset class: Property-led financial accumulation after the crisis. *Economic Geography, 94*(2), 118–140.

Fligstein, N. (2021). *The banks did it: An anatomy of the financial crisis*. Harvard University Press.

Fligstein, N., & Habinek, J. (2014). Sucker punched by the invisible hand: The world financial markets and the globalization of the US mortgage crisis. *Socio-Economic Review, 12*(4), 637–665.

Fohlin, C. (2007). *Finance capitalism and Germany's rise to industrial power*. Cambridge University Press.

Freye, S. (2015). Professional socialization and institutional change: German corporate leaders in transition. *Competition & Change, 19*(5), 406–426.

Frost, R. (2009). *Wünsche werden Wirklichkeit: Die Deutsche Bank und ihr Privatkundengeschäft*. Piper.

Frost, R., & Raab-Rebentisch, A. (2005). *Die Deutsche Bank in Frankfurt am Main*. Piper.

Froud, J., Haslam, C., Johal, S., & Williams, K. (2000). Shareholder value and Financialization: Consultancy promises, management moves. *Economy and Society, 29*(1), 80–110.

Gabor, D. (2015). The IMF's rethink of global banks: Critical in theory, orthodox in practice: The IMF's rethink of global banks. *Governance, 28*(2), 199–218.

Gabor, D. (2016a). A step too far? The European financial transactions tax on shadow banking. *Journal of European Public Policy, 23*(6), 925–945.

Gabor, D. (2016b). The (impossible) repo trinity: The political economy of repo markets. *Review of International Political Economy, 23*(6), 967–1000.

Gabor, D. (2018). Goodbye (Chinese) shadow banking, Hello market-based finance. *Development and Change*, *49*(2), 394–419. https://doi.org/10.1111/dech.12387

Gabor, D., & Ban, C. (2016). Banking on bonds: The new links between states and markets. *JCMS: Journal of Common Market Studies*, *54*(3), 617–635.

Gabor, D., & Kohl, S. (2022). *My home is an asset class; Study about the financialization of housing in Europe*. TheGreens / EFA.

Gall, L., Feldmann, G. D., James, H., Holtfrerich, C.-L., & Büschgen (Eds.). (1995). *Die Deutsche Bank, 1870–1995*. C.H. Beck.

Gammelin, C. (2019). Warum Olaf Scholz die Gründung einer Superbank gut fände. *Süddeutsche Zeitung*.

Germann, J. (2013). State-led or capital-driven? The fall of Bretton Woods and the German Currency float reconsidered. *New Political Economy*, 1–21.

Germann, J. (2021). *Unwitting architect: German primacy and the origins of neoliberalism*. Stanford University Press.

Gerschenkron, A. (1962). *Economic backwardness in historical perspective: A book of essays*. Belknap Press of Harvard University Press.

Gibadullina, A. (2023). Rent and financial accumulation: Locating the profitability of American finance. *New Political Economy*, *28*(2), 259–283.

Gindin, S., & Panitch, L. (2012). *The making of global capitalism the political economy of American empire*. Verso.

Godechot, O. (2016). Financialization is marketization! A study of the respective impacts of various dimensions of financialization on the increase in global inequality. *Sociological Science*, *3*, 495–519.

Golin, J. L. (2006). *Covered bonds: Beyond Pfandbriefe: Innovations, investment and structured alternatives*. Euromoney Books.

Goodfriend, M. (1998). *Eurodollars* (pp. 48–49). Federal Reserve Bank of Richmond.

Gorton, G., & Metrick, A. (2012). Securitized banking and the run on repo. *Journal of Financial Economics*, *104*(3), 425–451. https://doi.org/10.1016/j.jfineco.2011.03.016

Green, J. (2016). Anglo-American development, the Euromarkets, and the deeper origins of neoliberal deregulation. *Review of International Studies*, *42*(03), 425–449.

Grünbacher, A. (2004). *Reconstruction and Cold War in Germany: The Kreditanstalt für Wiederaufbau (1948–1961)*. Routledge.

Guill, G. D. (2016). Bankers trust and the birth of modern risk management. *Journal of Applied Corporate Finance*, *28*(1), 19–29.

Hackethal, A. (2004). German banks and banking structure. In J. P. Krahnen & R. H. Schmidt (Eds.), *The German financial system* (pp. 71–105). Oxford University Press.

Haldane, A. (2014). *The age of asset management?* [Speech to the London School of Economics]. www.bankofengland.co.uk/-/media/boe/files/speech/2014/the-age-of-asset-management.pdf?la=en&hash=673A53E92A9EB43E5689ED7BE33628F62C4871F1

Hardie, I., & Howarth, D. (2009). Die Krise but not La Crise? The financial crisis and the transformation of German and French banking systems. *JCMS: Journal of Common Market Studies*, *47*(5), 1017–1039.

Hardie, I., & Howarth, D. (2013a). A peculiar kind of devastation: German market based banking. In I. Hardie & D. Howarth (Eds.), *Market-based banking and the international financial crisis* (pp. 103–127). Oxford University Press, Oxford.

Hardie, I., & Howarth, D. (Eds.). (2013b). *Market-based banking and the international financial crisis*. Oxford University Press.

Hardie, I., Howarth, D., Maxfield, S., & Verdun, A. (2011). Zysman thirty years on. The political economy of finance revisited. *Unpublished Manuscript*. https://pdfs.semanticscholar.org/fb5f/67186f663cdb84070e17b3fa453f7b8a2c7c.pdf

Hardie, I., Howarth, D., Maxfield, S., & Verdun, A. (2013). Banks and the false dichotomy in the comparative political economy of finance. *World Politics*, *65*(04), 691–728.

Hardie, I., & Macartney, H. (2016). EU ring-fencing and the defence of too-big-to-fail banks. *West European Politics*, *39*(3), 503–525.

Hardie, I., Verdun, A., & Maxfield, S. (2013). Introduction: Towards a political economy of banking. In I. Hardie & D. Howarth (Eds.), *Market-based banking and the international financial crisis* (pp. 3–18). Oxford University Press.

Hart, J. (2002, January 31). 'Toxic' synthetic CDOs balloon to pounds 92 billion: [C Edition]. *Evening Standard, West End Final Ed.*, 41.

Hassel, A. (2003). Wer beherrschte die Gemeinwirtschaft? Unternehmenskontrolle in politischen Unternehmen. In W. Streeck (Ed.), *Alle Macht dem Markt?: Fallstudien zur Abwicklung der Deutschland AG* (pp. 93–118). Campus Verlag.

Heires, M., & Nölke, A. (Eds.). (2014). *Politische Ökonomie der Finanzialisierung*. Springer VS.

Helgadóttir, O., & Ban, C. (2021). Managing macroeconomic neoliberalism: Capital and the resilience of the rational expectations assumption since the great recession. *New Political Economy*, *26*(5), 869–884.

Helleiner, E. (1994). *States and the reemergence of global finance: From Bretton Woods to the 1990s*. Cornell University Press.

Hendrikse, R. P., & Sidaway, J. D. (2014). Financial wizardry and the Golden City: Tracking the financial crisis through Pforzheim, Germany. *Transactions of the Institute of British Geographers*, *39*(2), 195–208.

Hilferding, R. (1981). *Finance capital: A study of the latest phase of capitalist development* (T. Bottomore, Ed.). Routledge & Kegan Paul.

Höpner, M. (2001). Corporate governance in transition: Ten empirical findings on shareholder value and industrial relations in Germany. *SSRN Electronic Journal*.

Höpner, M., & Jackson, G. (2006). Revisiting the Mannesmann takeover: How markets for corporate control emerge. *European Management Review*, *3*(3), 142–155.

Höpner, M., & Krempel, L. (2004). The politics of the German company network. *Competition & Change*, *8*(4), 339–356. https://doi.org/10.1080/1024259042000304392

Howarth, D. J., & James, S. (2023). *Bank politics: Structural reform in comparative perspective*. Oxford University Press.

Howarth, D., & Quaglia, L. (2013). Banking on stability: The political economy of new capital requirements in the European Union. *Journal of European Integration*, *35*(3), 333–346.

Hudson, M. (2010). *The monster: How a gang of predatory lenders and Wall Street bankers fleeced America – and spawned a global crisis* (1st ed.). Times Books/Henry Holt and Co.

Hüfner, F. (2010). *The German Banking System: Lessons from the Financial Crisis* (OECD Economics Department Working Papers 788).

Hughes, M. (2016). *The peculiarities of universal banking* [PhD Dissertation]. University of Sussex.

Hyman, L. (2013). *Debtor nation: The history of America in red ink* (3. printing, and 1. paperback print). Princeton University Press.

IMF. (2011). *Germany: Technical Note on the Future of German Mortgage-Backed Covered Bond (Pfandbrief) and Securitization Markets* (11/369; Country Report, p. 37). International Monetary Fund.

IMF. (2018). *Global financial stability report*. International Monetary Fund.

Jackson, G., & Deeg, R. (2012). The long-term trajectories of institutional change in European capitalism. *Journal of European Public Policy, 19*(8), 1109–1125.

Jackson, G., & Sorge, A. (2012). The trajectory of institutional change in Germany, 1979–2009. *Journal of European Public Policy, 19*(8), 1146–1167.

Jäger, C. F. (1831). *Ulms Verfassungs, bürgerliches und commercielles Leben im Mittelalter: Meist nach handschriftlichen Quellen samt Urkundenbuch*. Löflund.

Janssen, S. (2009). *British and German banking strategies*. Palgrave Macmillan.

Judson, R. A. (2012). Crisis and calm: Demand for U.S. currency at home and abroad from the fall of the Berlin Wall to 2011. *Board of Governors of the Federal Reserve System, 1058*.

Kaltenbrunner, A., & Painceira, J. P. (2017). Subordinated financial integration and financialisation in emerging capitalist economies: The Brazilian experience. *New Political Economy, 0*(0), 1–24.

Kantrow, Y. (1994, August 29). John Rolls' Grand Plan. *Investment Dealers' Digest*.

King, M. A., & Kay, J. A. (2020). *Radical uncertainty: Decision-making for an unknowable future*. The Bridge Street Press.

KfW. (n.d.). *70 years of Marshall Plan*. Retrieved 29 March 2019, from www.kfw.de/KfW-Group/Newsroom/Press-Material/Themen-kompakt/Marshallplan/

Klein, D. K. R. (1995). *The banking systems of the EU member states*. Gresham Books.

Knafo, S. (2022). The power of finance in the age of market based banking. *New Political Economy, 27*(1), 33–46.

Knafo, S., & Dutta, S. J. (2016). Patient capital in the age of financialized managerialism. *Socio-Economic Review*, 771–788.

Knafo, S., & Dutta, S. J. (2020). The myth of the shareholder revolution and the financialization of the firm. *Review of International Political Economy, 27*(3), 476–499.

Kobrak, C. (2007). *Banking on global markets: Deutsche Bank and the United States, 1870 to the present*. Cambridge University Press.

Kocka, J. (1988). German history before Hitler: The debate about the German Sonderweg. *Journal of Contemporary History*, 23(1), 3016.

Koddenbrock, K., & Sylla, N. S. (2019). *Towards a political economy of monetary dependency: The case of the CFA franc in West Africa* (Working Paper 19/2). MaxPo Discussion Paper.

Kohl, S. (2015). The power of institutional legacies: How nineteenth century housing associations shaped twentieth century housing regime differences between Germany and the United States. *European Journal of Sociology / Archives Européennes de Sociologie, 56*(2), 271–306.

Kohl, S. (2017). *Homeownership, renting and society: Historical and comparative perspectives*. Routledge.

Konings, M. (2008a). European finance in the American mirror: Financial change and the reconfiguration of competitiveness. *Contemporary Politics, 14*(3), 253–275.

Konings, M. (2008b). The institutional foundations of US structural power in international finance: From the re-emergence of global finance to the monetarist turn. *Review of International Political Economy*, *15*(1), 35–61.

Konings, M. (2009). The construction of US financial power. *Review of International Studies*, *35*(1), 69–94.

Konings, M. (2010). Neoliberalism and the American State. *Critical Sociology*, *36*(5), 741–765.

Konings, M. (2011). *The development of American finance*. Cambridge University Press.

Krahnen, J. P., & Schmidt, R. H. (Eds.). (2004). *The German financial system*. Oxford University Press.

Krippner, G. R. (2005). The financialization of the American economy. *Socio-Economic Review*, *3*(2), 173–208.

Krippner, G. R. (2011). *Capitalizing on crisis: The political origins of the rise of finance*. Harvard University Press.

Lanchner, D. (1998). The trouble with Germany's big banks. *Global Finance*, *12*(4), 33–37.

Lane, C. (2003). Changes in corporate governance of German corporations: Convergence to the Anglo-American model? *Competition & Change*, *7*(2–3), 79–100.

Lane, C. (2008). National capitalisms and global production networks: An analysis of their interaction in two global industries. *Socio-Economic Review*, *6*(2), 227–260.

Lassen, T. (2005). Specialization of covered bond issuers in Europe. *Housing Finance International*.

Lave, R., Mirowski, P., & Randalls, S. (2010). Introduction: STS and neoliberal science. *Social Studies of Science*, *40*(5), 659–675.

Lazonick, W., & O'sullivan, M. (1997). Finance and industrial development: Evolution to market control. Part II: Japan and Germany. *Financial History Review*, *4*(02).

Lea, M. J. (1996). Innovation and the cost of mortgage credit: A historical perspective. *Housing Policy Debate*, *7*(1), 147–174.

Lee, P. (1998, July). Deutsche dumps its investment bankers. *Euromoney*; London.

Lee, P. (2023, June 30). BlackRock expands private credit platform into venture debt. *Euromoney*. www.euromoney.com/article/2bv3dphun9yzqfh8ikphc/capital-markets/blackrock-expands-private-credit-platform-into-venture-debt

Lehrer, M., & Celo, S. (2016). German family capitalism in the 21st century: Patient capital between bifurcation and symbiosis. *Socio-Economic Review*, *14*(4), 729–750.

Levich, R. M. (1984). *Securities Activities of U.S. Commercial bank affiliates: Lessons from the international financial markets* (1428; NBER Working Paper Series, p. 69). National Bureau of Economic Research.

Levingston, I., Dunkley, E., Aglionby, J., & Morris, S. (2023, April 28). Deutsche Bank signals confidence in London with £410mn Numis deal. *Financial Times*.

Lewis, M. (2011, August 10). *It's the Economy, Dummkopf! Vanity Fair*. www.vanityfair.com/news/2011/09/europe-201109

Lockhart, J. A. (1969). The Eurobond market today: Some facts, some fancies. *Financial Analysts Journal*, *25*(2), 128–132.

Louch, W., & Mourselas, C. (2023, July 21). EU tightens rules on leverage for private credit funds. *Financial Times*. www.ft.com/content/2ab74817-5b14-4110-9815-a7549621b521

Lütz, S. (1998). The revival of the nation-state? Stock exchange regulation in an era of globalized financial markets. *Journal of European Public Policy*, *5*(1), 153–168.

Lütz, S. (2000). From managed to market capitalism? German finance in transition. *German Politics*, *9*(2), 149–170.

Lütz, S. (2004). Convergence within national diversity: The regulatory state in Finance. *Journal of Public Policy*, *24*(2), 169–197.

Lütz, S. (2005a). The finance sector in transition: A motor for economic reform? *German Politics*, *14*(2), 140–156.

Lütz, S. (2005b). Von der Infrastruktur Zum Markt? In P. Windolf (Ed.), *Finanzmarkt-Kapitalismus* (Vol. 45, pp. 294–315). VS Verlag für Sozialwissenschaften.

Lysandrou, P., & Shabani, M. (2018). The explosive growth of the ABCP market between 2004 and 2007: A 'search for yield' story. *Journal of Post Keynesian Economics*, *41*(4), 526–546.

MacKenzie, D. (2015, June 3). Dark markets. *London Review of Books*, *37*(11).

Mai, H. (2015). *Money market funds – an economic perspective: Matching short-term investment and funding needs*. Deutsche Bank. www.dbresearch.com/PROD/RPS_EN-PROD/Money_market_funds_%E2%80%93_an_economic_perspective%3A_Matc/RPS_EN_DOC_VIEW.calias?rwnode=PROD0000000000435631&ProdCollection=PROD0000000000441776

Massoc, E. C. (2019). Banks, power, and political institutions: The divergent priorities of European states towards 'too-big-to-fail' banks: The cases of competition in retail banking and the banking structural reform. *Business and Politics*, 1–26.

Massoc, E. C. (2022). Banks' structural power and states' choices on what structurally matters: The geo-economic foundations of state priority toward banking in France, Germany, and Spain. *Politics & Society*, *50*(4), 599–629.

Massoc, E. C., & Benoit, C. (2023). A tale of dualization: Accounting for the partial marketization of regulated savings in France. *Review of International Political Economy*, *0*(0), 1–26.

Massoudi, A., Storbeck, O., Crow, D., & Morris, S. (2019, May 2). How the dream of creating a German banking champion died. *Financial Times*. www.ft.com/content/6d0f86f8-6c25-11e9-a9a5-351eeaef6d84

Mattli, W. (2019). *Darkness by design: The hidden power in global capital markets*. Princeton University Press.

Maxfield, S., Winecoff, W. K., & Young, K. L. (2017). An empirical investigation of the financialization convergence hypothesis. *Review of International Political Economy*, *24*(6), 1004–1029.

Mayer, M. (1976). *The bankers*. Ballantine.

Mazzucato, M. (2019). *The value of everything*. Penguin.

McCauley, R. (2018). The 2008 crisis: Transpacific or transatlantic? *BIS Quarterly Review*, December, 39–58.

McCauley, R. N., McGuire, P., & Sushko, V. (2015). Dollar credit to emerging market economies. *BIS Quarterly Review*, December, 27–41.

McCauley, R. N., & Schenk, C. R. (2020). *Central bank swaps then and now: Swaps and dollar liquidity in the 1960s*. BIS working paper, No 851

McGuire, P. (2004). A shift in London's Eurodollar market. *BIS Quarterly Review*, September, 64–78.

Mertens, D. (2015). *Erst sparen, dann kaufen?: Privatverschuldung in Deutschland*. Campus Verlag.

Mertens, D. (2017). Putting 'merchants of debt' in their place: The political economy of retail banking and credit-based financialisation in Germany. *New Political Economy*, *22*(1), 12–30.

Mertens, D., & Thiemann, M. (2018). Market-based but state-led: The role of public development banks in shaping market-based finance in the European Union. *Competition & Change*, *22*(2), 184–204.

Montgomerie, J. (2006). The financialization of the American credit card industry. *Competition & Change*, *10*(3), 301–319.

Montgomerie, J., & Büdenbender, M. (2015). Round the houses: Homeownership and failures of asset-based welfare in the United Kingdom. *New Political Economy*, *20*(3), 386–405.

Morris, M. D., & Walter, J. R. (1998). Large negotiable certificates of deposit. In T. Q. Cook & R. K. Laroche (Eds.), *Instruments of the Money Market* (pp. 34–47). Federal Reserve Bank of Richmond.

Morris, S., Crow, D., & Storbeck, O. (2019, March 4). Deutsche and Commerzbank: Why Berlin is backing a merger. *Financial Times*. www.ft.com/content/fd55d086-3b52-11e9-b856-5404d3811663

Morris, S., Storbeck, O., & Smith, R. (2018, September 10). Deutsche Bank struggles with rising funding costs. *Financial Times*. www.ft.com/content/b2f071bc-b28c-11e8-99ca-68cf89602132

Moschella, M., & Tsingou, E. (2013). Regulating finance after the crisis: Unveiling the different dynamics of the regulatory process. *Regulation & Governance*, *7*(4), 407–416.

Mülhaupt, L. (1977). *Einführung in die Betriebswirtschaftslehre der Banken*. Gabler Verlag.

Neebe, R. (2004). *Weichenstellung für die Globalisierung: Deutsche Weltmarktpolitik, Europa und Amerika in der Ära Ludwig Erhard*. Böhlau.

Nesvetailova, A. (Ed.). (2018). *Shadow banking: Scope, origins and theories (1 Edition)*. Routledge, Taylor & Francis Group.

Nolmans, E. (2006). *Josef Ackermann und die Deutsche Bank: Anatomie eines Aufstiegs*. Orell Füssli.

Noonan, L. (2020, March 2). The rise and dramatic fall of European investment banks in the US. *Financial Times*. www.ft.com/content/68f8d7a6-56fb-11ea-a528-dd0f971febbc

Noonan, L. (2023a, March 16). European regulators criticise US 'incompetence' over Silicon Valley Bank collapse. *Financial Times*. www.ft.com/content/5e4a8dde-c053-4510-8cd9-8aecb9082a6e

Noonan, L. (2023b, September 5). Global financial watchdog warns of 'further challenges and shocks' ahead. *Financial Times*. www.ft.com/content/8f16ea1e-f926-4e23-b627-f22e58d0abbb

Norfield, T. (2017). *The City: London and the global power of finance*. Verso.

Norrlof, C. (2010). *America's global advantage: US hegemony and international cooperation*. Cambridge University Press.

Norrlof, C. (2014). Dollar hegemony: A power analysis. *Review of International Political Economy*, *21*(5), 1042–1070.

Oermann, N. O. (2013). *Tod eines Investmentbankers: Eine Sittengeschichte der Finanzbranche* (1st ed.). Verlag Herder.

Orhangazi, Ö. (2008). Financialisation and capital accumulation in the non-financial corporate sector: A theoretical and empirical investigation on the US economy: 1973–2003. *Cambridge Journal of Economics*, *32*(6), 863–886.

Ost, F. (1970). International activities of German Banks. *Intereconomics, 07*, 3.

Ott, J. C. (2014). *When wall street met main street: The quest for an investors' democracy*. Harvard University Press.

Pagliari, S., & Young, K. (2015). The interest ecology of financial regulation: Interest group plurality in the design of financial regulatory policies. *Socio-Economic Review*, mwv024.

Palan, R., & Nesvetailova, A. (2014). Elsewhere, ideally nowhere: Shadow banking and offshore finance. *Politik, 16*(4), 26–34.

Panitch, L., & Gindin, S. (2005). Finance and American Empire. *Socialist Register, 41*.

Pape, F. (2022). Governing global liquidity: Federal reserve swap lines and the international dimension of US monetary policy. *New Political Economy, 27*(3), 455–472.

Partnoy, F. (2009). *Infectious greed: How deceit and risk corrupted the financial markets*. PublicAffairs.

Paul, S., Sattler, F., & Ziegler, D. (Eds.). (2020). *Hundertfünfzig Jahre Commerzbank 1870–2020* (Erste Auflage). Siedler.

Paul, S., Schmitz, F., & Liedtke, F. (2020). Die Commerzbank 1989–2019: Zwischen Expansion und Konsolidierung. In S. Paul, F. Sattler, & D. Ziegler (Eds.), *Hundertfünfzig Jahre Commerzbank 1870–2020* (Erste Auflage, pp. 415–604). Siedler.

Pauli, C. (1999, June 21). Deutsche Bank: Amerikanische Sitten. *Der Spiegel*.

Pfeiffer, H. (1987). *Das Imperium der Deutschen Bank*. Campus Verlag.

Piketty, T. (2014). *Capital in the twenty-first century*. The Belknap Press of Harvard University Press.

Pistor, K. (2020). *The code of capital: How the law creates wealth and inequality (First paperback printing)*. Princeton University Press.

Pohl, M. (1998). Deutsche Bank in London 1873–1998. In M. Pohl & K. Burk (Eds.), *Die Deutsche Bank in London: 1873–1998* (pp. 11–112). Piper.

Pozsar, Z., Adrian, T., Ashcraft, A., & Boesky, H. (2010). Shadow banking. *Federal Reserve Bank of New York Staff Reports, No. 458*, 82.

Prokesch, S. (1989, November 28). Germans to Buy Morgan Grenfell. *The New York Times*.

Quinn, S. (2017). 'The Miracles of Bookkeeping': How budget politics link fiscal policies and financial markets. *American Journal of Sociology, 123*(1), 48–85.

Quinn, S. L. (2019). *American bonds: How credit markets shaped a nation*. Princeton University Press.

Quint, M. (1992, May 6). Deutsche Bank Pursues Diversity for Its U.S. Unit. *The New York Times*.

Rademacher, I. (2021). One state, one interest? How a historic shock to the balance of power of the Bundesbank and the German government laid the path for fiscal austerity. *Review of International Political Economy, 0*(0), 1–23.

Ramm, U. (2002). German banks and the American challenge. In S. Battilossi & Y. Cassis (Eds.), *European banks and the American challenge: Competition and cooperation in international banking under Bretton Woods* (pp. 177–199). Oxford University Press.

Rethel, L., & Sinclair, T. J. (2012). *The problem with banks*. Zed Books.

Rixen, T. (2013). Why reregulation after the crisis is feeble: Shadow banking, offshore financial centers, and jurisdictional competition. *Regulation & Governance, 7*(4), 435–459.

Roberts, A. (2013). Financing social reproduction: The gendered relations of debt and mortgage finance in twenty-first-century America. *New Political Economy, 18*(1), 21–42.

Roberts, R. (2001). *Take your partners: Orion, the consortium banks and the transformation of the Euromarkets*. Palgrave Macmillan UK.

Rodgers, K. (2016). *Why aren't they shouting?: A banker's tale of change, computers and perpetual crisis*. Cornerstone Digital.

Röper, N. (2018). German finance capitalism: The paradigm shift underlying financial diversification. *New Political Economy*, *23*(3), 366–390.

Ross, D. M. (1998). European banking clubs in the 1960s: A flawed strategy. *Business and Economic History*, *27*(2), 353–366.

Sablowski, J. W. (2008). Towards the Americanization of European finance? The case of finance-led accumulation in Germany. In M. Konings & L. Panitch (Eds.), *American empire and the political economy of global finance*.

Saeidinezhad, E. (2023, April 1). Banks as Hedge Funds? | Elham Saeidinezhad. *Phenomenal World*. www.phenomenalworld.org/analysis/banks-as-hedge-funds/

Sanford, C. (1996). *Managing the transformation of a corporate culture: Risks and rewards* [Speech delivered as part of the 1996–97 Musser-Schoemaker Leadership Lecture Series at the Wharton School, University of Pennsylvania]. www.terry.uga.edu/about/history/sanford/managing-transformation

Sattler, F. (2010). 'Investmentsparen' – ein früher Durchbruch der Geschäftsbanken zu breiteren Privatkundenkreisen? In R. Ahrens & H. Wixforth (Eds.), *Strukturwandel und Internationalisierung im Bankwesen seit den 1950er Jahren* (pp. 35–70). Steiner.

Sattler, F. (2020). Die Commerzbank 1945 bis 1989: Neuanfang, Wirtschaftsboom aund Internationalisierung. In S. Paul, F. Sattler, & D. Ziegler (Eds.), *Hundertfünfzig Jahre Commerzbank 1870–2020* (Erste Auflage, pp. 219–414). Siedler.

Schelkle, W. (2012). A crisis of what? Mortgage credit markets and the social policy of promoting homeownership in the United States and in Europe. *Politics & Society*, *40*(1), 59–80.

Schelkle, W., & Bohle, D. (2020). European political economy of finance and financialization. *Review of International Political Economy*, 1–14.

Schenk, C. (2002). International financial centres 1958–1971: Competitiveness and complementarity. In S. Battilossi & Y. Cassis (Eds.), *European Banks and the American challenge: Competition and cooperation in international banking under Bretton Woods* (pp. 74–102). Oxford University Press.

Schenk, C. (2005). Crisis and opportunity: The policy environment of international banking in the city of London, 1958–1980. In C. Youssef, & B. Eric (Eds.), *London and Paris as international financial centres in the twentieth century*. Oxford University Press.

Schenk, C. R. (1998). The origins of the Eurodollar market in London: 1955–1963. *Explorations in Economic History*, *35*(2), 221–238.

Schenk, C. R. (2020). Globalisation and crisis, 1989–2020. In W. Plumpe, A. Nützenadel, & C. R. Schenk (Eds.), *Deutsche Bank: The global Hausbank, 1870–2020* (pp. 461–660). Bloomsbury Publishing.

Schieritz, M., & Nienhaus, L. (2019, February 8). Industriepolitik: Jetzt wird wieder in die Hände gespuckt. *Die Zeit*. www.zeit.de/2019/07/industriepolitik-bundesregierung-schutz-konzerne-china-amerika-peter-altmaier

Schmidt, R. H., Hackethal, A., & Tyrell, M. (1999). Disintermediation and the role of banks in Europe: An international comparison. *Journal of Financial Intermediation*, *8*(1), 36–67.

Schmidt, R. H., & Tyrell, M. (2004). What constitutes a financial system in general and the German financial system in particular? In J. P. Krahnen & R. H. Schmidt (Eds.), *The German financial system* (pp. 19–68). Oxford University Press.

Schnabel, I. (2019, March 26). A merger between Deutsche and Commerzbank is a bad idea. *Financial Times*. www.ft.com/content/d25ef54c-4fa7-11e9-8f44-fe4a86c48b33

Schreiber, M., & Willmroth, J. (2018). Tosender Applaus für Mutmach-Parolen. *sueddeutsche.de*. www.sueddeutsche.de/wirtschaft/deutsche-bank-christian-sewing-stellen abbau-1.3991330?sc_src=email_138166&sc_lid=16288810&sc_uid=JtWSSm6NH6&sc_llid=2916&utm_medium=email&utm_source=emarsys&utm_content=

Schwan, M. (2021). Weathering the storm? Financialisation and German savings banks. *New Political Economy*, *26*(3), 422–438.

Schwartz, H. (2008). Housing, global finance, and American hegemony: Building conservative politics one brick at a time. *Comparative European Politics*, *6*(3), 262–284.

Schwartz, H. (2010). *Subprime nation: American power, global capital, and the housing bubble*. Cornell University Press.

Schwartz, H. M. (2019). American hegemony: Intellectual property rights, dollar centrality, and infrastructural power. *Review of International Political Economy*, *26*(3), 490–519.

Schwartz, H. M. (2020). Covering the private parts: The (re-)nationalisation of housing finance. *West European Politics*, *43*(2), 485–508.

Schwarz, F. (2003). *Die Deutsche Bank: Riese auf tönernen Füßen* (1st ed.). Campus Verlag.

Seabrooke, L. (2001). *US power in international finance*. Palgrave Macmillan. https://doi.org/10.1057/9780230513365

Seabrooke, L. (2007). Everyday legitimacy and international financial orders: The social sources of imperialism and hegemony in global finance. *New Political Economy*, *12*(1), 1–18.

Sgambati, S. (2019). The art of leverage: A study of bank power, money-making and debt finance. *Review of International Political Economy*, 1–26.

Shin, H. S. (2012). Global banking glut and loan risk premium. *IMF Economic Review*, *60*(2), 155–192.

Shonfield, A. (1965). *Modern capitalism: The changing balance of public and private power*. Oxford University Press.

Singleton, J. (2009). The Euromarkets and the New Zealand government in the 1960s. *Australian Economic History Review*, *49*(3), 252–275.

Sissoko, C. (2015a). The bank-centered view of the money market, part I: Why banks are different. *USC CLASS Research Paper, CLASS15-4*.

Sissoko, C. (2015b). *The bank-centered view of the money market part II: Re-Evaluating the real bills approach to macro-prudential regulation* (SSRN Scholarly Paper 2578408).

Sissoko, C. (2017). The plight of modern markets: How universal banking undermines capital markets. *Economic Notes*, *46*(1), 53–104.

Sissoko, C. (2019). Repurchase agreements and the (de)construction of financial markets. *Economy and Society*, *48*(3), 315–341.

Skyrman, V. (2023). Why didn't Europe securitise more? The institutionalisation of covered bonds as an efficient instrument for financialisation. *New Political Economy*, *0*(0), 1–15.

Snowden, K. A. (1987). Mortgage rates and American capital market development in the late nineteenth century. *The Journal of Economic History*, *47*(3), 671–691.

Spangler, M., & Werner, R. (2013). *German covered bonds*. Springer.

Statistisches Bundesamt. (2019). *Gesamtentwicklung des deutschen Außenhandels 1950 bis 2018*. (Destatis).

Stigum, M. L. (1983). *The money market* (Rev. ed.). Dow Jones-Irwin.

Stigum, M. L. (1990). *The money market* (3rd ed). Dow Jones-Irwin.

Stockhammer, E., Sgambati, S., & Nesvetailova, A. (2021). Financialisation: Continuity and change – introduction to the special issue. *Review of Evolutionary Political Economy*, *2*(3), 389–401.

Storbeck, O. (2019, March 14). The eight men who will decide the future of German banking. *Financial Times*. www.ft.com/content/6633bc0e-44e4-11e9-b168-96a37d002cd3

Storbeck, O., & Morris, S. (2019, March 18). The hurdles in a Deutsche Bank and Commerzbank merger. *Financial Times*. www.ft.com/content/8690eb72-48d9-11e9-bbc9-6917dce3dc62

Storbeck, O., Morris, S., & Jenkins, P. (2019, February 14). Top investors call on Deutsche to cut back US investment bank. *Financial Times*. www.ft.com/content/6bb5777c-2ec7-11e9-8744-e7016697f225

Story, J. (1996). Finanzplatz deutschland: National or European response to internationalisation? *German Politics*, *5*(3), 371–394.

Strange, S. (1986). *Casino capitalism*. Blackwell's.

Strange, S. (1987). The persistent myth of lost hegemony. *International Organization*, *41*(4), 551–574. JSTOR.

Streeck, W. (1991). On the institutional conditions of diversified quality production. In E. Matzner & W. Streeck (Eds.), *Beyond Keynesianism: The socio-economics of production and full employment* (pp. 21–61). Edward Elgar Publishing.

Streeck, W. (2009). *Re-forming capitalism: Institutional change in the German political economy*. Oxford University Press.

Streeck, W. (2010). E Pluribus Unum? Varieties and Commonalities of Capitalism. *MPIfG Discussion Paper, No. 10/12*.

Streeck, W. (2011). The crises of democratic capitalism. *New Left Review*, *71*, 25.

Streeck, W. (2014). *Buying time: The delayed crisis of democratic capitalism*. Verso Books.

Streeck, W. (2016). *How will capitalism end? Essays on a failing system*. Verso.

Streeck, W., & Höpner, M. (Eds.). (2003). *Alle Macht dem Markt? Fallstudien zur Abwicklung der Deutschland AG*. Campus Verlag.

Streeck, W., & Thelen, K. (Eds.). (2005). *Beyond continuity: Institutional change in advanced political economies*. Oxford University Press.

Tagliabue, J. (1986, September 21). Germany's Goliath Bank. *The New York Times*.

Tanega, J., & Baklanova, V. (2018). European money market funds: A study of the market micro-processes. In A. Nesvetailova (Ed.), *Shadow banking: Scope, origins and theories* (pp. 122–142). Routledge.

Tett, G. (2012). *Fool's gold: How unrestrained greed corrupted a dream, shattered global markets and unleashed a catastrophe*. Abacus.

The Banker. (2001, November 1). Germany – Left on the shelf – Cross-border expansion has Eluded Commerzbank. *The Banker*, November.

The Economist. (1993, April 10). New tricks to learn, A survey of international banking. *The Economist*, 1. The Economist Historical Archive, 1843–2014.

The Economist (1999, January 7). After the deal. www.economist.com/special/1999/01/07/after-the-deal

The Economist. (2016, September 16). America's department of justice asks Deutsche Bank for $14 billion. *The Economist.*

The Economist. (2017, March 11). Blues in a different key; Deutsche Bank. *The Economist*; London, *422*(9031), 75.

Thelen, K. (2014). *Varieties of liberalization and the new politics of social solidarity.* Cambridge University Press.

Thiemann, M. (2012). 'Out of the Shadows?' Accounting for special purpose entities in European banking systems. *Competition & Change, 16*(1), 37–55.

Thiemann, M. (2018). *The growth of shadow banking: A comparative institutional analysis.* Cambridge University Press.

Thompson, H. (2015). Germany and the Euro-Zone crisis: The European reformation of the German banking crisis and the future of the Euro. *New Political Economy, 20*(6), 851–870.

Thompson, H. (2016). Enduring capital flow constraints and the 2007–2008 financial and euro zone crises. *The British Journal of Politics and International Relations, 18*(1), 216–233.

Tooze, J. A. (2018). *Crashed: How a decade of financial crises changed the world.* Viking.

Trampusch, C., Linden, B., & Schwan, M. (2014). Staatskapitalismus in NRW und Bayern: Der Aufstieg und Fall von WestLB und BayernLB. *Zeitschrift f?r Vergleichende Politikwissenschaft, 8*(2), 129–154.

Van der Zwan, N. (2014). Making sense of financialization. *Socio-Economic Review, 12*(1), 99–129.

van der Zwan, N. (2017). Financialisation and the pension system: Lessons from the United States and the Netherlands. *Journal of Modern European History, 15*(4), 554–584.

Van Gunten, T., & Navot, E. (2018). Varieties of indebtedness: Financialization and mortgage market institutions in Europe. *Social Science Research, 70*, 90–106.

van Meeteren, M., & Bassens, D. (2019). Chasing the phantom of a 'global endgame': The role of management consultancy in the narratives of pre-failure ABN AMRO. In M. Hoyler, C. Parnreiter, & A. Watson (Eds.), *Global city makers: Economic actors and practices in the world city network* (pp. 170–191). Edward Elgar Publishing.

Vitols, S. (1995). *German banks and the modernization of the small firm sector: Long-term finance in comparative perspective.* WZB Labor Market and Employment Working Paper No. FS I 95-309

Vitols, S. (1998). Are German banks different? *Small Business Economics, 10*(2), 79–91.

Vitols, S. (2003). *Changes in German finance: Introducing more 'market' into a bank-based system* (Working Paper 03–29). United Nations University.

Vitols, S. (2004a). Continuity and change: Making sense of the German model. *Competition & Change, 8*(4), 331–337.

Vitols, S. (2004b). Negotiated shareholder value: The German variant of an Anglo-American practice. *Competition and Change, 8*(4), 357–374.

Vitols, S. (2005). Changes in Germany's bank-based financial system: Implications for corporate governance. *Corporate Governance: An International Review, 13*(3), 386–396.

Vitols, S. (2009). Die Großbanken und die Internationalisierung des deutschen Finanzsystems. In A. Sorge (Ed.), *Internationalisierung: Gestaltungschancen statt Globalisierungsschicksal* (pp. 135–156). Edition sigma.

Vitols, S., & Engelhardt, L. (2005). *National institutions and high tech industries: A varieties of capitalism perspective on the failure of Germany's Neuer Markt*. WZB, Markets and Political Economy Working Paper No. SP II 2005-03

Wansleben, L. (2020). Formal institution building in financialized capitalism: The case of repo markets. *Theory and Society*, *49*(2), 187–213.

Wansleben, L. (2023). *The rise of central banks: State power in financial capitalism*. Harvard University Press.

Weber, A. (2009). *Pfandbriefmarkt und Finanzmarktkrise*. www.bundesbank.de/Redaktion/DE/Downloads/Presse/Reden/2009/2009_11_26_weber_pfandbriefmarkt_und_finanzmarktkrise.pdf%3F__blob%3DpublicationFile

Wieandt, A., & Moral y Santiago, R. (2006). Banking & finance. In K. Lucks (Ed.), *Transatlantic mergers and acquisitions: Opportunities and pitfalls in German-American partnerships* (pp. 85–96). Publicis; Wiley.

Wigan, D. (2010). Credit risk transfer and crunches: Global finance victorious or vanquished? *New Political Economy*, *15*(1), 109–125.

Wigglesworth, R. (2023, April 20). Blackstone ♡ private credit. *Financial Times*. www.ft.com/content/8b50cf70-b379-42a0-b373-18cd1afea8fe

Wijburg, G., & Aalbers, M. B. (2017). The alternative financialization of the German housing market. *Housing Studies*, *32*(7), 968–989.

Wijburg, G., Aalbers, M. B., & Heeg, S. (2018). The financialisation of rental housing 2.0: Releasing housing into the privatised mainstream of capital accumulation. *Antipode*, *50*(4), 1098–1119.

Willmroth, J. (2018, April 3). Kopflos durch die Führungskrise. *Süddeutsche Zeitung*. www.sueddeutsche.de/wirtschaft/deutsche-bank-kopflos-durch-die-fuehrungskrise-1.3928070?sc_src=email_82734&sc_lid=10078554&sc_uid=JtWSSm6NH6&sc_llid=53974&utm_medium=email&utm_source=emarsys&utm_content

Wilson, J. (2012, May 31). Ackermann defends record at Deutsche. *Financial Times*. www.ft.com/content/3924b236-ab03-11e1-b875-00144feabdc0

Wixforth, H. (2010). 'Global Players' im 'Europäischen Haus'? Die Expansionsstrategien deutscher Großbanken nach 1945. In R. Ahrens & H. Wixforth (Eds.), *Strukturwandel und Internationalisierung im Bankwesen seit den 1950er Jahren* (pp. 97–120). Steiner.

Wixforth, H. (2017). Das Universalbanksystem – Ein Erfolgsmodell auf den Finanzmärkten? *Jahrbuch für Wirtschaftsgeschichte*, *58*(2). https://doi.org/10.1515/jbwg-2017-0021

Woll, C. (2014). Bank rescue schemes in Continental Europe: The power of collective inaction. *Government and Opposition*, *49*(3), 426–451.

Wright, C. (2023, June 19). Deutsche and Barclays eye private credit opportunity in wake of Credit Suisse takeover. *Euromoney*. www.euromoney.com/article/2bteg9a8ql65l7kw6yqdc/banking/deutsche-and-barclays-eye-private-credit-opportunity-in-wake-of-credit-suisse-takeover

Wullweber, J. (2020). The politics of shadow money: Security structures, money creation and unconventional central banking. *New Political Economy*, *0*(0), 1–17.

Zysman, J. (1983). *Governments, markets, and growth: Financial systems and politics of industrial change*. Cornell University Press.

Index

www.ingramcontent.com/pod-product-compliance
Lightning Source LLC
LaVergne TN
LVHW091530200926
848483LV00002B/352

* 9 7 8 1 0 0 9 4 1 1 8 1 3 *